The PHOTOGUIDE to Lighting

THE ⓕ FOCALGUIDES TO

	Basic Photography
COLOUR	David Lynch
EFFECTS AND TRICKS	Günter Spitzing
EXPOSURE	David Lynch
LIGHTING	Paul Petzold
LOW LIGHT PHOTOGRAPHY	Paul Petzold
SLIDES	Graham Saxby
	Equipment
CAMERAS	Clyde Reynolds
FILTERS	Clyde Reynolds
FLASH	Günter Spitzing
LARGER FORMAT CAMERAS	Sidney Ray
LENSES	Leonard Gaunt
SLIDE-TAPE	Brian Duncalf
35 mm	Leonard Gaunt
THE 35 mm SINGLE LENS REFLEX	Leonard Gaunt
	Processing
CIBACHROME	Jack H. Coote
COLOUR FILM PROCESSING	Derek Watkins
COLOUR PRINTING	Jack H. Coote
THE DARKROOM	Leonard Gaunt
ENLARGING	Günter Spitzing
HOME PROCESSING	Ralph Jacobson
	Subjects
ACTION PHOTOGRAPHY	Don Morley
CLOSE-UPS	Sidney Ray
MOUNTAINS	Douglas Milner
PHOTOGRAPHING PEOPLE	Alison Trapmore
PORTRAITS	Günter Spitzing
	Movie
MOVIEMAKING	Paul Petzold
SHOOTING ANIMATION	Zoran Perisic

The FOCALGUIDE to Lighting

Paul Petzold

Focal Press · London

Focal/Hastings House · New York

ISBN (excl. USA) 0 240 50962 5
ISBN (USA only) 0 8038 2348 7

First edition 1977
Second impression 1978
Third impression 1979

Spanish edition
LA ILUMINACIÓN
Ediciones Omega, S.A., Barcelona

Text set in 10/12 pt Photon Univers, printed by photolithography and bound in Great Britain at The Pitman Press, Bath

Contents

Light:
What is it?

Light is a form of energy. It is a small section of the spectrum of electro-magnetic rays. Other rays found in that spectrum include infra-red radiation, radio waves, X-rays, ultra violet and gamma rays. Light is just like these other rays. But we regard it as distinct because our eyes can detect it. The other rays, though some of them can be felt, are invisible. Some of the other rays can be "seen" by a camera. You can take photographs by X-rays, or by ultra violet or infra-red radiation even though you can not see them yourself. Electromagnetic rays travel with a wave-like motion, vibrating the whole time. The wavelength – that is the distance between one peak (or trough) and the next – determines the kind of radiation. Wavelength ranges from hundreds of kilometres down to absolutely minute lengths. Light has a mid-range wavelength; but even this distance is so microscopic that it has to be measured in millionths of a millimetre (nanometres – nm).

As well as determining whether or not we can see the radiation, the distance between one wave and the next determines its colour. For instance, short wavelength light (around 400 nm) is blue-violet, and is found at one end of the visible part of the spectrum; whereas longer wavelength light (700 nm) is red. All the colours you see in between are, literally, the colours of the rainbow. In a rainbow, the colours are arranged in order according to wavelength.

If you take all the colours of the rainbow, including all the intermediate shades, and mix them together, you get white. At least, that is what happens when you mix *light* of those colours. Mixing coloured paints is another matter. The same works the other way round. A suitable light splitter (disperser) such as a prism, can break up a white light beam (such as sunlight) in to all the different colours of which it is composed.

If these coloured rays are then rejoined by a second prism, they combine to make white light.

To simplify thinking about it, the spectrum is normally considered to be divided into three equal parts. These three broad bands are known as the "primary" colours of light – red, green and blue. Mixed in equal proportion, they form white. If the mixture is altered in any way, it no longer adds up to white. White light can therefore be turned into light of a particular colour by removing some or all of the other colours that make up the complete spectrum. This may be done with colour filters.

A filter which allows only the primary colour red to pass through it, absorbs blue and green. Mixed together, blue and green form red's *complementary*, blue-green. The complementary of any colour is that which, when added to the other makes white light. Transparent substances (including filters) *transmit* light of their own colour and *absorb* the complementary colour. Opaque surfaces *reflect* their own colour and *absorb* the complementary – the remainder of the spectrum. If white sunlight falls on a red jersey, it reflects the red but absorbs the other component colours of the spectrum.

The way in which light is absorbed, transmitted or reflected is the essence of photography. Often, you can consider it as a whole – just white light, but its colour, too, can be a very important factor in photography. To take just the pictures you want – in black-and-white or colour, you must know how light behaves, and how its colour can be affected grossly or subtly.

Why do we need it?

We need light to see by. Without it we would be groping in a world of blackness, determining the shape, size and position of things only by touch, smell, taste or sound.

We see most things around us by the light that they reflect. The light reaching them bounces off and enters our eyes. This enables us to distinguish between one object and another, to help determine its shape and to note its texture and colour.

Although, at first thought, you might imagine that you see things "just as they are", in fact the quality of light greatly affects the way an object looks. Colour, intensity and direction of the light all change our ideas of what something really looks like. However, if we know what we expect to see – a familiar face, a house, the rolling landscape, or whatever – our eyes and brain make allowances for the lighting. We see what is really there. But the camera is far more sensitive to small differences. In fact, it is utterly dependent on the evidence of light. It does not have a brain with which to sift the visible evidence before it and make a judgement as to what it is actually seeing. So it is more easily cheated than we are.

Having only one "eye", a camera cannot normally see in three dimensions as we can with our two eyes. So it is far less able to record the depth, roundness, distance and scale of objects. A photograph can only hint at scale or distance by apparent perspective and the relative sizes of different objects in the same scene.

In the two-dimensional flat pictures from a camera, the illusion of depth or distance must come from other reference points. One important one is the modelling effect of light and shadow.

It is therefore up to you as a photographer to provide the right quantity of light and in the right place to let the camera do its job properly. Often, you have to provide all the light, otherwise there will be no pictures. At other times you may augment what is already there. There are advantages in providing all the light yourself. For one thing, you have complete control. You have a means to overcome some of the problems that the process does, admittedly, have. Having achieved success, the control gained by doing your own lighting enables you to repeat it time and again. Further, you can explore other possibilities using your familiar working methods as a departure point.

The camera and the eye are often compared. There are similarities. In place of the light-sensitive retina on the back wall of the eye there is, in the camera, a piece of light-sensitive film. But the way in which it responds to light is not exactly the same as with human eyesight. Once the light-sensitive material has responded you see your eye's view immediately. However, on film, the series of steps before you have the final picture take time. You can control some of the steps to alter the picture, but this does not remove the importance of controlling the picture-taking light. Sometimes that is the only way to make adjustments or corrections.

What does it do?

You need a certain minimum level of light in order to see a subject or photograph it clearly. The brightness of the subject depends on two factors; how much light falls on it and how efficient it is at reflecting that light.

The intensity of the light reaching the subject depends largely on the power and design of the light source and its distance from the subject. Obviously, if you move a light away from a subject less light falls on it; and if you bring it closer the light level is increased. There is a strict relationship between the intensity of light falling on a subject and the distance of the light source from it. This relationship is covered by the inverse square law.

With a point light source, the intensity of the illumination falling on a subject is *inversely* proportional to the *square* of the distance between the light source and the subject. So, if a lamp is moved to double the distance, the light intensity is only a quarter of what it was. If it is moved to three times the distance the illumination is nine times weaker. If, on the other hand, the lamp is moved to half the distance the light is four times brighter. Light intensity alters with distance much more than you would think.

The law relates to point sources of light, and although most ordinary lamps or flash units are not such, the law still works well enough for them. It does *not*, however, apply to focused sources such as spot lights or projectors, which have near-parallel light beams and far less fall off in power with distance.

When light strikes a surface, one of three main things can occur, it can be absorbed, reflected or transmitted. Absorption is obvious, for example, with an almost totally non-reflecting surface such as black velvet. But it happens to a greater or lesser extent with most other surfaces. The darker the surface, the more light is absorbed, the lighter, the less. Shiny surfaced objects tend to absorb less light than those with a matt or rough texture. A surface that absorbs strongly needs more light on it to be seen or photographed as easily as one which does not absorb so much.

Reflection can be either regular, as with a mirror or polished object, or diffused, as in the case of a surface which is patterned, textured or uneven, however light in colour that surface may be. It is by the light reflected from them that we see and photograph most things. Light that is neither absorbed nor reflected is transmitted through objects. This, too, can be in a regular (relatively unimpeded) diffused

way. We see objects between us and a light source if they do not transmit the light perfectly.
Let us look again at the behaviour of light under these conditions. They have considerable bearing on the way in which light can be used in photography.

Absorption

On the face of it, absorption of light would seem to have few applications. The subject or surface is apparently destroying the light you are providing for it and making the job of taking a photograph quite difficult.
But suppose you want to differentiate strongly between a bright object in front of the camera, such as a coin, and its surroundings. You have to light the coin reasonably well to photograph it but you don't want anything else in the picture, even a texture. Put it against a matt black surface which is totally absorbant, and the problem is solved – the coin, which reflects light well, stands out clearly against the background which is totally absorbing the light falling on it.
Another case of light absorption is seen where the light travels *through* a transparent medium such as glass or liquid. Some of the light may be absorbed by the density of the glass or liquid. White light may emerge as a particular colour because the glass has absorbed the complementary colours that make up the full spectrum. This is what happens with the stained glass windows of a church. The white skylight falling on them has some of its wavelengths (colours) absorbed, allowing only the colour that we see to emerge from the other side. Colour filters used for photography do precisely the same thing.

Reflection

Objects all around us reflect light – that is how we know they are there without actually touching them. Those with a dull surface

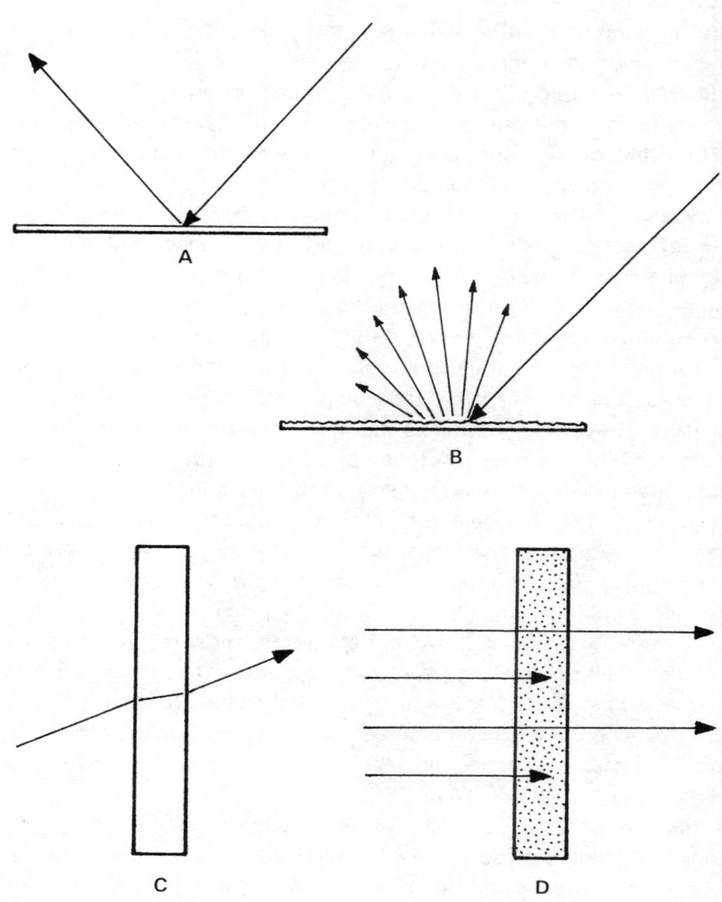

Light striking a surface. A. reflection: light striking a smooth surface is reflected at an angle equal to the angle of incidence. B. Light falling on a rough surface is scattered more or less haphazardly. C. Transmission: light passing at an angle through a transparent medium of differing density is bent (refracted) at its surfaces. D. Transmitting materials may absorb some light rays and allow others to pass through.

absorb more than others which are more shiny. Some polished surfaces give off bright, specular reflections, and all things look different according to the way the light falls on them.

Then there is the question of colour. Some objects look coloured when seen by ordinary white light because they reflect only part of the spectrum which is their own colour, and absorb the complementary colours. The apparent colour is altered when we view an object by another light source. The suit that a customer selects under shop lighting can look quite a different colour when he walks off down the street wearing it. If he is wise he takes the garment to the window to be quite sure that the colour still looks good in daylight.

Coloured objects change their colour under different light sources because the sources are made up from different proportions of colours. However good the object may be at reflecting a particular colour, if it does not receive that wavelength of light it cannot reflect it. We will now look more closely at the ways in which a surface may reflect light. But bear in mind that the light that falls on the surface or the light that is reflected from it may not necessarily be white light. Both white and coloured light have their uses in photography.

Light is reflected accurately from a smooth, shiny surface, such as that of a mirror, polished metal or smooth water. If light strikes perpendicular to the surface, it is reflected directly back. If it strikes at any other angle, it is reflected at the same angle on the other side of the perpendicular, so that the angle of reflection always equals the angle of incidence.

If the surface is not polished but has a rough or irregular finish the incident light, instead of being reflected at a particular angle becomes scattered and diffused in all directions. Surfaces vary all the way down from shiny to matt, but most reflect part of the light directly and scatter the remainder.

These properties of reflection are of immense importance in lighting for photography as they determine not only the appearance of a subject when light falls on it but the way in which you can control that light before it gets there. Reflectors for lamps and other purposes can be suitably designed or positioned to make the light go where you want.

Transmission

If you shine a light on a wineglass most passes through, though some may be reflected internally and emerge only at the rim and other edges. If the glass is dirty, "smoked" or stained, some of the light, instead of passing through, is diffused at the surface and scattered inside the glass. If the surface is really rough as with ground glass, most of the light becomes diffused and is scattered within the glass, transmitting far fewer regular light rays through to the other side. With opal glass the diffusion is so great that virtually no regular, or directional light rays emerge from the other side at all. Everyday examples of these effects can be seen in domestic light bulbs. The clear ones transmit light rays straight from the filament – their light is hard, directional and gives sharp shadows. Light from the pearl or frosted type is far more diffused and gives softer shadows. The softest light comes from the opal type which diffuses the light so much that it can be used in the home without a shade.
When light passes obliquely from a medium of one density into another it alters its course. Head-on rays are not deviated. The greater the angle from the perpendicular, the greater the bend. You can see the bending, known as refraction, by putting a stick half-way into water. The amount of refraction at any angle to the perpendicular varies from substance to substance. The variety of properties is used in the construction of optical instruments. We won't go into detail, just note that light *can* be refracted, and by using lenses can be made to converge on a point, or focus. The choice of curvatures and materials determines just how a lens works. Some kinds of lenses are used to focus light or condense (that is, concentrate) it for photographic purposes. They afford another means of controlling light to give the desired effect.
Certain transmitting mediums have a crystal structure that allows light waves to pass through only if they are vibrating in a particular direction. We saw earlier how, normally, light waves vibrate in all directions about the axis of the direction of travel. Light which vibrates in one plane only is said to be polarized. If the light passes through such a medium, which may be a filter, it becomes polarized. All the other light waves, which are not vibrating in the right direc-

tion, are absorbed by the filter. Crystals, or filters made from suitably treated materials which are transparent in only one plane are said to be plane polarized.

Most non-metallic reflecting surfaces polarize light naturally, at a particular angle. With glass, which reflects and refracts light falling on it, if the angle of incidence is such that the angle between the reflected and refracted light is 90 degrees the reflected rays are plane polarized. In practical terms this means that the glass will polarize most light rays at about 56 degrees to the perpendicular of the surface. As we shall see later, that fact allows us to cut out some unwanted light reflections from the subject with the aid of a special filter placed over the camera lens (This filter can also be used to darken some areas of the sky because light which comes from the sky at an angle of about 90 degrees to the sun's bearing is strongly polarized.)

What can you make it do?

Light radiates in all directions from a point source. It travels in straight lines. So if you want to control it, you know to a large extent what you are dealing with.

You can control lighting to produce the picture you require. You can arrange it around a subject to give any effect of light and shadow on that subject, at any level of brightness, according to distance or the strength of each individual source.

The light can be diffused at source by different kinds of diffusers which, by varying degrees, soften the appearance of the subject being photographed. Or the light can be focused with lenses, fresnel screens or condensers to concentrate it, brighten it, sharpen the shadows or reflections, increase the contrast or make the light carry over a greater distance.

The light can be deflected with mirrors to change its direction or to increase the number of apparent sources by reflecting another image of the same lamp. It can be bounced off walls or ceilings to diffuse or spread the illumination. In this way it can cover a very wide area with great evenness. It can be bounced off reflectors of

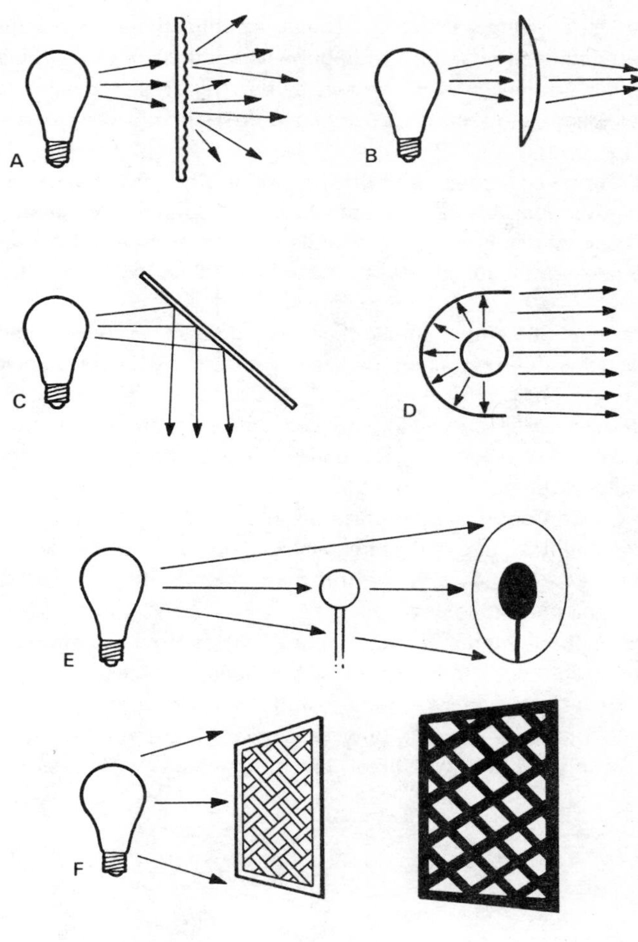

Controlling light. A Light is scattered as it passes through a diffuser. B. It is focused with a lens or condenser. C. It can be bent by mirrors and other reflectors. D. It is gathered and controlled by a bowl reflector. E. It is stopped by an opaque object. F. Or broken into a pattern.

many kinds giving soft, hard or coloured reflections. Or it can be gathered in bowl reflectors around the lamps themselves to be concentrated forward over a particular area. This makes the greatest use of a lamp's output and also allows full control over where the light falls.

Light can be broken up with prisms, or cut off in selected areas by placing opaque objects or shapes in its path. In such a way it can falsify the appearance of a subject by creating shadows that do not really exist and highlights that are not justified by the subject's own contours.

For really exotic effects the light can be coloured, striped, dotted or patterned with filters, screens or any kind of made-up device placed in the light beam.

It is always possible to add light, take some away or make it cover a wider or narrower angle. You can also make it come in a flash, many separate flashes or continuously.

The light can be in the picture itself, or outside it, or both. Or you may add light to that which already exists but is not quite adequate. Or your added light may be the main source, with the existing source just playing an ancillary role.

Some methods mentioned above may provide the basis for normal everyday lighting. Others would be for exceptional cases only – the odd special occasion, or difficult lighting situation.

The main thing is knowing how to exploit the potential of light for any circumstances in which you find yourself taking pictures.

Artificial Light

To take a picture, you need a certain minimum quantity of light. Exactly how much depends on the film, the camera, the subject and what kind of result your are after.

Sometimes you don't actually need to provide any light – you can use what is already there. This may be daylight coming through a window or home lighting which is quite bright in the room where you are taking a photograph. You may need to move a particular lamp a little nearer to the subject, or place the subject closer to the window and that "existing" light is enough.

Is it needed?

In many cases the existing light is not strong enough, it is coming from the wrong direction, or it is wrong for the particular colour film in your camera. Whatever the reason, it is very convenient, and sometimes essential to provide the light yourself – in the form of lamps or flash.

There are special advantages in having your own lighting. You can always be sure to get your picture. An automatic camera, for instance, can refuse to function if there is insufficient light for it to work by. With your own lighting you can avoid that problem by stepping up the light level to the required amount. You also have more control with your own lights; you can move them about wherever you like, changing their angle or distance to suit the subject and the situation. You don't have to move the subject to suit the light. You can use your light to reinforce the existing light coming through a window. There are also occasions when it is useful to have your own light outdoors, in daylight or at night.

Your own light allows you to get brilliantly lit effects in your pictures which are often hard to obtain with existing light, and also to create some other lighting effects which would otherwise be impossible.

For portraits, and pictures of people generally, your own lights enable you to illuminate a face or figure in the most favourable way or to draw out the best or most characteristic feature of a person. You can choose where the shadows are to fall. With flash, you can forget about problems of subject movement. The flash itself lasts for

so short a period that almost all subjects are "frozen" at the moment of exposure. This is very handy when taking pictures of children, animals and other active subjects.
But the main reason for using lamps or flash is that sometimes you find that you just can't do without them!
Any bright lighting that allows you to use a small aperture means all subjects in the same picture can be quite near to, or far away from the camera yet still remain sharp. The small aperture makes it easier to get a subject in sharp focus even if your were slightly inaccurate when setting the focus distance on the camera, using a rangefinder, or focusing the image on a screen.
The manipulation of lights for the interpretation of a subject in front of your camera or even for the effects of light for its own sake, is a most absorbing aspect of photography. It is very satisfying to be able to draw out from the subject with light what you can see with your eyes and so "present it to the camera" from your own point of view.

How much light?

The first requirement is to have enough light for correct exposure of the film in the kind of situation where you normally take photographs and need extra light.
Exposure these days is not the problem it used to be. Most cameras are equipped to take flash and are also suitable for all work at average light levels. So the particular camera you use does not really enter the question of how much light you need.
What does matter is the film. All modern films are fast, that is, very sensitive to light, by the standards of years ago. The average speed film of today is quite adequate for most purposes.
All other things being equal, there is a direct relationship between the speed of the film and the necessary brightness of the subject you are taking. The faster the film, the less light you need. Why not, then, use the fastest film at all times? Because you may want to take other subjects in bright sunshine using the same roll of film,

and for this the fastest film could be a disadvantage or may even prevent you from taking pictures at all. Another reason is that the image quality you can expect with the fastest films is not as good as that from medium speed films. Where considerable enlargement is needed, as with 35 mm film, the grain structure of the film can appear very prominent. Apart from being itself rather obtrusive in the picture, grain breaks up the outline in the subject, loses the fine details and coarsens the tone gradation. For instance, the skin on a child's face, instead of looking soft and even, may be peppered with small grains which are most unattractive. At great degrees of magnification such an effect can resemble a skin disorder.

For normal size pictures, choose a medium speed black and white or colour film. All but the fastest fast colour films, even today, are equivalent in speed to a medium speed black and white emulsion. Correctly exposed and processed, they do not produce images markedly lower in quality than those on medium speed film of the same type.

Film speed can be modified by processing, as can contrast and grain. But these techniques do not concern us here. They are discussed in detail in the Photoguides to *Low Light Photography* and *Processing*.

Having taken these factors into account, how much light do you need?

Whatever type of light you use, you are unlikely to need more than two units, that is, two sources of light. One provides the main light that illuminates and "shapes" the subject; the other is used to adjust the contrast by "filling" the shadow areas left by the main, or "key" light.

A third light may be handy to light the background separately or to provide a highlight or edge effect light in the subject, but this is not essential. In fact, the rather stylized approach, of which such highlighting is a feature, is these days somewhat out of fashion for ordinary day-to-day work.

You can often obtain adequate lighting with only one source – say, a single flash head or photographic lamp, used directly or bounced off a reflecting surface. This can be combined with a portable reflector of some kind to fill shadow areas. But one-lamp lighting is basically

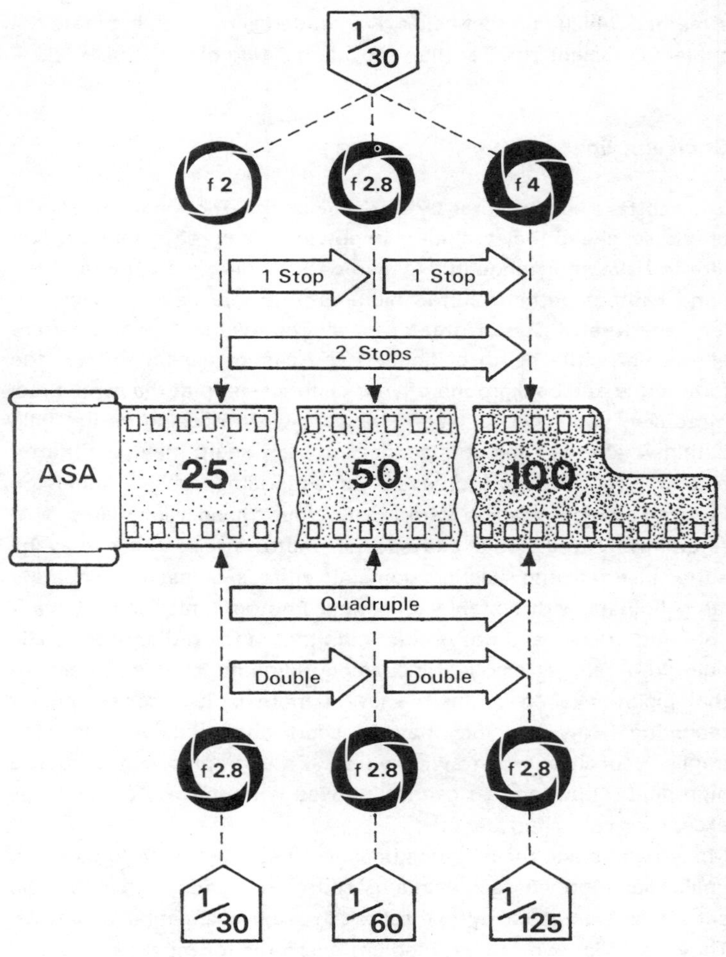

Effect of choosing different films. The film you choose determines the shutter speed and aperture you can set at any particular light level. With a film of twice the speed you may set the aperture one stop smaller for the same shutter speed, or set the shutter to give half the exposure. A film four times as fast allows you to set one stop smaller, or to halve the exposure time again, but such films give more grain.

a method which, in most cases, is intended simply to illuminate the subject sufficiently rather than provide exciting pictorial effects.

Choice of light source

You can take your pictures by domestic lamps. Though plentiful and, of course, cheap they are not very powerful. You require a fairly fast film to have short enough exposures for holding the camera in the hand without getting blurred pictures. And you need a maximum lens aperture of *f*2.8 or greater for average work. A wide aperture allows very little depth of field so you cannot expect to have the foreground and background of your pictures sharp at the same time. Moreover, you have to take extra care with focusing as the field within which the subject appears absolutely sharp may be a matter of only a few inches. Moreover, domestic lamps give a rather too "warm" a colour reading with most colour transparency films.

Alternatively you could use special photo lamps. These may be either inserted into existing domestic fittings or used in separate lamp holders with suitable reflectors. Photographic lamps have a light output several times greater than that of the ordinary domestic bulb. You can get colour transparency films matched for them, so that pictures taken by them show a more or less correct colour rendering. However, they have a short operational life and are fragile, especially when switched on. Photographic lamps have a high heat output and so cannot be used with ordinary lampshades except for very short periods.

Many people like these lamps because they are simple to use and, unlike flash, provide a continuous source of lighting which can be set up and adjusted by eye rather than by calculating distances. They also allow you to set medium apertures for most pictures.

Another type of lighting unit in use these days is the halogen lamp. Originally introduced for movie lighting, this lamp has also found applications in still photography. Halogen lights are suitable for all kinds of colour work, but are relatively expensive and still camera work alone seldom justifies the original outlay.

Flash is undoubtedly the most popular form of light in present day

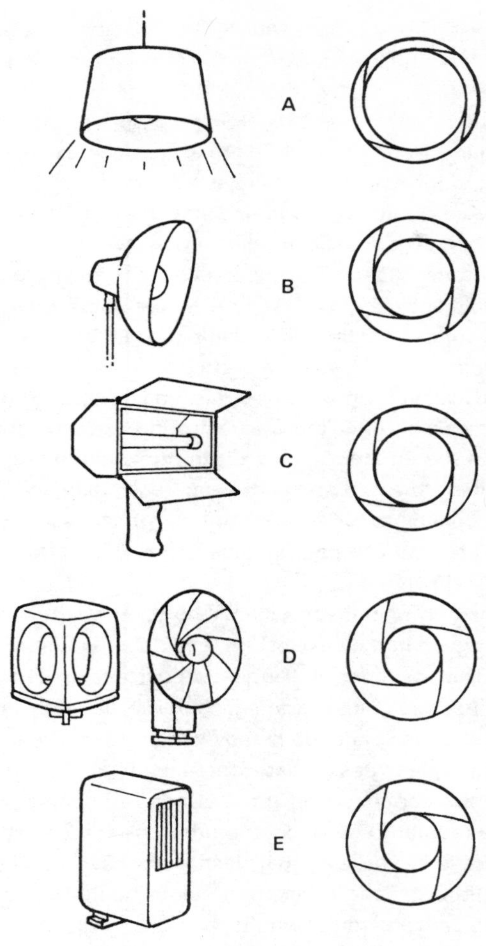

Brightness of the light source. A. Household lights usually demand the widest apertures or longest exposure times. B. Photo lamps are brighter, allowing medium apertures or shorter exposures. C. Halogen movie lamps allow medium apertures or shorter exposures. D. With bulb flash you can work at medium-small apertures. E. Likewise with the more powerful types of electronic unit.

amateur use. This is largely due to the availability of fairly low cost electronic flash units of quite high output for general purposes.

Flash is available in two forms, bulb and electronic. Bulb flash produces light from a bulb containing a self-consuming incandescent filament. One bulb is discharged for each exposure to give an immense output of light in a very short period. Enough to give a full exposure to a photographic film. Bulbs are often supplied in packs (cubes or bars) which discharge in sequence – one for each picture taken. By one means or another each new bulb is prepared automatically for the next shot, until all the bulbs are used up. More traditional forms of bulb flash take individual bulbs which must be inserted and rejected before and after each exposure.

Bulbs are available in various sizes and light outputs, the most powerful of which offer the greatest output of any form of lighting available to the amateur. The sizes in most common use, however, are equivalent to a fairly powerful electronic flash unit. Bulbs in any form are convenient for a small number of exposures or occasional use. They are also compact and comparatively trouble free, but not particularly cheap.

Flash bulbs may be fired by a simple battery or battery and capacitor circuit or, again, in the case of some combined packs without either of these. The triggering unit may be built into the camera. Or the bulbs are inserted in a separate flash unit which may be fitted on to the camera. Those units are mostly very inexpensive in themselves, and being simple in design and construction do not often go wrong.

Owing to the popularity on the one hand of simple cameras with flash circuits built in, and, on the other, of fairly inexpensive electronic units, conventional bulb flash guns have declined in usage. There are now far more electronic units offered for sale than the kind taking conventional flash bulbs.

Electronic flash has one enormous advantage over flash bulbs or cubes. The flash cube which is the source of illumination is capable of being discharged tens of thousands of times before needing replacement. In fact, in the majority of cases the tube never is replaced. The power for this flash usually comes from a small battery or batteries contained within the body of the flash. Some such batteries are rechargeable, making the unit very economical to run. In other respects the flash gun produces an effect very similar to bulbs. There are, however, fundamental differences in the kind of flash produced. These differences do not affect the quality of picture you can obtain with either method when used properly. But they do present a slight problem in synchronizing with the shutter. This and other complications of using the flash with the camera are discussed on page 63.

Flash units for amateur use are designed to be held in the hand or fixed to the camera. Floodlamps are normally used in a separate fitting which is free-standing, clipped to furniture or doors, etc. but not often held in the hand.

Flash units do not permit you to set the lighting arrangement by eye as the flash is far too short lived to be seen in this way. Lighting must be done by calculation. Only professional studio units combine with each flash "head" a separate modelling light which allows the photographer to work out his lighting visually before taking a picture.

The cost

The cost of providing light is not merely a question of the purchase price of lighting units. There is also the running cost, the reliability and the amount of use the equipment is likely to have with the kind of photography you do.

You may wish to spend nothing on providing special light. Your need for lighting may be only occasional and you might be prepared to make do with the ordinary lights found in the home. This does imply some limitations – you have to use wide apertures and slow shutter speeds. But you may *like* to work with this existing light. If you use fast film you may not need special lights anyway.

The next step up in power and economy from household lamps would be a No. 1 photoflood lamp (see page 74). This can be fitted into existing domestic sockets, and so would not require special reflectors, though they can be used.

The more powerful No. 2 lamp has a power consumption and heat output that makes it inadvisable for use in overhead household light fittings. So for these, and photopearl (studio) lamps which all have a higher wattage rating than domestic lamps, you need to buy proper photographic lamp holders.

There is also a special reflector photoflood or photopearl lamp available in wattages equivalent to the ordinary versions. Their mushroom shaped envelope incorporates a reflector so that a separate reflector is not needed. But this lamp has a higher replacement cost, being two or three times the price of conventional lamps.

Photoflood bulbs, because they are overrun, have a short working life – about 2 or 3 hours for a No. 1, and three times that for a No. 2. Photopearls, on the other hand, which are not overrun, last for around 100 hours.

Photoflood lamps are more fragile but cheaper than photopearls. Although they are given an estimated working life by the manufacturer, they tend to be very unpredictable in this respect. You can have one lamp working for only fifteen minutes and another giving you two or three times the rated life expectancy. This means that you should always have spares. If you use them away from home you will have to carry others around with you all the time. You can depend more on photopearls. One spare should be enough to take for a three-lamp set-up.

Unless you are going to use No. 1 photofloods in existing domestic sockets you will have to think of buying lighting units for your photographic lamps. These allow you to position the light where you wish and to control the way in falls, to some extent. The standard type of light fitting is a polished alloy reflector on a floor stand or clip unit for attaching to walls, doors, etc. There are various elaborations of these such as umbrella stands and boom lights. A reflector on its own, which you could fit to an existing tripod or music stand, for instance, would cost no more than the equivalent of a couple of rolls of colour film. The all-up cost of a complete unit, reflector and floor stand, could be about three times this.

You could use photographic and domestic lamps in the same reflectors. Both are available in either a standard screw or bayonet fitting in most countries, although those of higher output may only be available in the screw version.

The wide range of special fittings available for photographic lamps

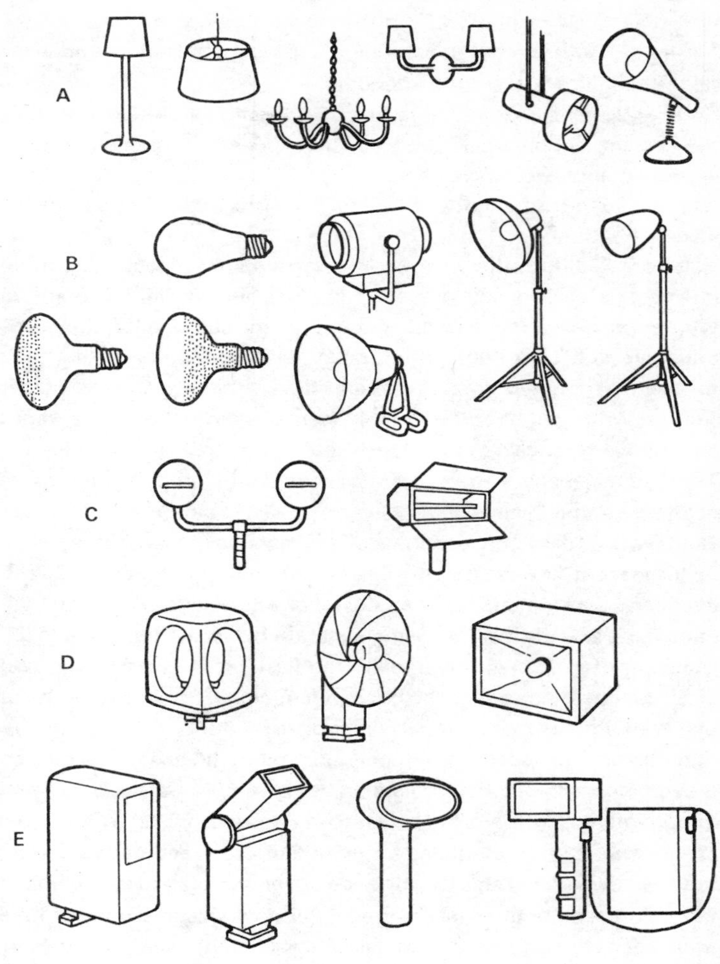

Types of lighting unit. A. Household standard, hanging, chandelier, wall, spot and reading lamps. B. Photo lamps – bare photoflood bulb, focusing spot, open flood, narrow angle flood, mushroom flood, mushroom fixed-focus spot, clip light. C. Halogen movie light – twin head, single head with barn doors. D. Bulb flash – cube, fan reflector, compact. E. Electronic flash – rigid, adjustable, grip, separate power pack.

would naturally involve you in greater outlay than these basic reflector lamps. But for most general work, including portraiture, conventional flood lights are quite adequate.

Spotlights, which allow you to focus the light on a particular area of the subject, are on the whole far more expensive to buy as they are of more complex construction.

A cheaper substitute, however, is the domestic spotlight, though this has a limited output.

Halogen lighting (otherwise known as tungsten halogen or iodine quartz) has certain advantages (page 31) but is a fairly expensive way to provide a continuous light source for still photography. The units are mostly designed for hand held use (though they can usually be mounted on a stand) and have a more elaborate holder than the ordinary photoflood. Replacement lamps (rated life about 12 hours) are considerably more expensive than a photoflood.

These days many people opt for flash, both on the grounds of economy and convenience.

Bulb flash is really only economical for occasional one-lamp lighting. The cheapest (lowest power) flash bulbs multiply the cost of each exposure considerably. These cost considerations apply to both cube flash and the method using separate bulbs. In fact, a whole roll of colour negative film used with bulb flash would work out at two or three times the cost of the original film alone. So, for this scale of use they are not really the wisest choice.

Then there is the cost of a unit or "gun" to fire the flash. This may be a separate unit. But simple cameras often incorporate a bulb firing arrangement and a socket for inserting a cube or bar so for these there is no need to purchase an extra unit. Even separate units are not, however, expensive, whether designed for flash cubes, bulbs or in some cases both. You can get a quite serviceable one for little more than the cost of a roll of colour transparency film. The battery it contains need be replaced only very infrequently. The main running cost is the supply of the cubes or bulbs themselves. A packet of half a dozen bulbs costs more or less the same as a black and white film. Flash cubes are slightly more expensive shot for shot.

Obviously if you are going to do much flash photography, then despite the low initial outlay for the flash gun, this method could run you to considerable expense, especially with more than one unit used at a time.

Electronic units, though mostly far more expensive than bulb flash soon repay the high initial outlay. For units which run off ordinary batteries the cost of each flash is equivalent to the cost of the battery divided by the number of flashes you get from it. Most units, however, can also be run directly off the home power supply. The cost of flashes in this case is negligible. There are also rechargeable batteries available for some units. These nicad (nickel cadmium) batteries cost about five times as much as the conventional type but have a very long working life if kept in reasonable condition.

Electronic units are most often used for one-lamp photography, though many models are available with extra "heads". Sometimes it is just as economical to buy a second flash gun.

The two basic types of electronic unit, manual and automatic (or computer) (page 47) do not vary widely in price, though the more versatile automatic units may cost two or three times as much as the simpler models.

If you use more than one flash you may need a stand for one. Flash units can be mounted in special reflectors but for most photography they are used as they are, so there is no further expense for ancillary equipment.

Studio flash units designed for professional use have several times the light output of the ordinary type. Each lighting head may operate from a central slave unit but whatever the arrangement, the cost per lighting head can be as high as that of a medium priced camera.

Their usefulness

Household lamps are satisfactory for photography provided that you do not require great depth of field in your pictures, or effects full of brilliance with broad areas of highlight and many specular reflections. The pictures are more likely to show large areas of heavy shadow, strongly modelled volumes and many extremes of contrast generally – especially when the subjects are placed near to light sources in order to shorten exposure times.

Lamps found in the rooms of an average house offer a wide range of lighting for photographers. Some lamps may be shaded, giving diffused light. Others may be open, offering hard, direct lighting. Some are close to the wall, reflecting light from a broad area, whereas others, placed on their own, may be more directional in their effect. If you take into account central fittings, standard lamps, table lamps, wall lights, decorative hall lights, fluorescent or daylight striplights, and domestic spot lamps you can see that there is a veritable arsenal of lighting units at your disposal – all free of charge.

Household lamps can be used for filling the shadow side of subjects photographed by light through the widows, provided you are shooting in black and white. They balance well in strength with daylight and give just the right amount of "lift" to the shadows without overpowering the daylight and giving effects that appear unnatural. But, being far warmer in colour than daylight, the mixture of the two sources in colour pictures looks rather odd, though some people find it acceptable.

Photofloods have a high enough light output to permit you to set medium apertures when using fast colour film yet give short enough exposures to hold the camera in the hand. Alternatively, they provide enough light to be used indirectly though this may require you to set a fairly wide aperture, and/or have the camera on a tripod.

There is enough output from a single photoflood to light quite a large area indoors. Several lamps could be used if necessary. This would still not be very expensive. With effective large-area lighting, the subject can move about freely and always be well lit without needing to be pursued with a lamp held at a certain distance. Photoflood light is warmer in tone than daylight but not as red as that from domestic lamps. You can get colour films suitable for use with floods, but, whatever your film is balanced for, you get odd effects if you mix light of different colours. Photofloods are quite satisfactory for filling the shadow areas of window-lit subjects in black and white though they have to be kept at a distance or used indirectly to avoid overdoing the effect.

The wide variety of reflectors available for photofloods and indeed all continuous source lamps (except halogen units) allows an incomparable measure of control over the lighting. The light can be built up by eye using the conventional approach – key-fill-effect-background, and minor adjustments made at will to any of these lamps.

Halogen lamps, though sometimes fitted with barn doors (hinged shades) do not otherwise offer any special advantages this way. Those with the more versatile fittings tend to be expensive. Light from halogens, though bright, is sometimes rather uneven, being concentrated in a narrow angle more suitable to the angle of view of a movie camera lens than that on a still camera.

All continuous sources have the disadvantage of trailing leads to power sockets, which are liable to be tripped over. The maximum length of the lead can also restrict the placing of a light. Photofloods are normally on stands and leads hanging from the tops of these are a special hazard. Lamps dependent on a main power supply are, of course, largely restricted to use indoors.

Bulb flash units are very compact and light in weight. They may even be built in to the camera. If so, you need only carry a packet of bulbs or cubes with you, yet have all the light you need for most general snapshooting. The AG1 or AG3B bulb, for instance, has the equivalent output of a medium power electronic unit. Used directly (undiffused) they allow medium apertures to be set with average speed black and white and fast colour film for almost any indoor pictures. The on-camera position which many units compel you to use places limitations on the quality of the lighting you get. But it is a simple and effective expedient if you are only seeking enough light for the job and nothing else. (This position is quite good for filling shadows, however, when the main light comes from the other side of the subject.)

Ordinary bulb flashes can be bounced off light coloured surfaces if the subject is not too far away. But for real versatility with indirect illumination, bounced or diffused, you need the more powerful PF5 bulb. The biggest bulbs are the most powerful light sources available and compare in output only with powerful studio flash units. The PF5, for instance, used direct, allows small apertures to be set for most interior shots. The PF6 (same size as PF5), is designed to produce light over a much longer period, so that it can be used with focal plane shutter cameras. Effectively, then, it lets you use the same apertures as an AG3B bulb in the same circumstances. Bulb flash units are more mobile in use than photofloods, which have to be adjusted for distance with moving subjects unless they are covering the whole shooting area with sufficient light. The flash can move *with*, or be *on* the camera. It can be used with daylight as a fill-in or main light and matches correctly in colour with daylight balanced materials. Being always entirely free of external power sources bulb flash units may be used outdoors as main or shadow-filling sources, or at night for special effects and where the lamps in the picture do not give sufficient light for full exposure.

Although there are no leads to power sockets there is a synchronizing lead to the camera. The length of this naturally determines how far the flash unit may be placed from the camera position. Some on-camera units have a direct contact (hot shoe) with a triggering circuit in the camera. Others have a hot shoe or external sync lead, so you have a choice of methods. With all bulb flash units you have to work out the aperture to set in accordance with the distance of the subject from the flash and the speed of film you are using.

Electronic flash combines many of the advantages of bulb or cube flash with a good many of its own. However, the smaller manual units have a rather low power output, much less than a flash cube. They are useful only for direct lighting unless you are shooting in close up when they could be bounced off a suitable reflector placed nearby, or your own body. Such units are normally mounted on the camera or held in the hand.

Medium power electronic units are much more versatile and can be bounced off walls or ceilings provided that the subject is not too far off. Even those, however, are not suitable for the largest interiors where you might want a small enough aperture to give considerable depth of field in the picture. For this purpose a powerful unit is more or less essential.

Some of the better units are available with more than one lighting head, or two units can be used with a common sync lead to the camera. One head might be used direct and one bounced off the wall or ceiling.

An electronic unit takes only a few seconds after each flash to prepare itself for the next discharge. You are, of course, free from the chore of changing bulbs. Some units offer variable angles of lighting coverage, but any reasonably powerful electronic flash can be mounted on an umbrella unit, or at least put on a stand and fired at a reflector for this purpose.

Many modern units offer automatic light control, which obviates the need to make aperture/distance calculations for each shot. A sensor in the gun adjusts the amount of output from the unit by picking up light reflected back from the subject and cutting it off after a set amount has bounced back. In most cases this works quite efficiently but, as with many such devices, there are occasions when they can be misled by peculiarities in the scene. With non-automatic units you can use a flash meter instead (p. 251).

In the next chapter we will examine flash in greater detail.

Flash

One can compare flash and continuous light sources in a number of ways. No two lighting methods give the same light. Further, the mechanical side of any lighting method has certain points to recommend it, as well as limitations. The final choice may be for the method which seems most convenient for the purpose in hand. Or it may be the result of personal caprice!

Flash, however, is for many people the assumed light source. Often it is part and parcel of their photographic outfit. Many camera manufacturers make a flash unit with their own cameras specifically in mind. It may even be built in to the camera or at least designed in such a way that the two go together conveniently, but not so well with other partners – though this is more a feature of equipment of the past than the present. The only unifying factor today might be a high price!

Many manufacturers take it for granted that when the average camera owner needs extra light, he uses flash. Why should this be so? Flash has many things working in its favour and some of these were touched on in the previous chapter. Let us summarise them all:

A flash unit is portable, light and quick in operation. It can work independently of a power socket, though some can use one when convenient. It can provide light where you otherwise can't get it – indoors or out. It can arrest rapid action which many camera shutters could not. Nowadays it can give fairly reliable automatic exposures without taking readings or making calculations. It is simple to use. It mixes well in colour quality with daylight when the two sources appear in the same picture. It can be used on the camera for simple picture-taking, leaving both hands free to operate the camera controls. It is inexpensive if one head is used, and still relatively so when two flash units are necessary.

Now consider the main points ranged against the use of flash:

The actual lighting is not seen even at the moment of exposure because it is too fast for the eye. (With a single lens reflex camera you don't even see the flash as the mirror is up during the exposure, blocking off the viewfinder.) So it is not possible to adjust the lighting by eye (except with very expensive professional studio sets which have continuous tungsten modelling lights built in). It is also difficult to see disturbing reflections from objects in the scene, such as a window pane, gloss paint on woodwork or walls, a glass cabinet, mirror or TV screen. For normal operation the camera shutter must be synchronised for flash exposures (all modern ones are) but there are restrictions on the shutter speed that may be set on focal plane shutters.

Although there is the advantage of automatic flash exposure control on some equipment, it can be misled in certain conditions and cause errors in exposure. There are also shortcomings in the range and power of some electronic units compared with the claims made for them and many units are marketed which are suitable only for simple, direct use on the camera. The design or power output of many units, in fact, promotes frontal flash from the camera position with its attendant risks of poor modelling, black shadows forming a rim round the subject and the "red eye" effect. From an on-camera position even the angle adjustment for bounce flash provided on some models is a compromise solution – conceived more for the appeal of neat design than a genuine function for good lighting. Most flash units are intended for single lamp lighting, but there are methods for using more than one unit, though the need to synchronise additional heads increases the cost to more than just that of a second unit.

Weigh up these pros and cons and then decide whether flash is for you. We will now examine individual flash systems and their applications in greater detail.

Electronic units

Electronic flash is a method of obtaining a light sufficient for photography by causing a sudden discharge of electricity across the gap separating two electrodes. It has a distant antecedent in the early experiments in spark photography made by W. H. Fox Talbot in 1851.

In a modern electronic flashgun the flash is caused by the release of electrical energy through a gas filled tube with electrodes at either end. The energy, to be of sufficient force to flow in this way is first allowed to build up in a capacitor placed in the main circuit from the source of power, the batteries or accumulator. In its normal condition, the gas which is within the tube and forming the only link between the two electrodes, does not conduct electricity. When the flash is fired, a primary or "triggering" high tension charge is first released from a separate capacitor. This has the effect of ionizing the gas, so turning it into a conductor. The main charge may then flow through the tube causing the bright, but short lived flash by which you can take a picture. The triggering circuit acts like a valve for the main discharge, since immediately after each flash the gas returns to its normal non-conductive condition and will not allow electricity to flow until it is again ionized.

Closing of the triggering circuit may be effected either by an independent button release on the flash unit or through a synchronizing lead which is attached to the camera shutter. When the shutter is released, two small electrical contacts inside come together at precisely the right moment, to ensure that the brief flash can occur when the shutter is fully open. (The exact method of timing or synchronization with different shutter and flash methods is discussed below.)

Although the current from the main capacitor in such a flashgun is quite high, it is not this which passes across the contacts in the camera shutter, but the charge from the triggering circuit, which is far less. The camera contacts are not designed to cope with more than the demands of the average triggering circuit. (In arrangements where two guns are operated from the same synchronizing point on a camera the doubling up of the current puts an extra strain on contacts and may, after a period cause them some damage; see page 62. There are however, other methods of doing this without such a risk).

As the charge for the capacitors is commonly derived from a low voltage battery or accumulator source, it must pass via a transistor circuit, or transformer and rectifier, to emerge at a high voltage suitable for storage in the capacitor.

The actual period during which this process takes place and sufficient energy is stored in the capacitor for a flash discharge, can be a matter of several seconds from the moment the gun is switched on. The time it takes after each flash for the capacitors to fully recharge, ready for the next, is known as the recycling time. This

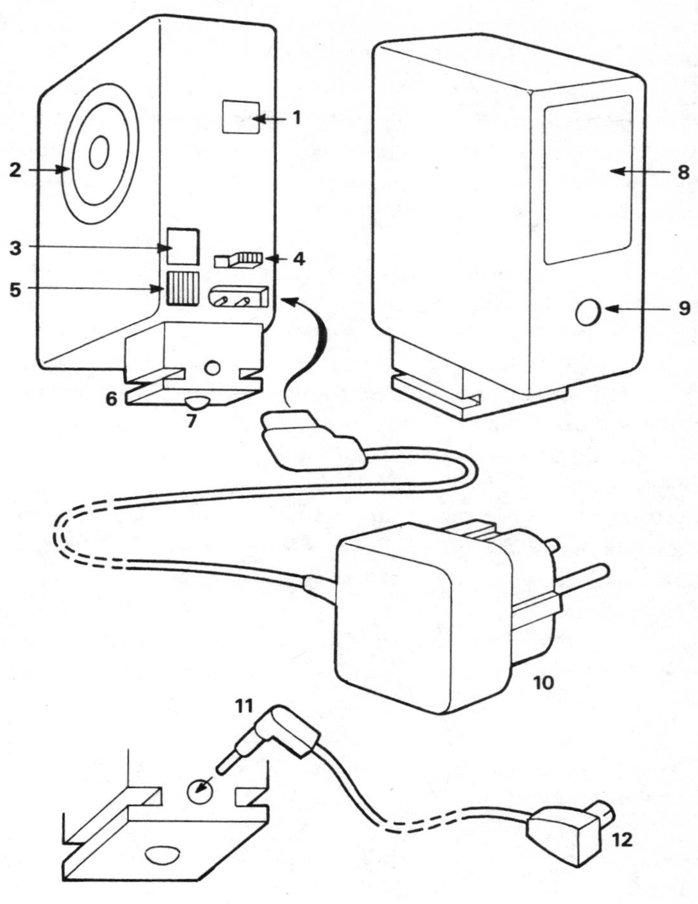

Electronic flash unit. 1. Film speed setting. 2. Exposure calculator. 3. Ready-to-shoot indicator. 4. On/off switch. 5. Open flash firing button (and/or auto/manual selector on auto guns). 6. Accessory shoe fitting. 7. Hot shoe flash contact. 8. Diffuser window. 9. Auto light sensor. 10. Charger unit. 11. Sync lead pin and socket with hot shoe contact cut-out. 12. Sync plug to camera shutter contacts.

recycling time depends on such factors as the design of the circuit and the type and condition of the batteries.

In some automatic units, recycling time also depends on how much of the energy from the previous flash was actually expended, since they have the provision to cut off the flash when only the required amount is released and leave the remaining unused portion of the charge in the capacitor. The requisite "topping up" of current from the power pack is therefore more quickly accomplished. With this method, energy is also conserved by the release for each flash of the exact amount needed, whereas with non-automatic units (and many automatics) the whole of the energy stored in the capacitor is released each time it is fired.

In the case of automatic units of this type the unwanted portion of the charge is "dumped" in a black-flash discharge tube arranged in parallel with the main tube. The charge is thus dispersed without effect.

The actual portion of the charge to be used by the flash tube in an automatic unit whatever the system, is determined by the built in light sensor as it reads the light from the flash which is reflected back by the subject (page 47).

Some units have full and half power settings which, besides their photographic uses also allow some economies in battery consumption.

Types of unit

Electronic flash units are made in several forms. There are small units, often rectangular in shape, which are designed to fit on the camera. These are usually of low or medium power and contain their own batteries.

A variation of this form is the so-called "professional" type fitted with a handle (in some cases battery compartment). This is primarily designed for hand holding, but may be mounted on a bracket alongside the camera. The design of such a unit obviously owes something to the traditional press-style flashgun. Although it is considerably more expensive than the average rectangular type most

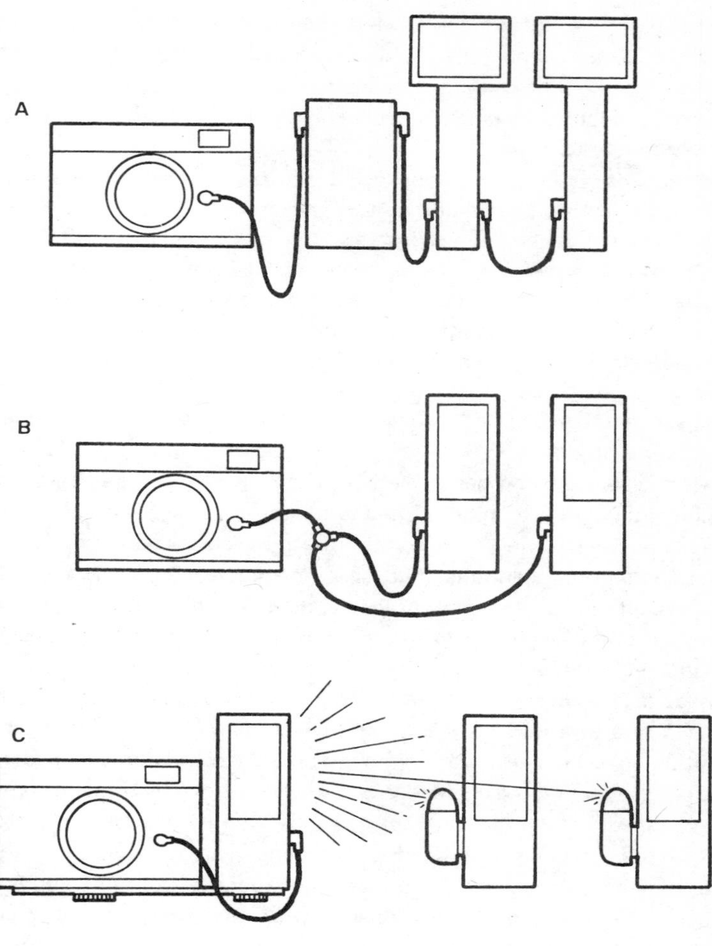

Multi-head flash. A. Units with independent flash heads operating off a separate power pack and synchronised via leads. B. Two units, each containing its own power source synchronised via a Y-connector lead from camera contacts. C. Main flash unit with a sync lead to the camera triggers additional units via light sensor slaves.

models do not offer much advantage if any, over those in terms of power. Again, although the unit sits in the hand more comfortably when used off the camera, it may prove less convenient for propping up on random objects when needed in a position which is out of the photographers reach.

Flashguns with higher output such as the standard professional type normally have a separate power pack which is relatively bulky because of the extra power storage capacity the gun demands. Such a power pack may use a rechargeable nickel cadmium accumulator. The flash head may be of the "press" type, but a further variation is the ring flash which is fitted to the front of the camera and provides shadowless illumination from the circular flash tube surrounding the lens.

These units can be fitted to (or adapted with rings to fit) most lenses of normal diameter.

More elaborate, and generally more expensive still, is the very high power studio flash unit designed to operate from a stand. The flash head may in some cases contain the power pack, or power may originate from a central source. Like most flash units, it may also be operated from main supply. These units allow adjustment of power output and have sufficient power to be used direct or indirect, say, reflected from an umbrella, and still allow small apertures to be set. A particular advantage of the studio flash set is the inclusion in each head of a tungsten modelling light which allows the lighting to be arranged in the same way as a normal continuous source by observing its effect on the subject. When the flash is fired the subject is lit in (approximately) the same way as seen with the modelling lights. As more than one flash head is commonly used for studio lighting each unit is normally fired from a central power pack or fitted with a flash triggering light sensor. The flash from one head is picked up by the sensor on another, and this then automatically fires the other unit.

Either arrangement avoids the need for more than one synchronizing connection to the camera shutter (page 62).

Studio flash units are available in the form of variable angle spotlights and floods, though such equipment is prohibitively expensive for most amateurs.

Automatic and manual flash

Four main factors govern the exposure of film by electronic flash; the speed of the film, the power output of the flash unit, the distance of the flash from the subject and the aperture set on the camera. (The question of shutter speed as a variable in exposure only enters in to flash photography where flashbulbs are used with M or FP synchronization, discussed on page 65, an arrangement which is wasteful of light.) All these factors work together to give the right exposure.

In practice, having selected the film to be used, correct exposure can be ensured by two methods of control. Either the camera lens aperture must be adjusted to suit the amount of flash light reflected from the subject, or the amount of flash light reaching the subject must be adjusted by varying the flash-to-subject distance or the quantity of light emitted by the flash unit. "Manual" flash units produce a fixed amount of light unless they can be used at a different power setting such as on "half power". Most manual units do not have this provision and therefore their power output is more or less constant and *known*. To vary brightness of illumination you must bring them closer or take them further away from the subject. The change in illumination of the subject can be exactly calculated. (You can also reduce the light by partially shielding it, filtering it or using it indirectly, but this is rather a hit and miss method as, without a flash meter you can not be sure by how much the light is reduced). Alternatively, you may adjust the aperture set on the camera to increase the amount of light from the subject reaching the film. It follows that each time a subject moves towards or away from the flash unit, or the unit itself is moved, an adjustment must be made to the lens aperture to compensate for the change. This must be calculated.

Manual guns (and most automatic ones) have a calculator disc incorporated in the body. This indicates the appropriate aperture settings at given flash distances when used with films of different ASA speeds (see Exposure, p. 248).

Automatic (or computerized) flash units eliminate this inconvenience by a device which controls the light output of the tube. When the flash is fired a tiny light sensor directed at the subject measures the amount of light it reflects and cuts it off when it has received enough for the aperture which has been set. The sensor may be a separate unit, or incorporated in the gun. Whichever is the case, it is much more convenient if it allows the measurement of light reflected from the subject even if the gun is used indirectly – i.e. bounced off a wall.

The amount of light reflected by the subject partly depends on its own tone. The light sensor on a flash unit works in something like the same way as an exposure meter reading the light reflected from the subject *as a whole*. While this is useful when it takes into account any light already falling on the subject from sources other than the flash itself, the sensor can also be misled by subjects containing wide variations of tone. If, for example, the main subject of interest is dark but most of the surroundings are light, the flash cuts out when the *whole area* has received enough light. It does not know that you are mainly interested in a dark subject. Consequently that dark subject may be underexposed. For different situations such as this compensations can be made in the way the unit is programmed to work. It is useful to have the additional facility of manual control and most automatic units have this.

Some "computer" units demand that you set one particular aperture for any given film speed. Others let you choose between two or more. As the automatic operation of the flash, in effect, shortens the exposure time as it quenches the flash, the wider the aperture set or the closer the subject the shorter the flash duration. Whereas the duration of flash on a conventional manual unit might be 1/500 sec, on an automatic unit in the right conditions (i.e. very close up) it can be as short as 1/40 000 sec.

Maintenance and cost

Some electronic units are designed to run off batteries, some off main power supply, and some off either. The batteries used may be expendable or suitable for recharging. These different methods vary widely in their maintenance demands and running cost. The most

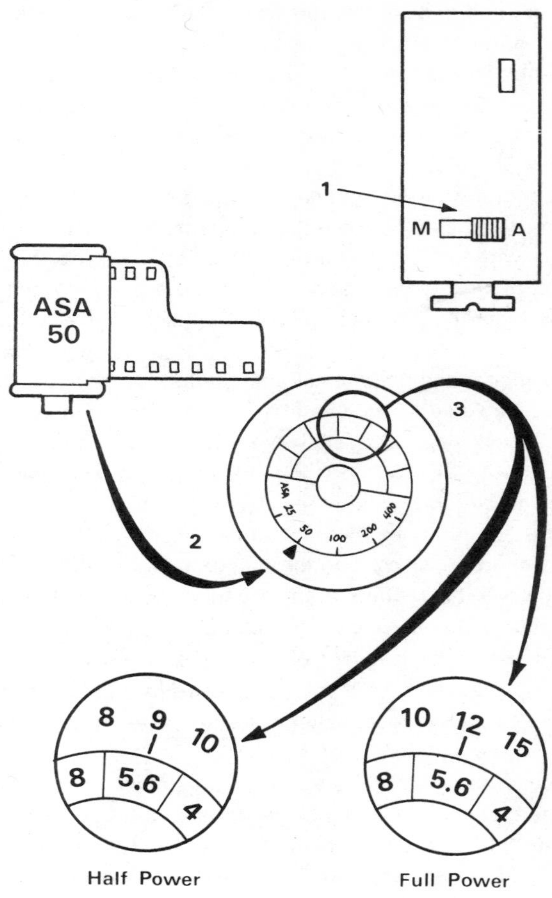

Electronic flash. Automatic: 1. Set 'automatic' on the mode selector. 2. Set the film speed on the calculator dial. 3. Read off the aperture to use for automatic operation. The maximum shooting distance is also indicated. Many guns offer auto operation on several apertures which are set according to your distance, range or depth of field requirements. Some powerful guns allow selection of full or half power operation.

economical method also depends on the type and frequency of use to which the unit is put.

Most low power and many medium power flash units are designed to run off two or more ordinary dry batteries such as pen cells or some of the other small sized varieties used in portable transistorized equipment.

The number of flashes you get depends on the power of the gun and the type of batteries. The rough estimates below apply to medium-sized guns without "energy-saving" circuits. Towards the end of battery life, though, recycling times increase. It is usually an impractically long recycling time that makes you change (or recharge) your battery.

The conventional carbon-zinc cell may be used, preferably the leak proof sort. They give something like 30–40 flashes per set.

Far more flashes (say, 100 with a typical flashgun) can be obtained from manganese alkaline cells which are widely available in the same sizes as carbon zinc batteries. Although much more expensive, their useful life is at least three times greater. They maintain a reasonably short recycling time through most of their life even when use is concentrated within a short period, but they tend to fail rapidly when they near exhaustion. Manganese alkaline cells are a better proposition for frequent use, but possibly carbon zinc cells work out more economically if the unit is used only intermittently. Carbon zinc cells do recover voltage to some extent if there are long enough intervals between use.

Mercury cells have often more consistent power delivery in continuous use than either of the above-mentioned types, and a longer storage life than any other type of battery. They do not have quite the working life of a manganese alkaline cell and are not so widely available. They are also fairly expensive.

Very popular for all types of electronic flash units these days are nickel cadmium (NiCad) rechargeable batteries. Unlike some other rechargeable units they are completely sealed in a leakproof case. Economically, this would seem very attractive, as the cells can be recharged from the mains (via a suitable transformer etc.) at low cost, and if properly maintained will last indefinitely. However the initial purchase price is extremely high, they give relatively few

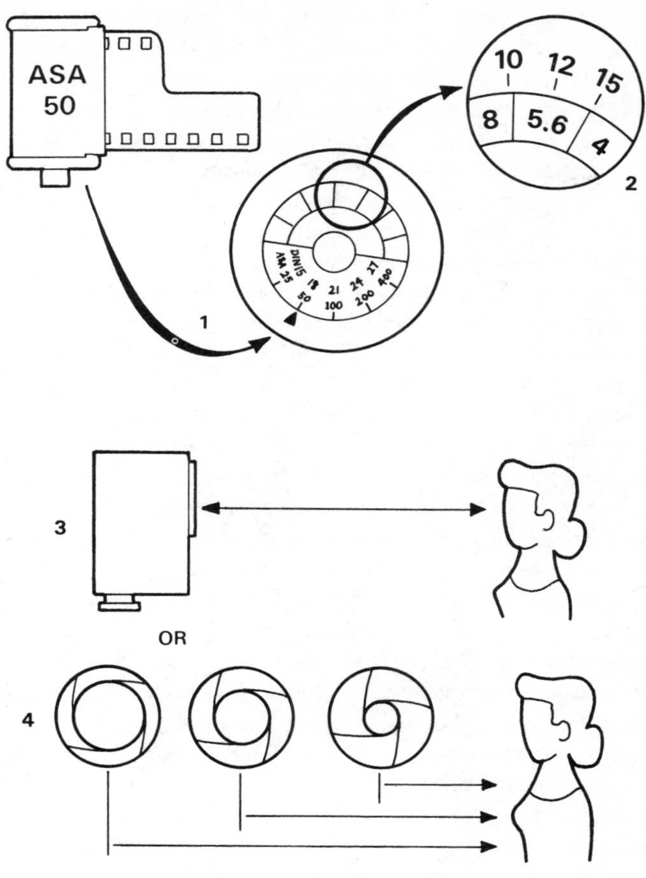

Electronic flash. Manual: 1. Set the film speed on the calculator dial. 2. Read off the aperture to be set for each flash distance. 3. Adjust the flash distance for the aperture set or, 4. Adjust the aperture to suit the flash distance.

flashes before they need recharging or replacement with fully charged cells and they need frequent recharging (every few weeks) *even when not in use* as they self-discharge quite rapidly. They are therefore best suited to more or less constant use and you need more than one set if you want a lot of flashes. Often the cells need up to 12 hours for recharging. The recycling time with NiCad cells lengthens after only a few flashes have been fired. So, all in all, they are something of a mixed blessing.

Some large flash units still use the older type of (wet) lead/acid accumulator for a power source, though for its operational convenience the NiCad type has replaced it in much equipment. Nevertheless the lead/acid type has advantages when compared with NiCads. Some lead/acid accumulators have about three times the storage capacity of the equivalent NiCad and it can maintain a short recycling time even with constant use. A large gun can be recharged in 12–16 hours (6 v). Many have a recycling time of 1–15 sec, and with a lead/acid accumulator may allow between 180–200 flashes compared with the 70–80 expected with a rechargeable NiCad cell.

Lead/acid accumulators must be kept in a reasonably well charged condition. Like NiCad cells, they lose the charge gradually with storage. Also, the dilute acid electrolyte must be occasionally topped up with the distilled water which is slowly consumed in the operation of charging and recharging. If left in a discharged state the plates accumulate a coating which renders the battery useless, and it must then be replaced.

The state of charge of a wet accumulator is often indicated by a visible signal in the side.

Clearly, whatever the type of cell or accumulators used there are always going to be some drawbacks, if only the need to replace the cells occasionally.

The life or charge of any cell can be greatly extended if the unit is used on a mains power supply wherever possible. This means having an extra trailing lead, unless you disconnect the unit just before each shot but this is often not too inconvenient provided it is kept out of the picture. It is a far more economical method of operation than any other, but is, of course, confined to indoor work.

Ready light

When the condensers are charged, this is indicated by a neon ready light. However, except with some professional equipment, the recycling time indicated can be deceptive. The light is supposed to indicate a fully charged capacitor, but many are deliberately set to come on before the capacitor is fully charged – probably to give the impression of a rapid recycling time of which the equipment is not really capable. If the unit is fired immediately the light comes on you may not obtain the full quantity of flash light you expect, but perhaps only three quarters of it. Resulting pictures could be underexposed. Therefore with all small units it is advisable to wait for a few more seconds to ensure that the capacitor is, in fact, fully charged for the flash.

Bulb flash

A flash bulb is an oxygen-filled sealed glass envelope containing a filament of fine zirconium, aluminium or magnesium wire or foil. The wire burns with a brilliant light when a primer also inside the bulb is ignited with a charge of electricity. The charge is introduced via two terminals in the base of the bulb which connect with a battery ignition circuit in the camera or flashgun. The filament disintegrates when the flash is fired and so serves for only one exposure. The bulb must then be discarded.

The flashbulb contains an indicator spot which, when blue, shows that the bulb is in useable condition, and when pink, that the bulb has deteriorated through leakage and should therefore not be used. Most flashbulbs have a blue laquer coating which serves the dual purpose of adjusting the light output to balance in colour quality with daylight type colour film and preventing the bulb from exploding from the intense heat of the burning filament. Such bulbs carry the designation "B" after the number. A few bulbs are clear-coated, and so do not balance with daylight.

Small bulbs have two kinds of fitting – the type found on AG3B bulbs and that found on PF1B and some other bulbs such as the more powerful PF5B and 6B. Neither has a metal "cap". Some flashguns or built-in flash units only accept either one or other of these bulbs but many will accept both. The bulb is fitted by just pushing it in. After firing, the hot bulb is ejected by pressing a button or lever in the unit.

Another type of bulb used on some Polaroid equipment and other flash units marketed in the United States is the M3. This is a clear bulb with a metal cap fitting. It has approximately twice the light output of an AG3B. (Comparative figures are, in fact, 7500 and 16 000 lumen seconds respectively). The light may be "blued" by positioning a suitably coloured screen in front of the bulb.

The largest bulbs, PF60 and PF100 have their own type of fitting and would not be used in the ordinary small flashguns designed for amateur work.

Cube flash

A flash cube is a transparent package containing four blue flashbulbs which may be fired in succession. It is designed for convenience. There is no need to remove each bulb after firing and replace it with another. The cube, with a bulb on each of four sides is automatically rotated in its socket on the camera as the film is wound on to the next frame. Separate cube flash units are also available. After the fourth flash, the whole cube is discarded and replaced with another.

There are two types of cube flash which vary in the method used for firing.

Firing bulbs and cubes

Flashbulbs are fired by an electric charge from a battery. The bulb may be in a simple circuit with the battery and contacts in the camera shutter. When the shutter is released these contacts close, the current flows and the bulb is fired – synchronized with the exposure. This system works well provided that the charge from the

battery is sufficient to fire the bulb. If it fails, that may be due to resistance to the current from poor (dirty) contacts, an over-long synchronizing lead or a nearly exhausted battery.
Another type of circuit is more reliable, though due to the efficiency of modern batteries may be dispensed with in some units. This uses a battery and resistor in circuit with the bulb and a capacitor. The capacitor is charged by a steady flow of current through the resistor and bulb. The current is insufficient to fire the bulb. When the shutter contacts close, the battery and resistor are shorted out and the capacitor placed in a circuit with the bulb, which it then fires. The capacitor is not recharged until another bulb is inserted. Thus, if no bulb is fitted the unit is in effect "switched off" and there is no drain on the battery. The battery fitted is usually of very small size but relatively high voltage, e.g.: 15 v or $22\frac{1}{2}$ v. In capacitor circuits it must be inserted the right way round only.
Ignition of the bulb may be via a synchronising lead to the camera flash socket or a direct contact in the camera accessory shoe.
It is possible to use some units independently of the shutter on "open flash". For this, you set the camera shutter on B, open it, fire the flash yourself and then close the shutter. (See page 224.)
Many flash units have a checking device which gives a small glow when the bulb is inserted or when a button is pressed. That indicates that the battery and circuit are in a condition to fire the bulb. A testing lamp is also available. This is a substitute for the flashbulb and is inserted in the usual socket. When the unit is fired, the testing lamp glows momentarily. That shows that the whole circuit, including the camera shutter contacts, is in working order.
Cube flash comes in two types. Ordinary flash cubes use the simple battery and shutter contact method employed by flashguns. Because in most cases the triggering circuit is in the camera itself and there is no lengthy synchronizing lead to the camera shutter, a simple circuit is reliable enough.
Magicubes do not use a battery, but are self-igniting. When the shutter is released a probe in the camera is driven in to the base of the cube. This activates a sprung latch which strikes a percussion cap. The cap ignites and fires the bulb.
Flash cubes and magicubes are not interchangeable and may only

be used in the sockets designed to accept either one type of cube or the other.

Another system of bulb ignition is the piezo-electric method where the bulb is triggered by an electric charge generated mechanically. When the shutter is released a tiny hammer strikes the piezo-electric ceramic element. This releases a small charge which activates a special priming-charge paste and fires the bulb. Piezo-electric flash was developed for use in suitably equipped pocket 110 cameras and is available as an 8-bulb cartridge which positions the bulbs far enough away from the lens axis to avoid the troublesome "red eye" effect (Page 136). The bulbs, though small, have an output equivalent to that of conventional flashbulbs.

Very little maintenance is required for bulb flash units of any type other than occasional replacement of the batteries. However, should the unit fail to fire, it would be as well to check that all the contacts inside, such as those on the battery and capacitor are clean, and that both these are making a proper connection.

With bulb flash, the initial outlay for the purchase of the unit is very low, the price of a roll or two of colour film. But the running cost is relatively high with 10 AG3B bulbs costing as much as a black-and-white film. This type of unit is definitely for the occasional indoor user.

It does, additionally, have the advantage of extreme compactness and light weight. Most units will slip easily into the pocket, even with a packet of bulbs.

Bulb fittings

Flash cubes (PF C4) fit a special socket either on the camera or a separate holder. Magicubes have a different socket. This can be on the camera or on an extender which is fitted on to the camera and simply holds the cube far enough away from the camera to avoid the red eye effect in direct flash pictures. Both types allow the cube to be rotated.

AG3B (all glass) bulbs have a flattened glass base without a cap. Most small bulb units accept this size. The fitting on type 1B, 5B

and 6B capless bulbs is larger but some flashguns accept this and the AG3B type with a quick adjustment of the socket.
Equivalent bulbs used in the US (apart from the all-glass AG3B which is uniform everywhere) have metal cap fittings. M213 and M313 have a small bayonet. 5B, 25B and 6B and 26B focal plane bulbs all have large bayonet caps. Small bayonet bulbs are intended for use in 3 inch reflectors and the large bayonet type in 4–5 inch reflectors.
The very largest bulbs, type 60, 60/97, 100 and 100/79 all have ES screw fittings and these can only be used in special large-socket guns.
Some flashguns designed to accept metal cap bayonet bulbs also have an adaptor for capless bulbs.

Lighting power

You can not judge the power of an electronic flashgun merely by its physical size – they are only vaguely related.
The output of a bulb flash unit depends on the sizes of bulb it uses and the efficiency of its reflector.
The output of the two types of unit may be compared in very general terms. For instance, you would expect the output of a low power electronic unit to be less than that of any bulb. Medium power electronic units (which can still be quite compact physically) have an output somewhere in the region of the smaller bulbs, such as the AG3B and 1B, M2B and cubes. The most powerful portable flash units match the more powerful 5B type bulb in output.
The type 60 bulb is only matched by fairly powerful studio flash and the 100 is the most powerful bulb of all. These bulbs are very expensive; three or four equal the price of a roll of 35 mm colour film. They provide the output of a very powerful and hefty studio flash set, but can be held in the hand! They are basically intended for professional use. The average person is unlikely to need anything like so much light, unless they want to illuminate a large hall full of people where a great light output allows a small enough aperture to get the picture sharp from a few feet away to infinity.

The light output of electronic units and flashbulbs is often stated in terms of power (so many joules or watt seconds) of flux (in lumen seconds). These figures are of little use except for making comparisons between one unit and another, provided they are compared in like terms.

There is, however, a method of gauging light output which is of direct practical value. This is the guide number, and can be applied to all types of flash equipment. A guide number is given by the manufacturer to each model of electronic unit or type of bulb when used with a film of a given speed. For instance, a certain electronic flash unit may be stated as having a guide number of 40 when used with a medium speed film – and the actual film speed may be quoted. The way in which the guide number allows you to control the light for correct exposures will be explained later (page 248). For the moment we are concerned only with its value as an indication of light output.

The higher the guide number quoted for film of a given speed the more powerful the flash. For instance, a low power electronic unit might have a guide number of around 35 with a 50 ASA film, a medium power portable unit about 65, and a high power portable unit approximately 130 with a film of the same speed. Studio flash sets can have a guide number in excess of 1000 with films of 40–50 ASA.

Guide numbers for bulbs (at shutter speeds of 1/25–1/30 sec) are:

AG1B, M2B, PF1B, MB	85
PC4 (Flashcube)	65
PF5B, M5B, 5B	130
PF6B, 6B	80
PF60/97	170
PF 100/97	215

The effective power of a flashbulb also depends on the efficiency of the reflector in which it is fitted. The guide numbers for bulbs are often quoted for optimum conditions where a reflector of suitable dimensions, say 5 in, is used. But the output is greatly reduced when the bulbs are fitted into a very compact unit with a small (2 in)

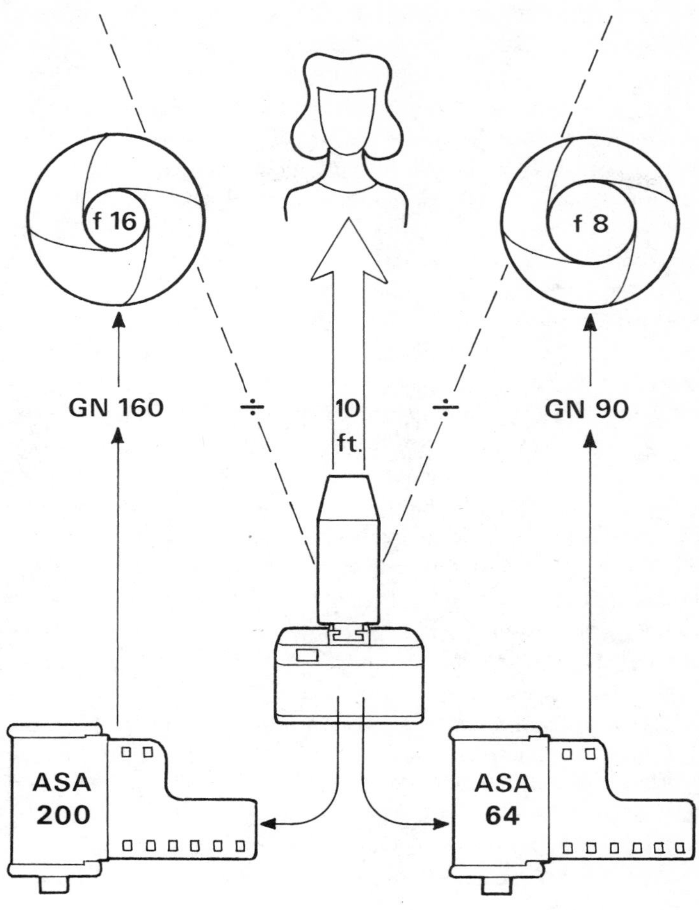

Guide numbers. The guide number varies with the film speed and the effective light output of the flash unit or bulb in use. The guide number (GN) divided by the flash-to-subject distance gives the aperture to be set (with shutter speeds that use the full power of the flash).

or very shallow reflector. Much of the light, instead of being reflected forward to the subject, escapes in other directions, and is wasted. (A 1B bulb, for example, with a guide number of 220 for a 4 in matt reflector, could be re-rated at 160 for a 2 in polished type.) Guide numbers for electronic units, are quoted for the unit working on full power. Each unit has a reflector of fixed dimensions and type, so in this sense the figures are more reliable than those quoted for bulbs.

Small and large units

In normal photography a low power unit would serve for direct flash (not bounced off ceilings, walls or other reflectors) with subjects photographed in average sized rooms at no more than say 10–12 ft, when using a slow speed film.

A medium power portable unit allows direct use in most circumstances and indirect (bounced and reflected lighting) in most. With indirect flash and with a slow film the camera would have to be set on fairly wide apertures for much of the time. A high power portable flash however, allows you to operate at medium or small apertures even when used indirectly. For direct use, without diffusers, it is handy to have some means of reducing power.

Bulb units used in average situations require AG3B or 1B bulbs. Cube flash, of lower output, is designed primarily for direct use, on or off the camera. AG3B bulbs can be used indirect, preferably for subjects within ten feet or so of the flash head. For large domestic interiors, or where small apertures or bounced lighting from darkish walls or high ceilings are anticipated, a 5B would be more than adequate. A 6B could be used with a focal plane shutter but the effective light output is nearer to that of a 1B than a 5B.

As stated earlier, the actual physical size of an electronic flash unit is no sure indication of its power output. But there remains the question of convenience, e.g.: whether you prefer a flashgun that you can slip in your pocket, or to sacrifice some portability for a very high output. Almost all bulb guns are pocketable, although you also have to carry a supply of bulbs. Some smaller electronic units are just

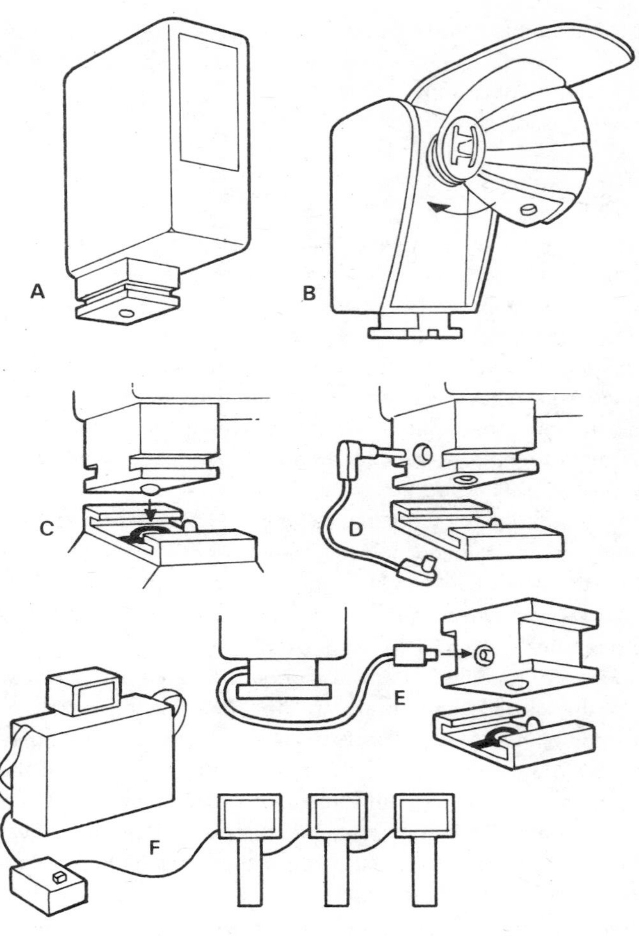

Flash equipment. A. Electronic unit with 'hot shoe' contact. B. Bulb gun with cable sync connector. C. Accessory shoe contact for 'hot shoe' equipment. D. Connector to convert 'hot shoe' to camera socket synchronisation. E. Converter to fit cable connector to accessory shoe contact. F. Large electronic unit with flash meter and extension heads.

about pocketable. The medium sized ones are not, and the more powerful portable units are heavy enough to need a shoulder strap for the battery pack.

Dual and multi-head flash

For anything but the simplest lighting arrangement more than one lamp or flash head is essential. Two or more flash units can be synchronized with the camera shutter.

With bulb flash this method becomes a very extravagant method of providing light, two or three bulbs being expended for each shot.

With multi-flash set ups one flash head at least is bound to be some distance from the camera. But with bulb flash the inherent resistance of a lengthy sync lead between the camera and the unit can result in a failure to fire.

Some electronic units are available as a two-head system, the second (extension) head deriving its power from the same power pack as the first. The disadvantage of this is the profusion of cables – for power and synchronizing – which connect the units and restrict their operating distances to some extent.

It is possible to connect more than one ordinary bulb or electronic unit to the same flash contact on the camera using a simple "Y" connector or multi-way type with extension leads. This however, can cause problems. The extra load passing across the small shutter contacts may, in the long run, cause them some damage. Dissimilar units can be difficult to arrange in this way. Due to a reversed polarity phenomenon one unit can fire the other without reference to the shutter contacts, making practical use impossible. This can however, be avoided by using a terminal with a built-in diode which allows completely different types of units to be synchronized from the same shutter contact.

Another method is to have one flash unit synchronized with the camera shutter and any other units operating completely separately, each triggered by a light sensitive "slave" connected to it. When one flash is fired by the camera the slave picks up the flash of light and almost instantaneously fires the unit to which it is connected. Slaves detect sudden changes in light intensity rather than register any particular intensity. So a slave unit can operate in any ambient light conditions, even direct sunlight, and still trigger from the light of another flash unit.

Some flash units do not function satisfactorily with slaves. The slave may set up a continuous discharging effect in the unit to which it is connected. As with all items purchased for use in conjunction with your existing equipment, it is advisable before making a final choice to set up a quick test and see that everything works together as it should.

An advantage of slave-triggered flash set ups is that the second or third units can be placed at any range from the camera without lengthy connecting leads of any kind. Each "head" has its own power source, so any number of slaves can be operated from a single camera flash. The slaves must be able to "see" the master flash unit, but this is not difficult to arrange as they are not directionally dependent on the units they trigger. A bulb or cube flash on the camera can be used to trigger an electronic unit or another bulb or cube flash on a slave, or an electronic unit may trigger a bulb or cube. But the slave in each case must be designed for use with the type of unit to which it is connected.

Flash synchronization

In the early days of flash photography exposures were made by the "open" flash technique. The camera shutter was opened, often simply by removing the lens cap, the flash powder was fired and the shutter was closed (or the cap replaced). The same method can still be used today with flashguns and modern shutters set on "B" but is really only suitable for stationary subjects. The advantage however, is that the whole of the flash is used, not just a part of it as with some present day methods.

But, with "open" flash, unless the subject is in totally dark surroundings there is a risk of producing more than one image of the subject on the film. This may occur if the subject or the camera moves during the exposure or the light existing in the scene is sufficiently strong to register an image independently of the flash while the shutter is open. Although it is possible to reduce the open-flash-close sequence of operations to the point where the shutter opens for no more than half a second, even this can often register a secondary image on the film. So, for most conditions, you need a mechanically controlled system, either with the flash occurring while the shutter is fully open, or the shutter opening and closing during the period of the flash. This simplifies shooting and allows such a short exposure that the likelihood of double images is reduced to the minimum. So flash can be used in any ordinary circumstances with existing light yet achieve good results.

Virtually all modern camera shutters have synchronizing contacts which, provided the flash unit is connected, ensure that the flash coincides properly with the opening and closing of the shutter. The connection may be made through a coaxial flash socket in the camera body or round the shutter casing; or via a contact in the base of the accessory shoe (hot shoe), with a complementary contact in the "foot" of the flash unit. Adaptors are available which convert one kind of contact to another. One or two older cameras have non-standard flash contacts or no flash synchronization at all. The former require the correctly matching plug (usually found only on the maker's own unit); cameras without synchronization can only be used with the open flash technique.

When the triggering circuit of an electronic flashgun is closed the flash occurs almost instantaneously. With bulb flash on the other hand, there is a period of delay before the bulb reaches its peak output of light. But it maintains that peak period for much longer than an electronic flash before dying away as the metal charge is consumed. Because of the two different timings needed for bulb and electronic flash two main types of shutter synchronization for them have come into existence. These are known as "X" and "M" synchronization.

Mainly because of the increase in popularity of electronic flash M synchronization is found far less often on cameras these days, and usually only as an alternative to X on a camera offering both. Most cameras made today offer only one type, and if not stated, it is sure to be X.

On leaf or blade shutters with M synchronization the bulb flash is triggered shortly before the shutter begins to open so that the peak output of the bulb coincides with the fully open shutter position regardless of what shutter speed is set. But the shorter the shutter speed, the smaller the part of the total light output is used and, naturally, the less exposure is given to the film. Electronic flash does *not* work with M sync because the flash fires before the shutter is open.

On leaf shutters with X synchronization the flash is triggered only when the shutter is fully open. So electronic flash can, in theory, be used with the shutter set to any speed; it fires instantaneously with the shutter reaching the fully open position. Bulbs, on the other hand, can only be used with the shutter set on 1/30 sec or slower speeds, otherwise the shutter begins to close again before the bulb has had enough time to build up to peak output, and most of the flash is wasted.

Focal plane shutters operate on a different principle which restricts their use for flash to some extent. Exposure of the film at all higher speeds is through a gap between the first and second blinds which travel quickly across the surface of the film. At any one moment therefore, only a part of the film area is uncovered. If a flash were to occur just then it would reach only part of the film. The rest would still be covered by the blind. Result: a partially exposed picture.

When focal plane shutters are used at the slower speeds however, the gap between the two blinds is so wide that the first, uncovering the film, has reached its destination before the second has started to move. Thus, for a brief moment the whole film area is uncovered. A flash exactly then exposes the whole film evenly.

With X synchronization on focal plane shutters normal bulb or electronic flash may be used only at certain shutter speeds which vary from one camera model to another.

Because X synchronization triggers the flash when the first blind reaches the end of its travel, the second blind must not have begun its travel when the flash fires. Bulbs have a momentary delay before reaching their peak, and by this time the second blind may have started to move, masking some of the film area. It is usual therefore when using bulbs on X sync with focal plane shutters to set the shutter on the next slowest speed to the maximum indicated for electronic flash.

On many cameras normal flash is possible at settings of up to 1/30 or 1/15 sec. On some, especially large format cameras, only at 1/8th sec. Most 35 mm shutters are designed to synchronize electronic flash at 1/60 sec and a few with vertical shutters at 1/125 sec. The maximum shutter speed for electronic flash is often indicated by a flash symbol ϟ or by the appropriate shutter speed being picked out in another colour.

Another type of synchronization found on some focal plane shutters is that marked F or FP, provided as an alternative to the normal X socket. This was at one time fairly common. It was intended for special FP long burning bulbs (such as the PF6B) designed for use with focal plane shutters. The FP bulb maintains its peak output for far longer than a normal bulb. This allows the focal plane shutter to be set on higher speeds where the narrow slit between the blinds exposes only a part of the film area at a time. The FP bulb maintains its output at more-or-less the same level throughout the time it takes the shutter to traverse the film. Ordinary flash bulbs do not maintain an even output for nearly so long a period, so if they are used on the FP setting the film will be unevenly exposed. With FP bulbs any shutter speed can be set. But the shorter the speed the less of the flash output is used – a wasteful method of working. FP bulbs are not nowadays used very often by amateurs.

Some confusion arises from the fact that as FP bulbs declined in popularity some cameras were instead (or additionally) given an F sync socket for use with ordinary flashbulbs, or even an M socket. But the exact function of such sockets on focal plane shutters can vary from one camera to another. It can be checked in the instruction book for the camera or by making tests on a spare roll of film using your own flash equipment.

Failure to synchronize flash with exposure in leaf shutters is indicated by underexposure, a faint image from ambient light or a blank frame. With focal plane shutters the tell-tale sign is a portion of the picture shade off by the blind, or where ordinary bulbs have been used, uneven exposure.

The main reason for wishing to avoid slow shutter speeds with flash is the possible inclusion of a second image on the film in addition to the main one from the flash exposure. This only happens when the existing light is bright enough for the film to respond even without the flash. It does not have to be anywhere near a full exposure. Long exposure times or quickly moving subjects can cause smeared highlights (reflected from the dying bulb after the peak flash period) or dark areas where the moving subject obscures the background for part of the exposure. Flash does not "arrest" rapidly moving subjects if they are light enough to register on the film without it.

Hand or stand

Most small bulb or electronic flash units have a "foot" which fits into an accessory shoe on the top or side of the camera. This should position the flash head as far as possible from the camera lens to avoid the red eye effect (page 41). If the camera has no shoe or had a detachable shoe which is lost, an accessory bracket may be screwed into the tripod socket in the base and the flash unit mounted on that. The sync cable however, must be long enough to reach the sync socket on the camera, whatever mounting arrangement is used. A flash unit on the camera "follows" the camera around but also places limitations on the quality of light obtained. Some units allow limited angle adjustment for bounced light, some require "hot shoe" connection.

The next stage is to use the flash off the camera but held in the hand, perhaps not far away. Any unit can operate in this way except the type that only synchronizes through contacts in the camera accessory shoe. If the flash unit has a standard coaxial plug but the camera has only a hot shoe, an adaptor may be available to convert the hot shoe contacts to work with the plug, thus allowing the flashgun to be operated off the camera. An extension to the sync lead is probably needed if the flash is to be more than a few inches away from the camera. From this position, held in the hand, the flash may be pointed in any direction or even made to bounce light off the photographer himself. The arrangement leaves only one hand free to operate the camera, however.

The flash unit may be placed on a piece of furniture or other support which is ready to hand. It is advisable to have a fairly generous extension sync cable, as one is apt to forget about it when moving quickly about with the camera.

You can buy clamps which allow you to fix a flash rigidly to any projecting surface, such as tables, doors, shelves or a mantlepiece. Highlight stands are available for photographic lighting. These can often be bought as interlocking items, including a counterweighted boom arm, umbrella reflectors etc. They allow you to position your flash at almost any height and angle. Music stands, camera or telescope stands may serve as a substitute though they do not normally offer the full height of the proper stand. Display stands, including floor-to-ceiling clamping poles are handy if you have some means of mounting the flash at the height you want.

Stand mountings can provide a fixed, predetermined flash set up which leaves you free to concentrate on camera angle, composition etc. Studio flash units are, as a rule, worked from adjustable stands and these are often designed for use with the particular equipment.

Diffusers and reflectors

Flash from small units is a relatively hard light source. It can be softened by diffusion or reflection. The diffusion may simply be a couple of folds of a handkerchief, or a sheet of translucent material placed in front of the flash cube or bulb. Most people improvise. They produce their own diffusers that soften the light to the degree they like.

Much the same applies to reflectors. Most flash units provide only the normal dish reflector. Further reflection, say for bounced illumination, would have to be from the surroundings or from separate reflecting surfaces treated with foil, paint etc. giving varying degrees of hardness to reflected light.

The umbrella is one form of reflector which has become fairly standardized, and is particularly applied to flash work. The flashgun is mounted facing the interior of the umbrella which itself forms a huge diffused reflecting surface. This produces a soft yet reasonably

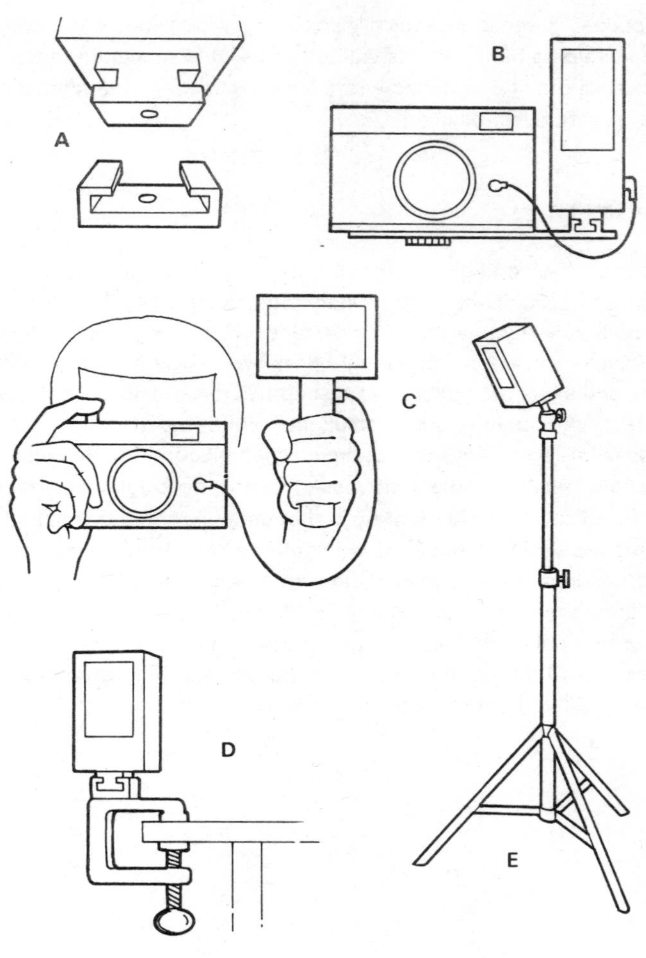

Ways to use flash. A. Foot fitting in to an accessory shoe on the camera. B. Mounted on a camera bracket. C. Off the camera but held in the hand. D. On a clamp bracket attached to a door, chair, table, etc. E. On a lighting stand.

directional illumination which gives some modelling to the subject while avoiding hard edged shadows and strong specular reflections. Umbrellas may be obtained with various reflecting characteristics – hard or soft, silver or gold.

Film and filter

Electronic flash and blue flashbulbs are suitable for use with daylight balanced colour films and all black and white films of any speed. Naturally, contrast can be a significant factor in any picture taking. But unless you are using a single flash well away from the camera angle and expect to get very hard shadows there is no need to go for the faster and usually softer black and white materials.

Colour films these days do not have very high contrast. So whatever may have been the case in the past, it is now no longer necessary to aim for particularly flat lighting – though sometimes this still gives the most pleasing colours. As we shall see later, the lighting chosen is determined by the subject rather than the film.

No filter is needed for flash photography unless you are using a colour film balanced for artificial light. In that case a correction filter (Wratten 85) should be fitted over the camera lens. Some drop in effective film speed then occurs (2/3 stop).

Lamps

The type, and number of lamps you need for any purpose depends on the subject you are shooting, and where it is located. With some situations, such as copying and shooting close-ups and static subjects you can make do with very little light. Ordinary house lights would probably do. For moving subjects, candid photography etc., you need much more powerful illumination.

The scale and power of lighting available to the ordinary photographer can cover virtually any need. There are special lamps designed for photographic work, available in various types and sizes, each with particular advantages.

These lamps differ from the ordinary domestic kind mainly in their light output. Even the least powerful has an output far higher than that of a domestic lamp. We are used to lamps in the home with power ratings within the range of 40–250 watts. Photographic lamps have an effective output of at least double the brightness of these – most of them considerably more. Such a great light output allows quite short exposures. Using photo lamps, there is no need to put the camera on a tripod and you do not have to shoot at the very wide apertures that can make focusing rather critical.

Even so, with fast films for much of the time you can avoid the extra expense of buying special lamps, and use instead the lamps you already have around you.

Domestic lamps

Domestic lamps are available in several forms, ordinary tungsten lamps, spotlights, and fluorescent tubes. Ordinary tungsten lights used in the home are generally diffused by some kind of shade. If you are using naked bulbs then the pearl or preferably white diffused or opal type are to be preferred as their light is fully diffused without a shade. Clear bulbs tend to give uneven illumination often with reflections or patterns from ripples in the glass envelope being clearly visible when the light falls on an even toned surface such as a background wall. If covered with a shade this is no less important. But clear bulbs can project an image of the shade joins, lacing holes or tassels on to the subject.

Any lamp in a shade takes on the colour of the shade itself and this shows up in colour pictures if the colour is strong enough.

Domestic lights are fine for black and white work. With most colour films however they give a rather "warm" or red (2600–2800 K; see colour temperature, page 234) cast to the picture which, though not always unpleasant, is quite noticeable. Colour films marked for use in tungsten light are intended to give correct colour rendering in the light from photo lamps which is "colder" or slightly more blue (3200–3400 K) than home lighting.

Domestic lamps in many fittings distribute their light in all directions. Photolamps on the other hand are mostly used in reflectors which concentrate the light over a smaller area. This allows control over where the light should fall and where there should be only shadow. Ordinary domestic light bulbs can be fitted in to photo lamp reflectors, and some lamps used in the home do just the same thing. In fact, the adjustable reading lamp on a stand that can be angled in various directions is ideal for photographic use. The only restriction is that these units often do not allow a lamp of more than 60 or 75 watts to be fitted. Even so, this is still quite handy for use at close range.

Domestic spotlights are also handy for photography. They may be the mushroom type with internal reflector, a dish reflector using a silver topped bulb, or the type with reflector and detachable shield taking ordinary bulbs. These lights have the same colour quality as ordinary domestic lamps (2600–2800 K) but deliver an intense and concentrated beam which casts shadows with fairly sharply defined edges. The light maintains its intensity over quite a distance but is not so evenly distributed as with a true photographic spot. The "hot" area in the centre of its light "pool" may not be of quite consistent shape.

Bulbs with clear envelopes must be used in domestic spotlights because the filament is focused by the reflector. Some models allow the light beam width to be adjusted by shifting the bulb position in the reflector. This provides a means of varying the intensity of light falling on the subject as well as increasing the area covered, without moving the lamp or subject. A few of these spotlights emit streaks, or spill light from the side which can dazzle a human subject or

cause flare in the picture. Domestic spots that accept ordinary bulbs can be fitted with coloured ones for special lighting effects. But coloured bulbs must be of the lacquered type where the filament is clearly visible, such as the red bulbs used in artificial coal fires.
Pencil light domestic spots are less useful because the light beam is too narrow except for inserting catchlights or other small scale effects in a picture lit by other sources.

Photoflood, photopearl

These special lamps designed for photographic work are manufactured as two distinct types – photofloods and photopearls, or studio lamps. They are both available either as the normal form of bulb or the kind with an internal reflector. The latter are mushroom shaped bulbs whose concentrated light beam acts like a slightly diffused spotlight with a high level of light emission from the sides.
A photoflood has a special filament which is deliberately designed for overrunning. This gives a far greater light output for the wattage rating of the bulb than one normally expects. The advantages of overrunning are that a high level of light can be obtained from a relatively low-cost bulb of small physical size and that several such bulbs can be run off a normal home power supply without exceeding the limited amperage capacity. The same output from conventional bulbs would require heavy duty power outlets such as those found in some studios.
The most widely used photofloods are the No. 1 (275 W) with an effective output of 750 W and the No. 2 (500 W) with an effective output of 1600 W.
Reflector versions are available in three main wattages: No. 5 (275 W) No. 6 (375 W) and No. 7 (500 W). All lamps are available with screw (ES) fittings and most are also available with the bayonet (BC) type.
Because the filament of these lamps is overrun, their working life is quite short – an estimated 3 hours for a No. 1 and No. 5, 4 hours for No. 6 and 6 hours for No. 2 and No. 7 lamps. The actual perfor-

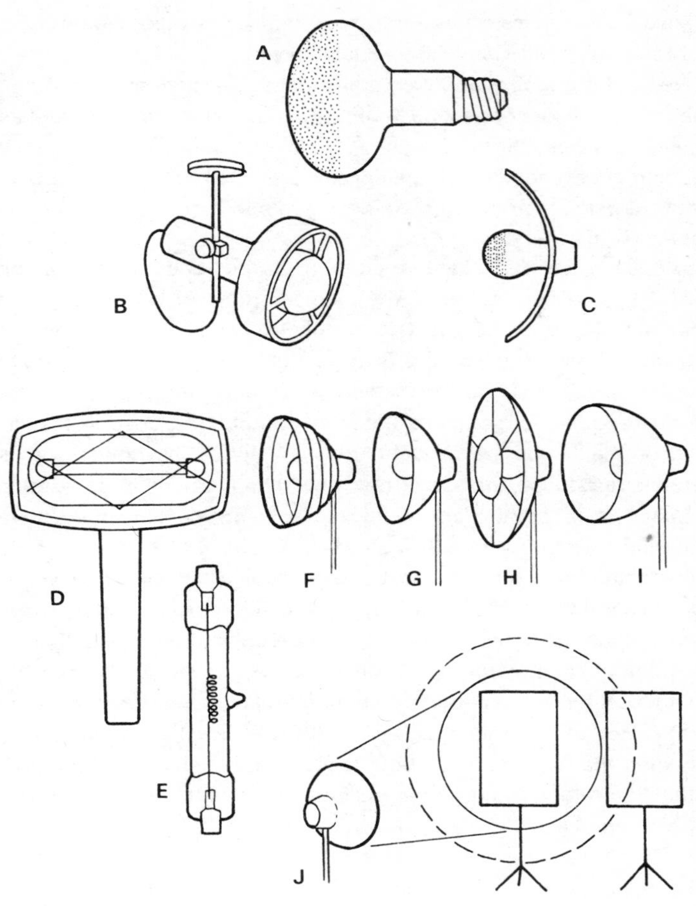

Lighting unit types. A. Mushroom type domestic spot or flood. B. Ordinary lamp in spot reflector with detachable shield. C. Silver-topped bulb in simple dish spot reflector. D. Halogen unit with E. Quartz envelope bulb. F. Photoflood in corrugated reflector. G. Smooth reflector. H. Shallow soft flood (skypan). I. Deep bowl. J. Separate reflectors can gather light from central 'hot', or penumbral areas.

mance can vary from one lamp to another and these figures give only a rough indication of life expectancy.
A No. 2 photoflood is approximately double the price of a No. 1 and the reflector types between two and three times the cost of ordinary equivalents.
All photoflood lamps are balanced for a colour temperature of 3400 K. Some colour films are designed specifically for use at this colour temperature.
Photopearls, or studio lamps, are high output photo lamps which give a light output equal to their consumption in watts. They are usually made with 500 W (No. 1) or 1000 W (No. 2) ratings. A reflector version, the No. 3, is 500 W. These lamps have an average working life of 100 hours if used correctly. Most lamps however can be made to last longer still if a surge-resistor is included in the circuit, or the lamps are brought up gradually to full power with a variable resistance, instead of being switched directly into the main supply. (It is advisable not to move lamps about more than necessary when switched on as the filament is at that time most vulnerable. They should also be kept clear of raindrops or water splashes which can cause a hot glass envelope to explode). These lamps are supplied with screw (ES and GES) fittings and emit light at a colour temperature of 3200 K, i.e.: slightly warmer than the photoflood type. Many colour films are balanced for use with such lamps. But the marginal difference (200 K) in colour temperature between these lamps and photofloods is not likely to cause objectionable errors in colour rendering when used with film designed for 3400 K sources.

Halogen lamps

Halogen lamps (otherwise known as tungsten halogen, tungsten iodine, quartz iodine or quartz lamps) were originally developed for moviemaking as a light source of very high output yet compact enough to be held in the hand if necessary. They have, since then, been adopted by some people for still photography, particularly if this avoids duplicating existing lighting equipment for only occasional use. A tungsten halogen unit however, may provide rather more light than is needed. A 600–1000 W halogen unit for example gives a light output equivalent to three No. 7 reflector photofloods, each of 500 W.

Halogen lights do not discolour with age as some tungsten lamps do. The lamp has a tungsten filament and the envelope is filled with a halogen gas such as iodine. As the lamp burns, particles from the heated filament, instead of forming a coating on the inside of the envelope (causing loss of light or a shift in colour temperature) are redeposited on the filament itself. This redepositing is not regular but it maintains the life of the filament for far longer than would otherwise be possible. The tremendous heat developed by these lamps requires the envelope to be made from special toughened glass. Quartz is sometimes used, but this tends to stain if touched with a naked finger.

Halogen lamps are made with the tubular bulb fitting in to a reflector or as a self contained "sealed-beam" glass reflector unit rather like a car headlamp.

Halogen lamps may have a short life, and replacements are fairly expensive. Some units take the bulbs in pairs. This arrangement can be very costly to run if there is no provision for one bulb to fail without automatically blowing the other.

Twin headed lamps of this type can produce troublesome double-outline shadows and it is best to avoid using these for still photography if possible.

All halogen lamps develop immense heat if used for prolonged periods. Although many are fitted with "barn doors" or shaders these after a while become too hot to handle. Filters placed over the lamp can easily buckle or burn. It is advisable to keep the lamp clear of walls and woodwork and to allow it sufficient ventilation. Halogen lamps have even been known to burn their own supply cables inside the unit!

The halogen lamps in most common use are the 650 W and 1000 W types. These are sometimes interchangeable in the same unit. If used in pairs with individual switching on each lamp there is (using pairs of identical lamps) a wide range of wattages: 650, 1000, 1300 and 2000 W.

Sometimes two lamps are included in a single reflector. In other cases the separate reflectors may be adjusted individually to a limited degree. It is however, preferable to use a single bar unit rather than a twin lamp type in order to avoid the double shadows. Typical halogen lamps statistics are as follows. The P2/21 type tungsten halogen lamp is rated at 250 W 30 V and has an output of 6500 lumens with a working life of 150 hours. P2/6 lamps rated at 650 W 125/130 V has an output of 18 500 lumens and a working life of 75 hours. P1/14 lamps running from full (UK) voltage 240/250 V have an output of 20 000 lumens and an average life of 15 hours. P1/15 lamps are 1000 W 240/250 V with an output of 33 000 lumens and average life of 15 hours. P2/12 lamps rated at 1250 W 240/250 V have a light output of 33 500 lumens and run on average for 200 hours.

Types P1/12, P1/14 and P1/15 are suitable for all black and white film and for Type A colour material balanced to 3400 K colour temperature. The other lamps are suitable for Type A colour film balanced for 3200 K.

For best results the lamps should be used only with films of the colour temperature indicated in each case. However, as with other photo lamps, the marginal shift in colour caused in mismatching by only 200 K should still give acceptable colour rendering.

Fluorescent lighting

Fluorescent strip lighting is very diffused, and can not be controlled or manipulated. As a general light source it is adequate but rather dull and lacking in character. The colour quality, or temperature, is rather unpredictable as it varies according to the tube coating. Tubes are available in a wide range of "whites" extending from near-pink to the coldest white. The majority range between 3700 and 4800 K.

One special problem exists, though. The light from most commonly available tubes is not evenly distributed throughout the spectrum. For this reason, it is very difficult to predict its effect on colour films. Often, you get an overall greenish cast. This can be ameliorated with a pale red or magenta filter on the camera lens. The only way to get successful results is to experiment with a particular combination of tubes and films.

With all pulsating lights such as fluorescent illumination there is a danger of strobing effects in pictures taken with the higher speeds on focal plane shutters. This can result in uneven exposure across the film as it is scanned by the slit in the moving blind.

Spot or flood

The most common type of floodlight has an open bowl-shaped reflector with the lamp fitted in the centre. Light emanating directly from the bulb mixes with light reflected from the inside of the bowl. But sometimes a small shield or back reflector is fitted over the bulb itself to cut off direct rays and ensure that all light is reflected via the bowl.

The bowl may be large or small, corrugated or smooth. It may vary in depth and in its surface finish. All these factors affect the quality of light that it gives – the area over which it is spread and the degree of diffusion obtained.

The larger shallower bowls give a wide spread of light. If the inside of the bowl has a matt white or satin chrome finish or a corrugated surface, the light reflected is more diffused. Flat shaped bowl reflectors are normally given a matt surface.

Reflectors with shielded bulbs give very soft illumination as the light originates wholely from a wide source. An unshielded lamp in a similar reflector would not give such diffused illumination because the light from the bulb itself always predominates, however efficient the reflector. These reflectors usually have a white or satin finish to maximize diffusion.

Narrow bowls restrict the spread of light to a smaller area. Sometimes these bowls, too, have a matt or corrugated surface to diffuse the light, but often the bowl has a highly polished finish. Such a bowl reflects a harder, more concentrated light.

Different subjects make different demands for lighting and there is no "best" lamp or reflector for all situations. But the main concern is to have a lamp and reflector that gives a wide enough evenly lit area to cover the subject. Most lamps light well enough centrally. But there is also an outer area where the light begins to drop in intensity before being cut off altogether by the edge of the reflector. That half-light area can be useful for making slight adjustments to cancel awkward shadows or for subtle shading or partial diffusion effects especially welcome in studio portrait work.

The floodlight is the basic source for most general work, including portraiture.

A spotlight emits a highly concentrated beam of light which can be thrown over a great distance and still retain much of its power. The light originates from a small bulb. This is backed by a spherical mirror positioned so that its focal length reflects an image of the filament in the same plane as that occupied by the real filament. A lens in front of the lamp focuses the filament and its reflection. These three main components are enclosed by a well ventilated tube.

Adjusting the distance separating the lens and the bulb (with its mirror) varies the width of the light beam. When the lens is placed near its focal length the light emerges from the lamp in more or less parallel rays. At less than the focal length of the lens, and when they are moved *towards* the lens the beam widens. (if they are moved away, beyond the focal length, the beam is more narrowly focused into a "hot" area.) The settings may be marked "spot" and "flood" on the adjustment control, but these are relative terms. All light from spotlights is highly directional and sufficiently focused to give deep shadows with hard outlines and sharp rendering of texture when striking an uneven surface from an oblique angle. Even when the lamp is set on "full flood" the light emitted is nowhere near as diffused as that from a true floodlight.

The lens, or condenser in a spotlight is normally the fresnel type, which can be made from a thinner section of glass than the equivalent spherical lens and is therefore less prone to breakage from expansion under heat. A fresnel lens is also much lighter in weight – an important consideration, since spotlights are generally far heavier than equivalent floods and may have to be supported by a heavy duty stand.

Spotlights of this kind use normal high wattage lamps which place

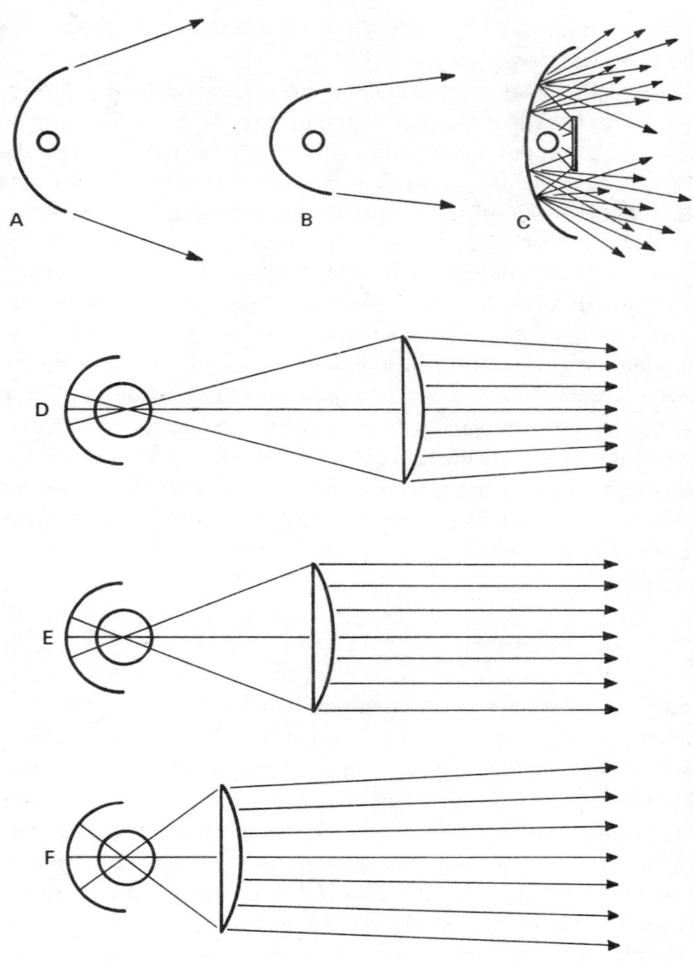

Spot or flood. A flood light reflector may give A. Wide, B. Narrow cone of light. C. With a front bulb shield or back reflector light comes only from the bowl, not directly from the bulb, giving very diffuse illumination. A focusing spot lamp can give D spot E, parallel or F (relative) flood effects by adjustment of the lens position.

the same limitations of load for house supplies as the non-overrun type of photographic lamp.
The spotlight though undoubtedly a useful piece of lighting equipment is not essential for good lighting. It rarely provides the main light in a set up but is commonly reserved for effects, such as the addition of highlights in subject or background, or as a controllable source for use with reflectors or diffusers. A great advantage is that it emits little "spill" light. Extra control, beyond that provided by the focusing adjustment, comes from adding various shaders, snoots, barn doors or other devices to the front. These allow small patches of light of any shape to be projected on the subject or into the scene. Spotlights are almost always expensive compared with floods. Luckily in many homes there is a good substitute ready to hand in the form of a slide projector. This, when not projecting a slide, functions in almost exactly the same way as a spotlight and provided it is not overpowered by other lamps, can be most effective. It has the additional possibility of allowing you to focus a slide on to the subject for special effects.

Reflectors and mirrors

A reflector can be used as a substitute for a lamp, casting light on to the subject in a number of ways. For example, the deep shadows resulting from lighting a subject with only one lamp may be filled with light from a reflector placed in a position to catch some of the light spilled from that lamp. Or, where the only lamp available gives a rather hard light for the particular purpose the subject can be lit instead by bouncing that light off a reflector. Many people do not believe how "powerful" reflected light can be until they try it.
Although reflectors are among the most useful photographic accessories, they are not normally manufactured items that you can buy in a shop. You have to make your own, and it is not difficult.
The simplest reflector is a sheet of paper, an open newspaper if it is to be a large reflector. This, or a large roll of paper reserved for the purpose, is fine where you only need a means of filling in shadows from time to time. But a white reflector has limited reflecting ability

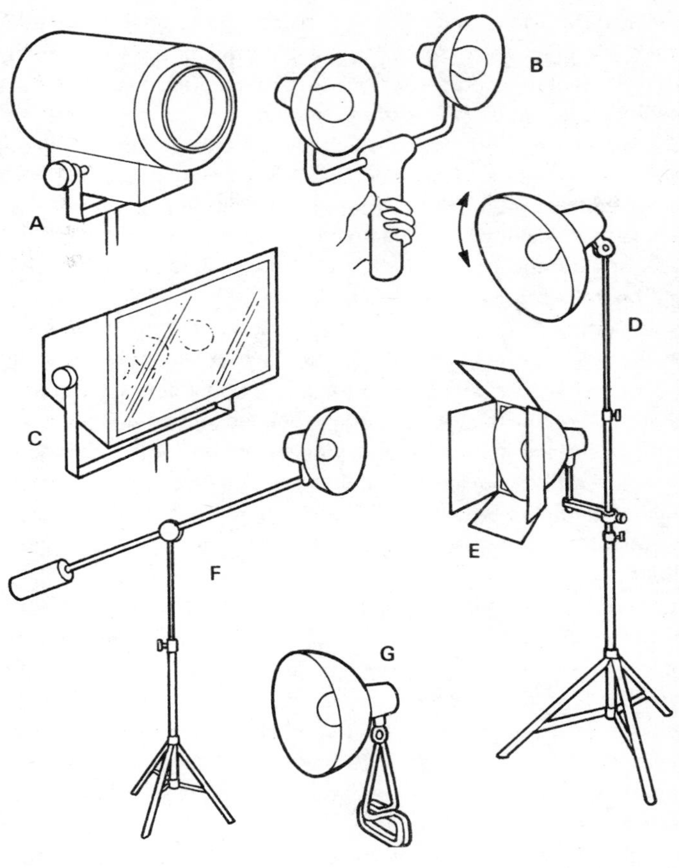

Special lighting units and supports. A. Spotlight in a ventilated tube. B. Special twin-head bar light using photofloods or photopearls. C. Enclosed trough or 'fish fryer' with front diffusing screen. D. Lightweight stand with adjustable reflector. E. Extension arm lamp fitted with adjustable shaders (barn doors). F. Boom lighting unit with counterweight. G. Clip-on lamp.

and must be placed quite close to the subject to have much effect. (There is a slight risk of including the reflector itself in the picture). It can have quite a marked effect on light toned areas in subjects such as the face or hands in a portrait. The light from a white reflector is very diffused and spread over a wide area. It is very suitable for bouncing directional light of sufficient power such as that from an electronic flash to convert it from hard to soft illumination.

A more permanent white reflector could be made by treating a sheet of ply or other thin board with a coat of matt white emulsion paint. A rigid board is more convenient to handle.

For a stronger effect you have to use a surface which is a more efficient reflector. A good reflector can be made by covering a sheet of plywood with aluminium cooking foil, shiny side upwards. The other side of the board can be roughened up by coating with a textured surface such as glued paper squeezed in to clumps and then covered by cooking foil with the matt side upwards. A second such reflector can be made with gold foil, or treated with varnish of different depths of colour to give warm reflections where desired in colour pictures.

The two-surface reflector offers a choice of two kinds of reflection. That from the shiny side gives a quite intense and directional light not unlike a floodlight, but which is controllable for different reflection effects by bending the board. Bending it inwards tends to concentrate a reflection in a small area of the subject, bending it outwards disperses the light. With directional reflectors there is a danger of concentrating unpleasant and often irregular highlights on the subject.

The other, roughened side of the reflector gives a diffused light, but of greater strength than that from a plain white reflector. The concentration can be varied by moving the board closer to, or further away from the subject. There is little risk of causing uneven light patches except when the reflector is too small to cover enough of the subject.

With diffusing reflectors the intensity of light reaching the subject falls off rapidly as the reflector is moved away. This is far less so with directional, polished reflectors.

A convenient way in which to construct a reflector is as a two-part board in plywood, hinged in the centre to fold conveniently and offer a choice of two reflector sizes. If sufficiently light in weight, such a reflector can be clipped or clamped to a stand or furniture or held in place by an assistant or the subject himself without too much cause to complain of the weight! It can also serve as a shader when placed in the light beam.

A mirror, used as a reflector becomes, in effect a second lamp. It reflects a bright image of approximately its own shape. The closer the mirror is to the lamp the larger is the reflected patch of light. The closer the subject is to the mirror the smaller and brighter is the area of the reflected light. When the mirror is very close to the subject the reflected area is very little more than that of the mirror itself.

Compared with diffusing reflectors mirrors are more convenient inasmuch as they can be much further away from the subject and still give a useful reflection.

But not all subjects can benefit much from the relatively small area of bright light that can be reflected by a hand mirror from any position other than one right next to the lamp.

Unless a fairly large mirror is used the mirror shaped reflection is likely to be too obvious. Polished metal mirrors have the obvious advantage of being more rugged but unless they are rigid the reflections are too haphazard and uneven to be of much use.

Concave shaving mirrors can act like a spotlight, concentrating flood illumination on a small area. This is mainly of use as an effect or for small objects photographed in close up. Used at greater range they tend to form an image of the lamp itself.

Plugs and sockets

There is little difficulty with using photo lamps in the average house though you have to take note of a few important points in the interests of safety.

Always take your power from an outlet in the room where you are actually shooting. Avoid long trailing cables which are dangerous, especially with children about, and get in the way of everyone's feet. Keep cables out of the way if possible and anchored to the bottom of lighting stands. With cables attached to the top, the slightest pull can topple the stand over. You can plug all lamps in to a distribution board, which then has only a single cable running to the wall socket.

Run all lamps from the power (wall) sockets not from the lighting circuit overhead which can not safely take the load of more than a single photoflood.

Make sure everything is switched off before fitting bulbs in sockets. Preferably switch on from the main switch on the wall.

Do not overload the power supply. You can quite easily work out how many lamps you may have on a socket of a given amperage. But note that the different sockets in a room, and sometimes even in different rooms may be on the same (ring main) circuit. If so, the circuit rating applies to the whole circuit and not just a single socket. So the power drawn from all sockets added together should not exceed that. The fuse fitted in the plug must of course be for the full power rating and not the low power type (such as 2A or 3A) intended for domestic lamps and other such items when running off the power circuit.

To determine how many lamps you may plug in to the power supply use the simple formula:

$$\text{watts} = \text{volts} \times \text{amps}.$$

Suppose you have a 13 amp (in the UK the square pin) power socket circuit and the supply is 250 volts.

The total wattage of all lamps you can safely run off that circuit is: $13 \times 250 = 3250$ W.

If you live in the USA where the household supply is usually 115 V you simply multiply this figure by the maximum amp rating for the circuit in use; e.g.: $14 \times 115 = 1725$ W.

You can find the maximum amp rating by looking on the plug. In the UK the square pin plugs, fitted with the right fuse, take 13A, some older large round pin circuits take 15A and smaller ones 5A. There are also 2A circuits which, like the lighting circuit are of limited use. In the USA there are flat pin plugs rated at 15A (max 125 V) and 6A.

A maximum load of 3250W allows a maximum of six 500W No. 2 photofloods to be used leaving a margin of 250W short of the maximum load. With photofloods the power is worked out on the actual wattage consumption of the lamp. On a 115 V power supply, with a 15A plug, three 500W photofloods can be used.

The efficiency of plugs and sockets varies from one to another and it is not uncommon for them to warm up when subjected to very heavy loads if the pin contact is not too good. In extreme cases there can be arcing inside the plug or socket. Replace any equipment that arcs. Otherwise it may form a permanent carbon track, overload the circuit and become a fire risk.

The main danger in exceeding the maximum load comes with using photo lamps in conjunction with existing appliances (such as electric fires) running off the same supply, or when using very powerful halogen lighting.

Stands and accessories

A lamp and its reflector must be supported by some means to hold it steady, preferably leaving both hands free to operate the camera.

Lamp holders are available to allow photo lamps to be held in the hand. Halogen lamp units are often designed with this idea primarily in mind.

Another type of lamp holder can be clamped on to any protruding surface such as the edge of a door or table or back of a chair using spring jaws. Some also have a standard mounting screw which will fit onto a tripod head. So that the tripod provides a substitute for a lamp stand. Other supports that can double for the real thing are microphone or music stands, projection screen stands and even household drying rails etc.

The most versatile kind of support is the one designed for the job. Photo lamp stands offer strength, light weight, stability, flexibility in application and compactness when folded. The typical modern stand has a telescopic column of light alloy draw tubes with three rubber-footed legs projecting from the base. Studio lamp stands are of heavier construction with wheels and very old fashioned types often have a solid metal casting for a base. Wheeled stands usually

allow for the wheels to be locked off once the stand has been moved in to the required position.
Lightweight stands are available with simple extending centre columns that accept a variety of arms. These can take the form of an extension hinged from the top which can be angled at will and locked with a wing nut. A variation of this is the counterweighted lighting boom with the fulcrum at the point where it is jointed to the telescopic light stand. The counterweight can be moved to compensate for the particular reflector and bulb fitted at the other end, and it can actually be locked at the hinged joint so that it remains in any position chosen.
Sometimes a small lamp bracket can be attached at any point on the column of a lighting stand.
This is handy for inserting lamps at any level (even just clear of the floor) instead of, or in addition to, the lamp at the head of the stand.
Lighting stands can also be used to hold shaders, reflectors or mirrors.
Some models are available as part of a kit of interlocking parts, so that you can make a variety of supports by adding small accessories to existing basic units. On all such lighting units the angle of the lamp reflector may be adjusted individually so that the light can come from virtually any direction. A few can also be "focused" by means of a sliding bar which moves the bulb back or forward in the floodlight bowl.
Some lamps have provision for attaching barn doors or filters. Barn doors are hinged shaders that fit in the front of the lamp. They cut off the light with a reasonably diffused edge, or narrow it down to cover only a small area of the scene being lit. The filters are large colour "gels" – pieces of coloured plastic sheeting which can be cut to any size or shape and can therefore be made to fit over any lamp to colour the light it gives out. Special diffusers are available which may be used in the same way.

Lighting the Subject

Before you consider the lighting needs of a particular subject or situation you have to understand what use can be made of the lights so that when you move or add a lamp you know exactly what is going to happen.
Lights are arranged for more purposes than just that of providing illumination. They can be made to stress the shape or volume of the subject, to influence its colour, or to suppress certain aspects of it in favour of others.

To illuminate

The lighting must be of sufficient strength to illuminate the subject for the exposure you have in mind. If not, you must adjust the exposure, move the lamp or change it for another of different power.
The character of lighting alters with its power. Although there is a relationship between the strength of light reflected from a subject, and exposure in the camera, it is more or less mechanical.
A dimly lit subject can not be made to look as if it is flooded with light simply by giving it more exposure. The highlights get brighter and there may be more detail visible in the shadows, but the contrast range is not extended very much. The full range of contrasts of a well-lit average subject are missing. It is merely a light picture of a dull scene.
Low-key effects are impossible to achieve with a subject which is obviously under brilliant lighting. A well-lit subject, even when underexposed, has too wide a contrast range and leaves too much detail visible everywhere for the picture to look as if it were taken in poor light. A generally well lit scene also lacks the particular highlights necessary to give the impression of a real low-light situation.
Alterations in brightness by exposure should therefore only be slight; the main change should be made by modifying the brightness of the light source.
Increasing the light by moving the lamp towards the subject is often the answer but on occasions may cause some concentration of light in particular areas which are closer to the source.

In most situations the light on a subject must seem to fall reasonably evenly all over it. If not, there will be arbitrary shading off in parts of the subject with no visible reason for why that should be. Or, at least, the cause will be outside the picture and therefore unknown to the person looking at it. This can be done intentionally for an effect; but in normal cases uneven lighting is to be avoided. It may cause problems in colour rendering, shape and tone representation of the subject.

Even if it is on a negative and can be corrected in printing, this requires time and some skill.

Unevenness of illumination is chiefly noticeable where the lamp is positioned well away from the camera axis, lighting a broad subject of even tone.

Subjects in which the tones are well broken up are less prone to showing this defect.

If you are likely to get this trouble; don't move the lights too close, increase the exposure. Note, however, that variations in the exposure time given can affect the contrast of the resultant picture, though not critically.

Also, exposures of greater than 1 sec duration can cause underexposure and problems with colour rendering due to reciprocity law failure (see page 247). Long exposure times also tend to increase the image contrast.

To reduce the power of the lighting you can move the lamp further away. The only objection to this, provided there is sufficient space to do it, is that a wider spread of light bouncing off more of the surroundings may alter the nature of the light reaching the subject.

The lighting must be sufficient for both subject and background. As the background is further from the lamp than the main subject it receives less light from it. (This is more so with unfocused lamps such as floods, than with focused spots). The closer the lamp, the darker the background appears in relation to the subject. If you want the background to appear nearer in tone to the subject you must move the lamp further away (in accordance with the inverse square law, page 13). That is assuming that the background is being lit by the same light as the one used for the subject. Other methods will be described shortly.

To shape

The light can be used to give a suggestion of solidity in a subject and separation from its background even though it is only reproduced as a flat two dimensional print or slide. This is especially necessary in black and white pictures, where subjects, parts of a subject, or subject and background can not be distinguished from one another by their different colours.

Modelling is achieved by lighting an object with a source placed at an angle away from the camera viewpoint. A shadow appears on the side furthest from the light, following the shape of the object and gradually diminishing towards the angle of the light, according to the curvature of the object or the undulations of its surface. So the object is divided up in to highlights, mid-tones and shadow areas. The illusion of roundness varies according to the angle of the light to the camera axis. When the lamp is at a greater angle and the shadow area is consequently larger, the subject is more "strongly" modelled. When it is close to the camera angle the modelling is less pronounced. Lit from a head-on position the object appears to have no depth. Lit from extreme angles modelling may indeed be stronger though it is fair to say that the actual illusion of roundness in the subject is not necessarily increased – so much depends on the particular subject, its shape and situation, and the impression you are aiming to create.

When the light is at oblique angle to a surface, any textural detail is more strongly rendered. Texture is little solids modelled individually, on a tiny scale. Each has its highlight and mid-tone area, and also throws a shadow.

Part of the modelling effect of light is to create a small highlight or specular reflection at certain points favourably angled to the camera viewpoint – i.e. where the angle of incidence of the light equals the angle of reflection towards the camera. The light behaves in much the same way as that shown in the typical cartoon rendering of a soap bubble where the four panes of a window are seen reflected as a highlight.

A subject can be modelled "naturally", or "abnormally". That is to say, the modelling is derived from a source which is coming from a

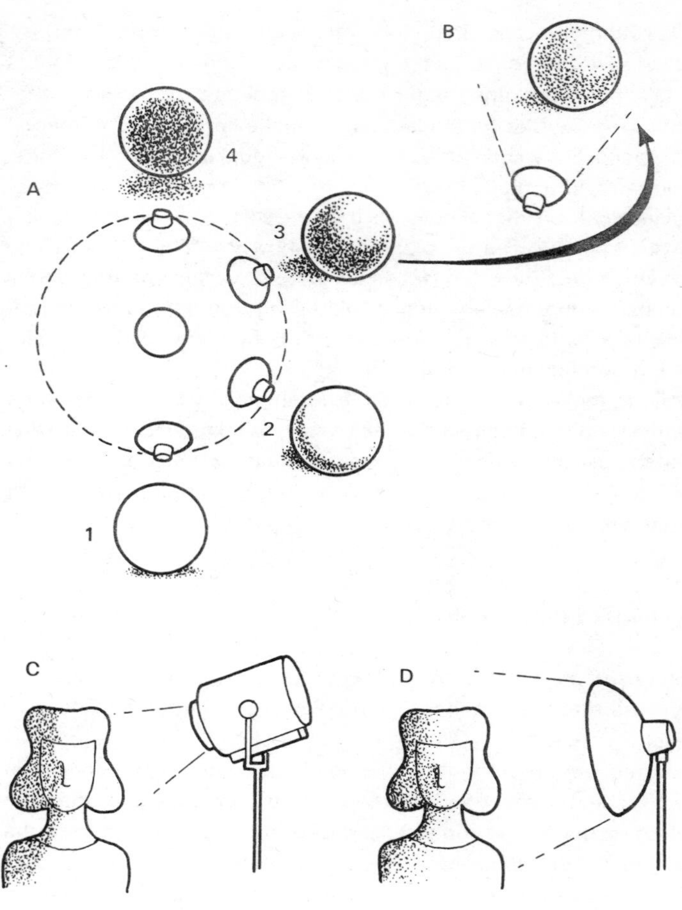

Light on the subject. A. As you move the light round a subject, the modelling changes. 1. Head-on flat frontal light, no shadows. 2. Side light gives small shadows and feeling of roundness. 3. Side lighting increases the shadow area and gives most modelling. 4. Backlight gives shadow with some modelling. B. Best modelling with high side or front/side lighting, plus frontal fill light. C. Spot gives hard edged shadows. D. Flood gives soft edged shadows.

familiar angle – one that we would normally expect and we associate with it – such as a typical angle of the sun. If the light is coming from some other angle, say almost directly underneath, that is apt to look a little theatrical and we make corresponding mental connections. So a subject, however well modelled, looks odd if it is lit from an odd angle.

A subject can be modelled with hard or soft light, relating to the equivalent effects in nature of direct sunlight, or sunlight obscured by cloud. Any effect from similar causes therefore seems natural, and is associated with those conditions, Modelling from strong direct light seems warm and cheerful, whereas soft light seems dim, suffused, cool and perhaps even damp.

Soft light makes the graduation from highlight to shadow area smoother and less detailed. Surface detail, or texture, is restrained in its effect as the diffuse light bounces about between the tiny crevices and weakens the shadows within them. Hard light emphasises those shadows.

To colour, or render colour

Lighting for good colour rendering follows a course that deviates slightly from the normal approach to lighting for modelling the solid subject.

Colour registered on the film changes in saturation (i.e. intensity of colour present) according to the amount of exposure the film receives. If the film is correctly exposed for a particular area of the scene the colour will resemble what you see in the original object or scene. If however, it is overexposed (on transparencies, even slightly) the colour content is weakened. Underexposure, on the other hand, deepens the colour. Our eyes and brain make partial adjustments for a colour seen in conditions of light or shade. The film does not. It is therefore the policy of some photographers to avoid shadows or large areas of highlight in their colour pictures wherever possible. This can be done with flat lighting, frontally placed (i.e. close to the camera viewpoint) and diffused if possible. When colour film first became widely available the materials then made tended to develop excessive contrast, and it was usually recommended that very flat lighting be used with them. This remedy is not really necessary with modern film, but the tradition of "flat lighting for colour" lingers on.

The feeling nowadays is often that if the colour in the subject is clearly shown (such as with flat lighting), that alone will differentiate it from the background. This however, can result in a certain uniformity of approach and in extreme cases the subject may resemble a figure or shape cut out of coloured paper and stuck on a background of a different colour.

The basic value of chiaroscuro (light and shade) and its manipulation for modelling remains completely valid, even in colour. A flatly lit subject lacks a feeling of solidity even if it differs in colour from the background. Such flat lighting often calls for an additional back or rim light to give the subject relief from the background.

Any deviation from the recommended colour temperature for a film caused by using a mis-matched light source causes an overall drift either in the direction of warmth (orange/red) or coldness (blue). Colour can be rendered in this way deliberately, for example, to "warm up" a scene. The same effect can be obtained by upsetting the correct colour balance with a filter placed in front of the camera lens or over the light source. Such filters, even when weakly tinted, have a strong effect.

Lights can be filtered with strongly coloured gels – pieces of sheet plastic placed over the lights. Or white light can be bounced off a coloured surface to reflect coloured light at the subject. Coloured filters such as those designed for black and white work can be placed over the camera lens. Filtering the camera lens colours the whole scene. But filtering a lamp colours it selectively, and only in those areas where that light happens to fall. Bouncing the light does the same, but in a more general way.

To outline and silhouette

Another function of lighting is to give a clear outline of a subject against its background. This technique seems absolutely false when compared with typical lighting we see in objects around us in everyday life.

How often does one see an object outlined against its background by light conveniently striking it from the rear? Rarely.

But the artificiality of the device compensates for something lacking in the two-dimensional image; anything which *subtly* assists in separating the planes in a subject or scene implies depth and thereby imparts clarity and realism to what we see.

A subject can be outlined by backlighting which gives a restrained highlight around the outer edges of the figure. Alternatively, extra light can be put on the background if necessary to differentiate it from the subject. Some of this background light may spill on to the subject and give slight "rim" lighting. An exaggerated form of outline, or rather an outline only, can be obtained by lighting the background fully and keeping all light off the subject itself – forming a complete silhouette.

Residual rim lighting reflected from the background can be cancelled by carefully positioning the background lamps behind the subject (if the subject is large enough) but turned away from it and towards the background.

Another outlining effect occurs if the lamp is placed behind the subject *facing* it, and the background and the front of the subject remain dark.

Light falling just on the edges of the subject "draws" it as a simple outline in light against a dark ground.

Distance and contrast

The contrast between the light and shadow areas in a subject lit by a single lamp does not alter substantially with the distance of the lamp unless some light is reflected from the surroundings.

If, by moving a flood lamp further away, more light is reflected off walls or ceiling, then with the lamp at a greater distance, overall picture contrast may be reduced.

The normal case in photography, however, is that a single modelling or key lamp produces too much contrast for sufficient subject detail

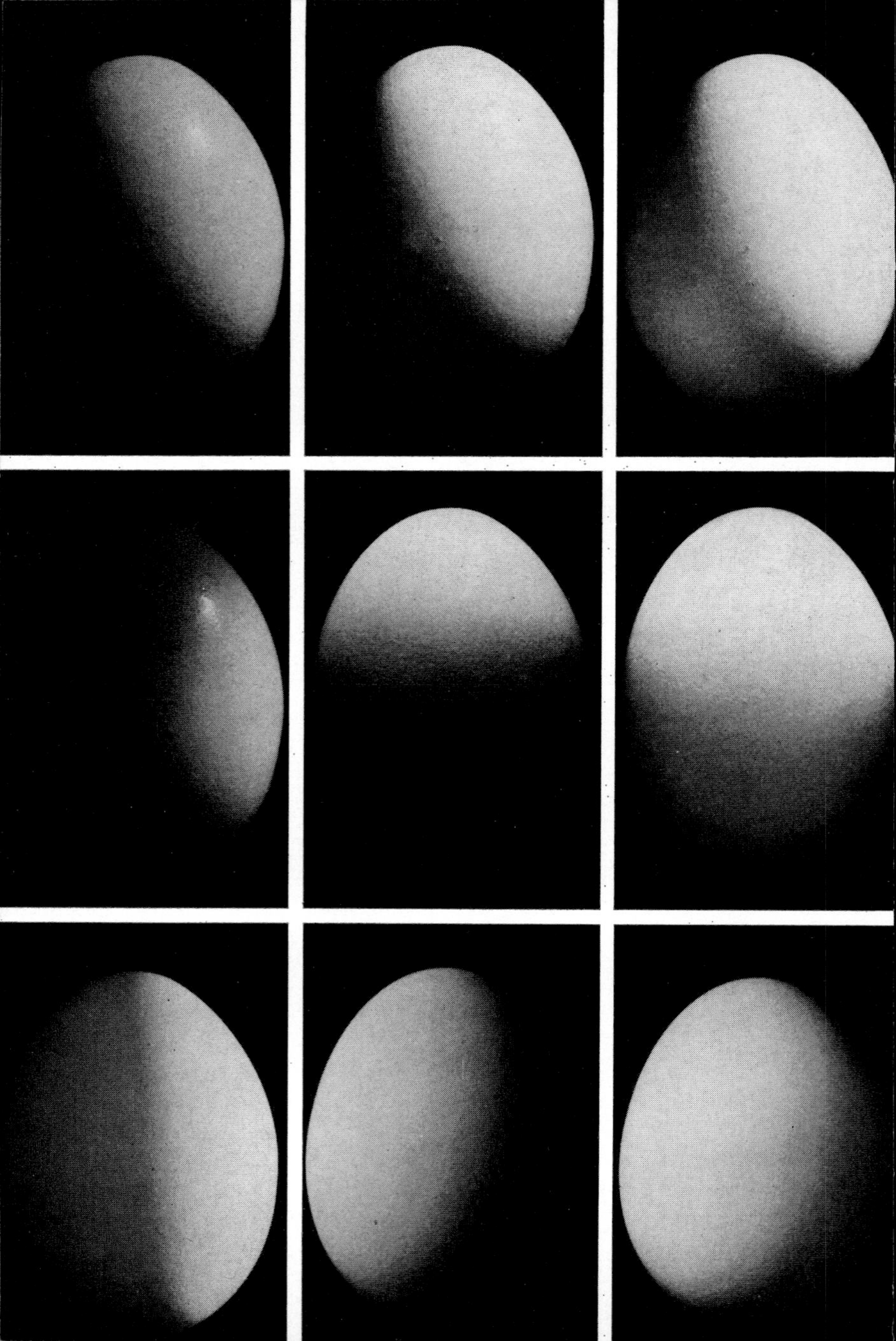

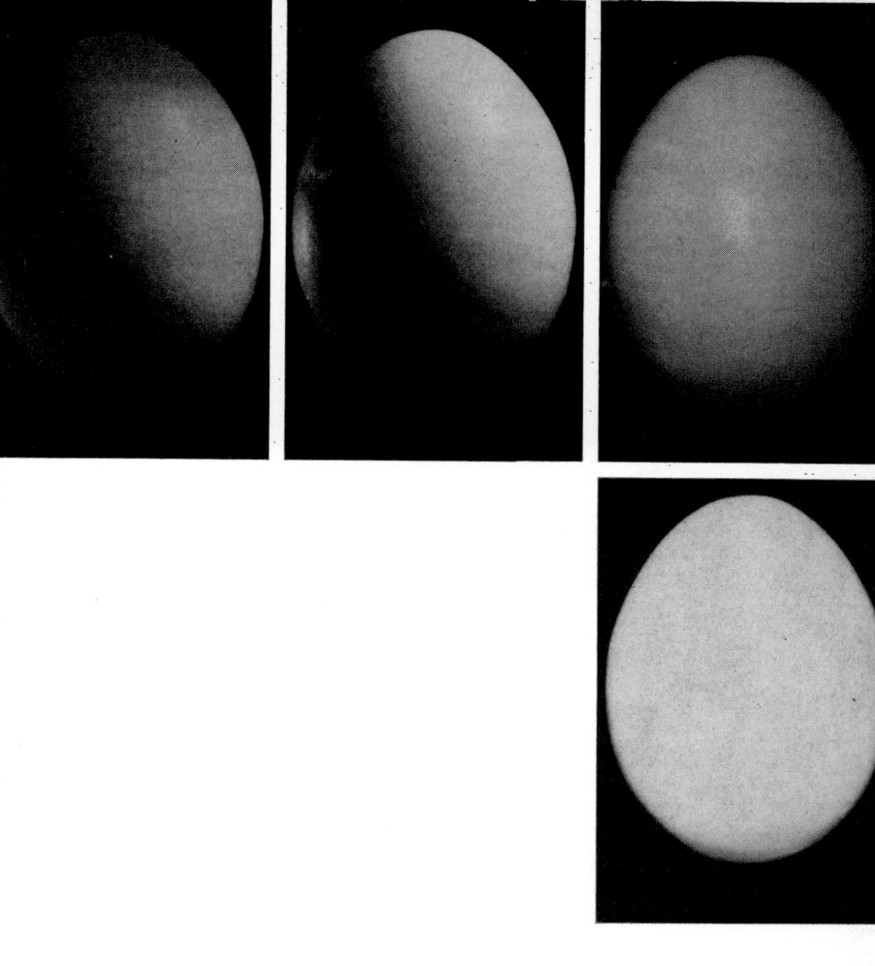

Page 97: Old wine bottles by reflected and transmitted light. These 18th century bottles are made from black and dark brown glass. *Top:* The rough surface of each is seen by frontal reflected light. *Bottom:* With the light behind transmitted through the glass, the varying thickness, joins etc become visible.

Left top: Modelling. High side lighting from one lamp; shadow filled by front lamp; shadow filled by reflector facing lamp. *Centre:* Shaded light alters apparent shape; top lighting; and with reflector from below stresses width or roundness. *Bottom:* Side/back lighting stresses length or narrowness; sweeping shadow line from high side light; followed round with second light models the solid form. *Right top:* High side light and rim lighting from rear side reflector; reflector replaced by second lamp; single direct lamp over lens giving shape and slight modelling plus highlight. *Bottom:* Front diffused source surrounding lens giving shape only, no modelling, no highlights.

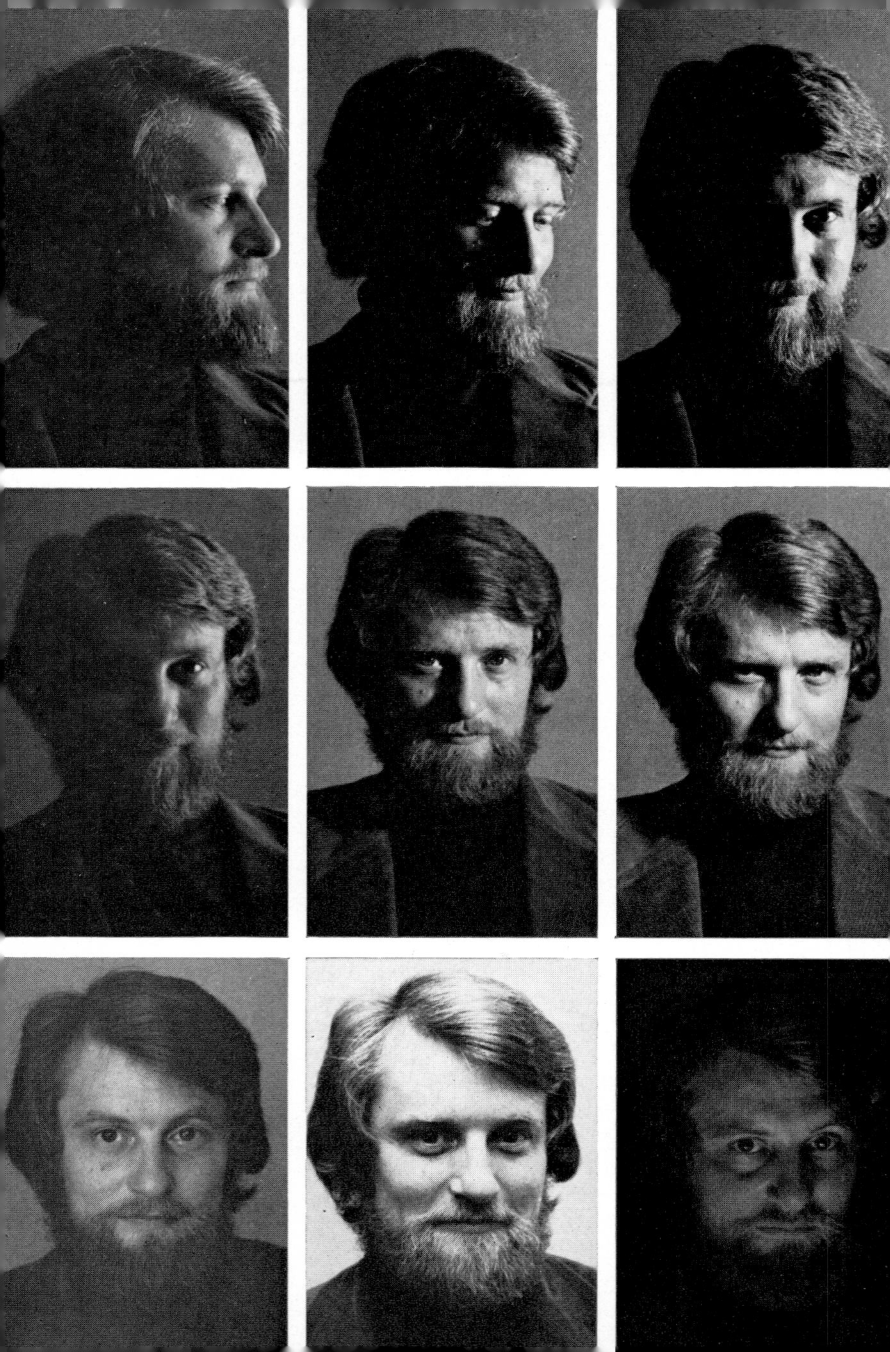

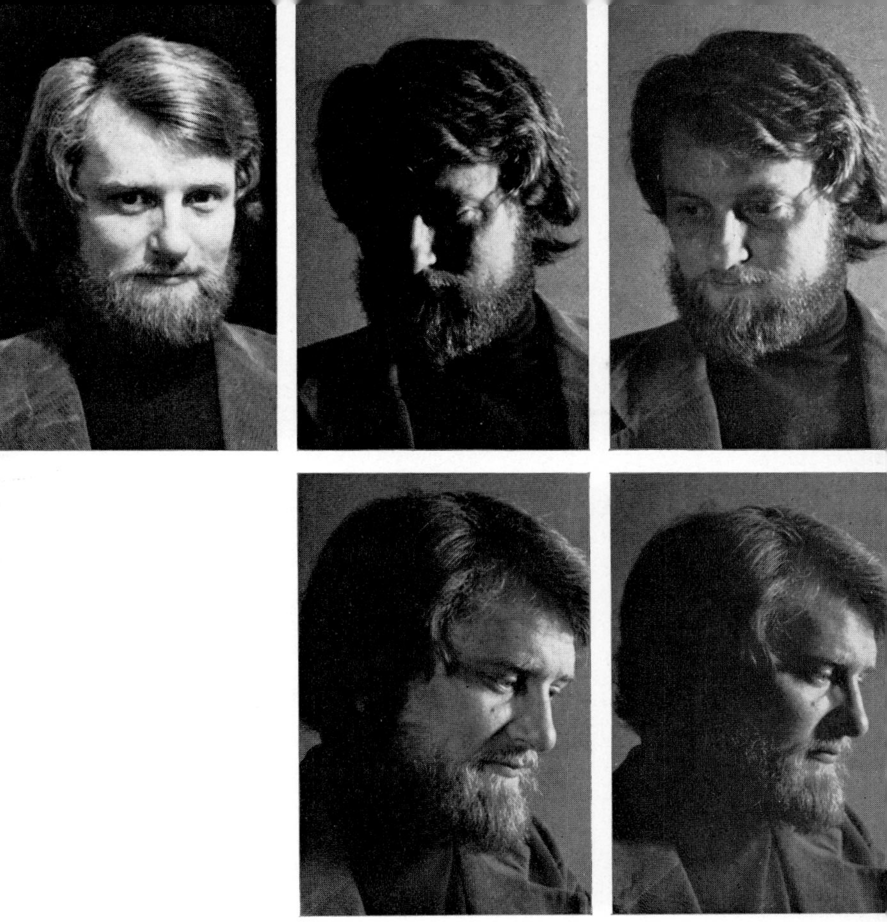

Left top: Light on the face. Rear side lighting. Profile view; three quarter view; front view. *Centre:* Front view. Rear side lighting; side lighting; front side lighting. *Bottom:* Indirect front side lighting; indirect overhead lighting; indirect lighting from below.

Right top: High side key with weak direct frontal fill. Side back lighting; and fill lamp opposite below giving modelled shadows. *Bottom:* High side key; with frontal reflector giving flat shadows.

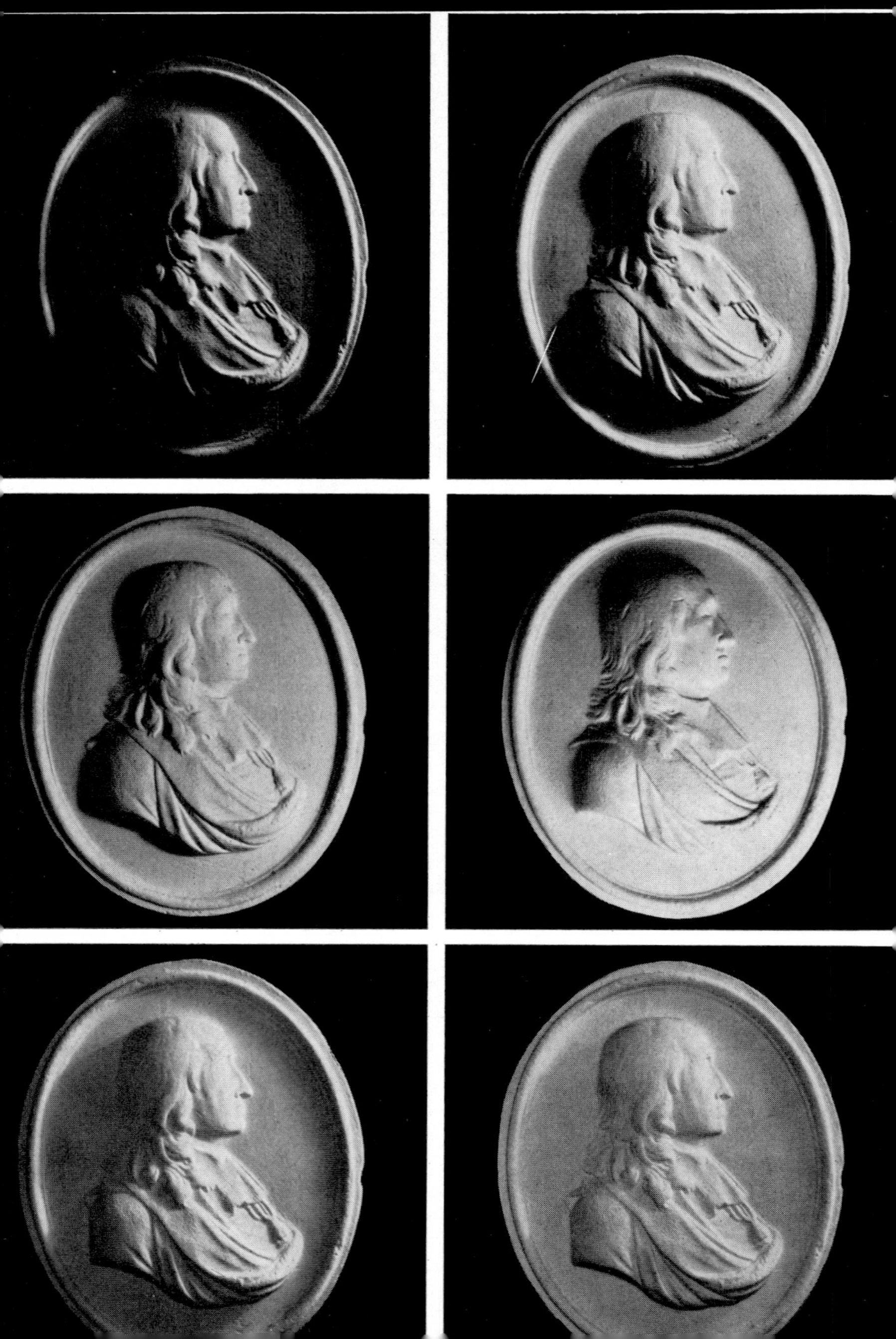

Left top pair and centre left: Lighting relief medallion (of John Milton). Lit with a key light only at decreasingly oblique angles to the surface. *Centre right:* Lit from beneath. *Bottom pair:* Same as top left but with weak, and stronger diffused frontal light for shadows. *Right:* Corresponding to centre pair opposite but with diffused frontal fill light added.

Page 104: Clown by single concentrated overhead lamp. A very complete portrai achieved with very high contrast lighting. Due to the precise positioning of lamp and subject, the light describes all aspects of the face despite partial concealment by heavy shadows – *Marcel Imsand.*

Page 105: Semi-profile using side key and backlight only with no fill from the camera position. The key is a soft fill umbrella flash at right angles to the camera. A second (un-diffused) flashhead backlights the hair. This set-up contrasts glowing flesh tones against a completely unlit background – *Colin Ramsay.*

Very soft frontal fill light on the face to complement the use of a diffusion disc over the lens. The blonde hair is teased out so that in the spot backlight it becomes iridescent – *Colin Ramsay.*

Right: Cat. Single small electronic flash head positioned slightly off centre from the camera viewpoint – a case where the texture of the subject can absorb such frontal lighting without giving a flat effect – *John Rocha.*

Page 108: Near-silhouette. By lighting the background only and avoiding any reflection from the front, most of the figure is kept in darkness. But because the background lit area is wide, light creeps round the sides of the figure. A narrow background area would give total or 'cut-out' silhouette effect – *Colin Ramsay.*

Page 109: Apostle teaspoon handles seen close up. They are lit from one side by an ordinary domestic reading lamp. Some texture is visible but the features are mainly highlighted by direct reflection from the polished metal – *Raymond Lea.*

Page 110: Not the head of a flower in close-up but a nylon brush! The base transmits the light but the bristles are less efficient at this – *Raymond Lea.*

Page 111: The light itself in the picture. Abstract pattern made from cocktail sticks laid on thin paper placed on a glass sheet above an ordinary torch – *Raymond Lea.*

Page 112: Leaves in the rain, shaped by single oblique side light which also gives each droplet its own catchlight – *Peter Rowe.*

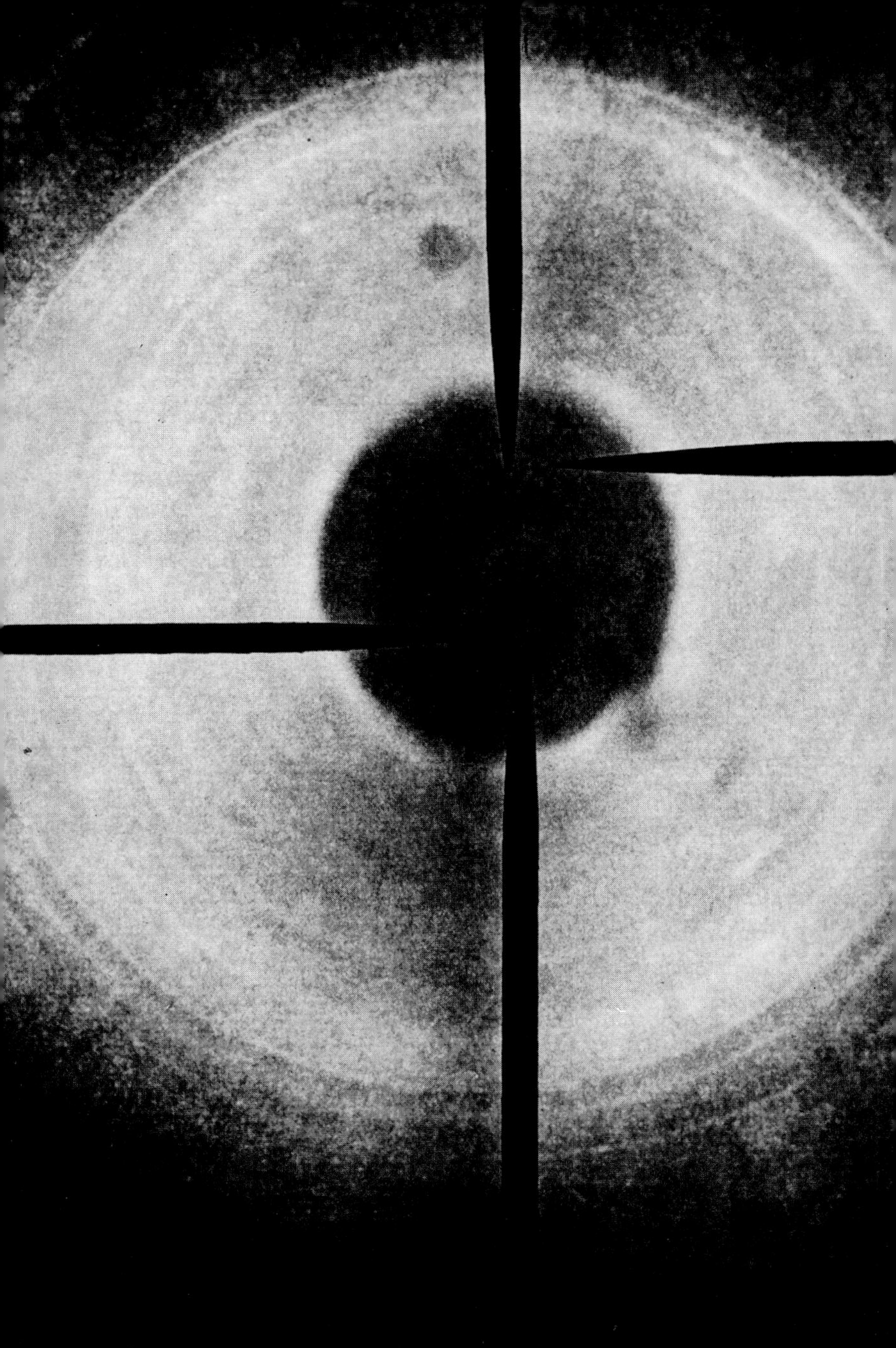

in the shadow area to register on the film. This is usually corrected by introducing a separate lamp – a fill light to lighten the shadows. In a basic lighting set up this is placed either at the camera position, giving full, frontal illumination, or slightly to the side of the camera – the side opposite to that of the key. Any adjustment of the distance from the subject of either lamp alters contrast between the highlight and shadow areas. It is usually more convenient to adjust contrast with the fill light.

The key light is the principal, and forms the basis of the modelling and composition in light and shade. It strikes the subject from a particular carefully adjusted angle. You determine the angle before the fill light is switched on.

The fill light on the other hand has a very secondary role. It comes from a very general direction and the exact angle is not critical. As a basis from which to work or experiment with contrast, start with a ratio of 4 : 1 in favour of the key light. For this, you place the fill light at twice the distance of the key light from the subject (inverse square law), assuming that the two lamps are of equal power.

A 4 : 1 ratio is, of course an arbitrary figure. "Ideal" lighting for individual subjects can vary over a wide range of contrasts. Or you may chose a particular lighting ratio to secure a certain mood. If you alter contrast you also change the appearance of a subject to some extent.

The law governing brightness and lamp distance depends on squares (see page 13), so does the aperture scale. The direct relationship between the systems allows you to make an exact exposure adjustment to compensate for the increase or decrease in subject illumination, without taking further exposure readings. If, for example, a lamp is moved to twice its original distance (giving only a quarter of the illumination) you can compensate by giving four times the exposure.

You open up the aperture by two stops by doubling the *f*-number, e.g. from *f*8 to *f*4.

Alternatively, you could make the adjustment with the shutter (if you are working with a continuous source) setting a speed of 1/60 sec instead of 1/250. Or, the adjustment could be made with one *f*-stop and one shutter speed, i.e. 1/125 at *f*5.6.

Background and foreground

The closer a subject is to the light source the more light it receives. As lights are usually set to favour the subject there is a tendency for the background to appear darker, or at least slightly underlit. This is no bad thing in many cases, as it helps to differentiate the subject and background in tone if they are anywhere near one another in colour or tone to start off with.

When you shift a light back or forward you change the relative distance from lamp to subject compared with that from lamp to background. This alters the brightness of each in relation to one another giving a separation in tone in the picture. The further away the lamp, the closer to one another in tone, or brightness, are the subject and background both lit by that lamp. The closer the lamp the greater the difference.

If the background is inherently lighter and you are shooting in black and white there is a risk that the fall off in light reaching the background will make up the tone difference so that the subject appears to merge with the background, so losing any firm outline. This can be corrected by moving the light source closer to, or further away from the subject, without altering the style of lighting set up you have chosen. If the blending effect occurred on the key lit area and you have moved the key light to cure it you have to re-establish the contrast within the foregound by shifting the fill light by an equivalent amount. If the blending occurs on the fill-lit areas you can shift the fill light only and just settle for a change in contrast. Again, you could re-establish the contrast range by moving the key light in unison.

There are other ways to alter the relative brightness of subject and background.

You can move the subject further towards, or away from the background or vice versa, so that, without moving the lights, the relative brightnesses are altered. You can shade light off the background without quite shading the light off the subject. This depends for success on the set up; a fairly high lamp position is best. Or, you can place the lamps so that the key light does not reach the background. This could mean moving the background further away.

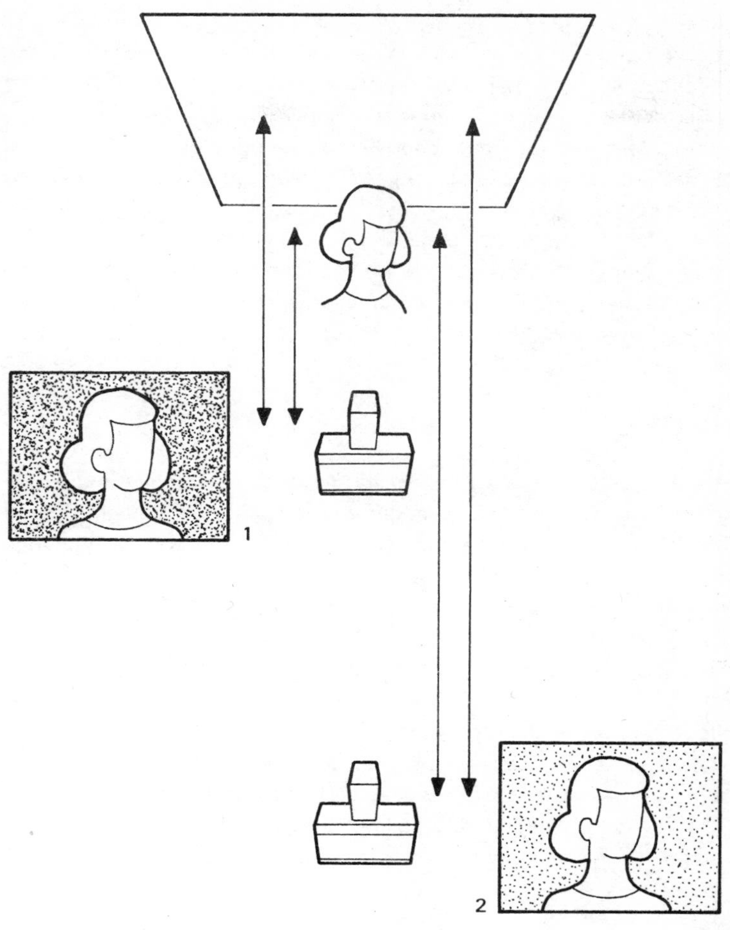

Background and foreground. 1. The closer the light source is to the subject, the greater the difference in tone between the subject and background. 2. The further away the lamp the closer in tone the subject and background become.

Another method to achieve separation is to illuminate the background with a second lamp, carefully angled to strike the background only. Separate lighting for backgrounds is discussed later with other multiple lamp techniques.
As a last resort you could choose a background of a different tone. Problems with merging subject and background are largely confined to black and white photography. In colour pictures it is unlikely that they will be of exactly the same hue. This does not mean that you can forget about backgrounds when shooting in colour. Varying the brightness changes the saturation of colours. Their balance is largely what determines the attractiveness of the picture.

One lamp

One lamp lighting is equivalent to the effect of sunlight. It is highly directional and gives sharp-edged shadows as with sunlight though that depends to some extent on whether or not the surroundings reflect light efficiently.
Another comparison can be made with sunlight. The sky is a vast, diffusing reflector.
If the sun shines from a clear sky its direct rays are mixed with soft illumination from the atmosphere. This is very much like receiving light from a bare bulb hanging in a white room.
When the sun is clouded over we receive diffused light only, but from the whole sky. It is rather as if the bare bulb were fitted with a shield that cuts off its direct rays from us and instead reflects the light onto the ceiling. Artificial light dispersed like this is seldom very bright.
So that none of the power is wasted, a photo lamp is usually made to concentrate its light with a fairly narrow angle. Even an ordinary floodlight is quite directional. So if any light is to be reflected into shadow areas of the subject it mostly comes from its immediate surroundings. The comparisons with the sun and skylight end there. Reflection from skylight is an all-pervading illumination; from a lamp it is localised. Skylight or sunlight does not diminish with distance: but light from a single lamp falls off in power very rapidly.

One lamp lighting has many uses, and some limitations. It is fine for flat frontal illumination of a subject with virtually no (or small) shadows. It works well for hard modelling with deep shadows. A spotlight gives the hardest effect.

You can use one lamp for flat copying only if the area to be photographed is very small or the lamp is far off, or its reflector is carefully angled to compensate for uneven lighting. (This doesn't work with all reflector bowls.)

A single lamp can be used with one or more reflectors, throwing some of the light in to the shadow areas. Or a mirror could throw a harder, brighter reflection like a second lamp, but not as bright as the first.

A single lamp may be combined with an existing source, in a supporting or a dominant role. Either source may be direct or reflected, hard or soft.

The remarks that follow relate to rounded or plane subjects in general. Special criteria apply to portraiture which is therefore discussed in greater detail in a later chapter.

Most people choose frontal lighting when working with a single lamp, in order to "cover" the subject in light in all areas.

If you are using the lamp for flat frontal illumination for best results in general situations have it diffused (with a handkerchief perhaps) or bounced off a reflector (your own body, provided you have near-white clothing).

Direct unreflected frontal lighting both strengthens and spreads the catchlights (direct highlights, specular reflections) to the maximum. The effect on the face is most unflattering, with large "greasy" patches appearing on the skin (see page 138).

Frontal illumination from a single source is almost always improved by raising the lamp by a small amount. This gives shape to a rounded subject yet retains fairly full illumination in all areas, with one or two catchlights at specific points.

One lamp off-axis giving full modelling, and (with no relief from reflectors) must be very carefully positioned to give a good result. You must be able to do this visually, so avoid the technique with a flash set which is not equipped with modelling lights unless you can reliably substitute a flash head for a continuous source (in *exactly*

the same position) immediately before shooting. Otherwise with flash you have to take a chance.
For maximum articulation of light and shadow the single lamp should ideally be positioned to give a feeling of roundness and sufficient penetration of light in all areas to clearly suggest the shape of the subject.
The opposite approach is to light for the maximum contrast so that all parts of the subject are either highlight or total blackness. Some people call this "bad" lighting. Some do it for effect.
You can place your single lamp *behind* the subject to give it a highlight outline and throw a shadow forward towards the camera. The light could come from directly above or almost directly below, or from a low angle to suggest an unorthodox origin outside the picture.
Reflectors can be positioned on the shadow side of the subject following the shadows round (see page 126, *Using reflectors*).

Two lamps

The most common use for a second lamp, as already described, is to adjust contrast by raising the light level in the shadows given by the first lamp. For this, a well diffused and preferably large lamp could be placed at the camera position or fractionally to one side.
The advantage of a second light for the shadows is that it gives you the freedom to light as you wish with the modelling lamp. You can concentrate on the weight and distribution of highlight areas and the shaping of the shadows and, when you have done that, use the second light to adjust the tone and modelling in those shadows.
The modelling in shadow areas is controlled by the same method as with the key, by adjusting the angle at which the light strikes the surface of the subject. Its strength is, of course, controlled by distance, diffusion or indirect use.
If the second lamp, instead of coming from the camera position, is placed at an angle between this and the key light it can give a more gradual transition from light to shade. This broader mass of graduated tone is richer in contrast because the final small edge-

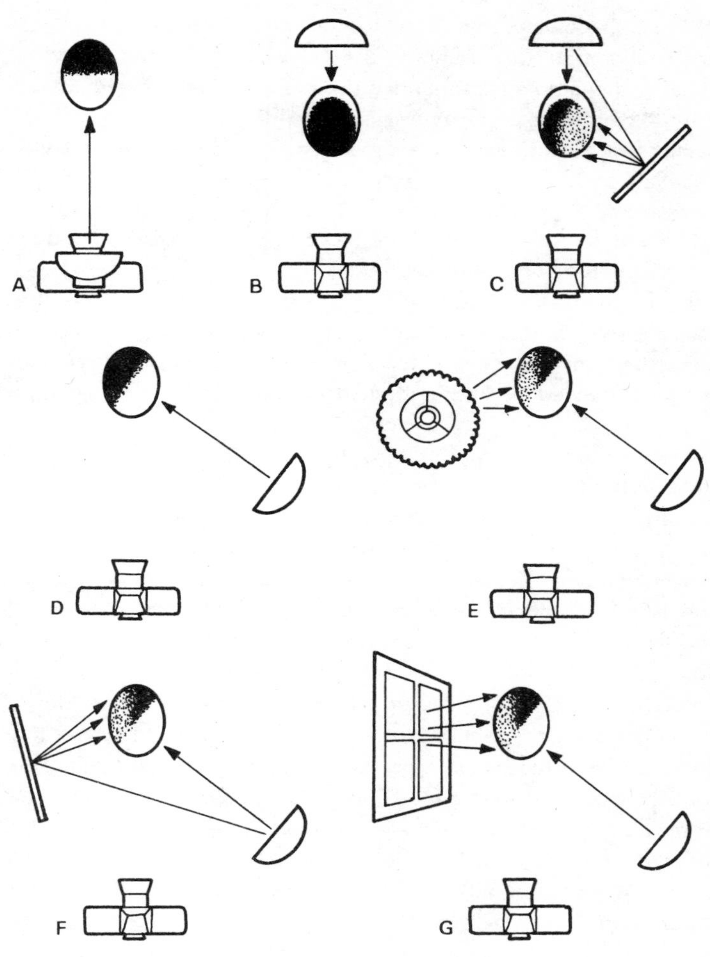

One lamp lighting. A. Flat frontal illumination. B. Lamp behind subject giving halo outline. C. Same with frontal reflector giving soft or hard frontal fill. D. Front/side lighting giving hard modelling. E. Front/side lighting plus existing household lamp filling shadow side. F. Front/side lighting plus reflector outlining spill light and directing it in to shady side. G. Front/side light with shadow filled by existing window light.

areas of shadow furthest from the lamps are almost unlit. Other modifications to the shadows are made possible by raising or lowering the lamp and graduating the shadows towards the bottom or top of the subject respectively.

Placing the second lamp on the opposite side to the key increases the likelihood that its own set of shadows will become visible, overlaid on those from the key. This unpleasant effect can be reduced by heavy diffusion of the fill light. Using a weak light does not in itself remove the cross shadows.

Even a very well diffused fill light opposite the key creates the classic cross-lighting effect and a dark river of shadow appears down the centre of the subject. This becomes both broader and more pronounced the further round the subject either of the lamps is moved.

The second lamp can be reflected from the ceiling, wall or floor, or via special reflector, to fill the shadows.

The second lamp does not just have to be relegated to filling shadows caused by the first. It can also join with the other lamp in creating lighting effects.

Two lamps placed frontally, but on different sides of the subject, give the cross lighting just mentioned. The subject is strongly lit on either side, but a darker area runs down the centre. There are also cross shadows but these disappear as the lamps are moved further round towards the back of the subject. The highlight areas also diminish (though catchlights increase in intensity) until the subject is rim lit from behind with a hard edge of bright light down each side juxtaposed directly with deep shadow areas spreading forward. This rim lighting may be combined with reflected light from the front, the two lamps would be hitting a frontally placed reflector head on so reflected light must be carefully regulated if it is to blend with the other light. It is easy to overdo the reflected light effect.

Cross-lighting lamps may be revolved about the "axis" of the subject, as it were, always facing one another. This gives modelling on one side and rim lighting opposite.

In cases where the subject itself is lit by only a single lamp (plus, perhaps, a reflector) the second lamp can be used just to light a background. This is more often the role of the third lamp.

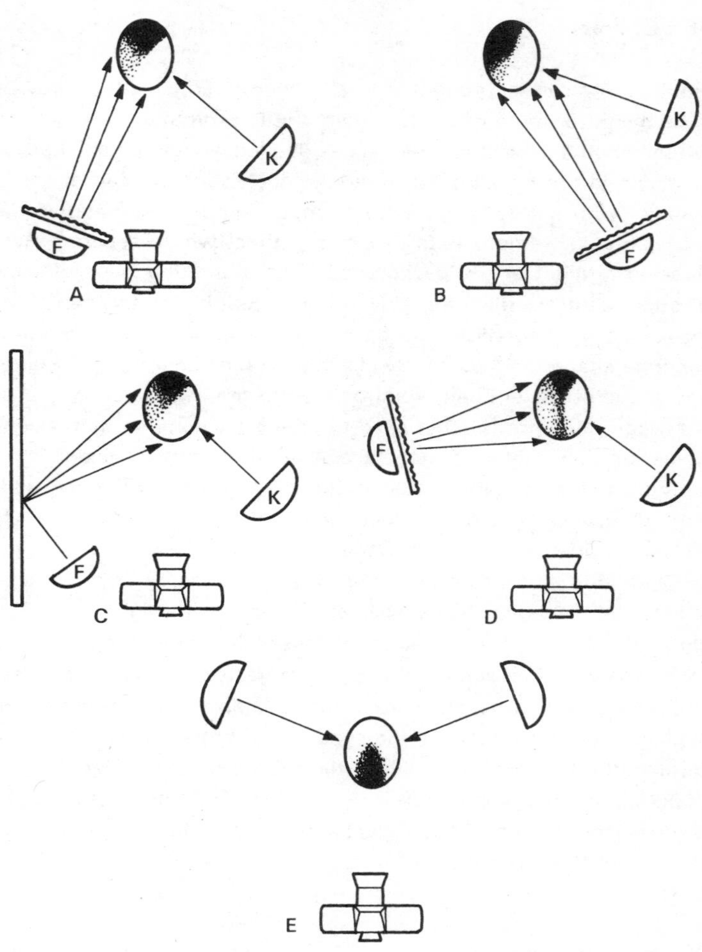

Two lamps. A. Front/side key with frontal fill light diffused for weak soft shadow filler. B. Side key with front/side fill on same side as key and diffused to soften hard edged key shadows and increase roundness. C. Front/side key with shadows filled by soft incident filler opposite, bounced from wall or ceiling. D. Front/side key with diffused filler from opposite, cross lighting causing dark central shadows. E. 'Rim' backlighting with lamps equidistant either side of subject.

Three lamps

A third lamp can be brought in to a lighting arrangement to provide a catchlight or more often, to modify the background.
Often, when a subject has been lit as desired, an unwanted shadow is visible in the background. Although such shadows can often be avoided with side, or high enough angled lighting, sometimes the most practical remedy is to overwhelm them with a separate light directed straight at the background. This also offers scope for individual control; the background light can be strengthened or weakened or shaded off with barn doors, a snoot on the lamp or a separate shader on a stand. By placing an object in front of the lamp any shape or pattern can be introduced to the background.
A background light is often used to adjust the tone so that it contrasts strongly with the subject and so throws the subject in to stronger relief. In some instances the background is flooded with light to give a "cut out" effect, where the subject is seemingly suspended in space with no shadow or support.
Background light can be restricted to small areas by barn doors or snoots on the lamp, or by shaders placed in the light path. The closer the shader is to the lamp the less well defined are the edges of its shadow. The same applies to "projected" shadow patterns. Conversely, the further they are from the lamp and the closer to the background the sharper are the shadows of projected objects.
Directed from behind the subject, the third light gives edge lighting or additional catchlights appear. A small spotlight or projector light is ideal for this effect. The catchlights enliven the image and can give it a little sparkle.

Playing with shadows

Shadows in a subject need just as much thought as the main lit area. A shadow is not just a "hole" in the picture, or something left out that can take care of itself.
It is not often that shadows are required to be black masses totally void of detail. Usually they are complementary to the lit areas and

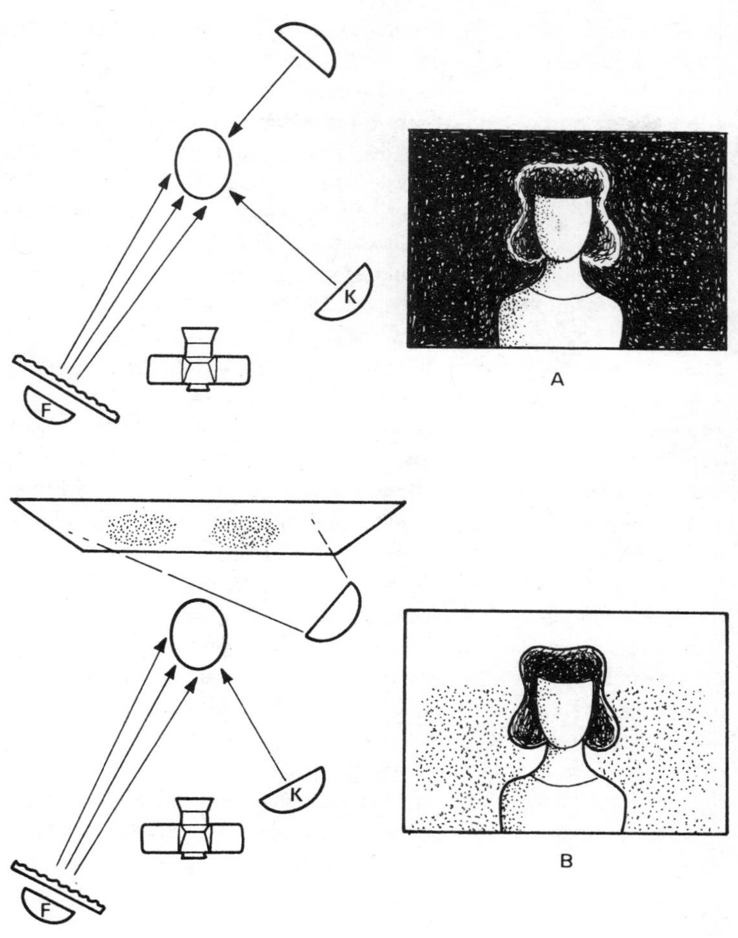

Three lamps. A. Front/side key light with weaker diffused filler close to camera on opposite side, and backlight outlining subject with rim highlight effect. The background in the picture is unlit and could be darker than the subject. B. Front/side key with weaker diffused fill and light on background to kill shadows from main lights. The background is lighter than the subject.

often have just as wide gradation of tone. It is true that they rarely contain important detail, but they can still be troublesome.

Poorly controlled shadows spoil many a picture. Even in printing nothing can be done to abate the effect of heavy shadow; if the detail is not present in the negative it can never be put in the print. If any generalized statement about shadows can be of value it is this: It is better to have too much detail visible in the shadow areas than too little. If it is there, you can always suppress it in printing. Even if you shoot transparencies, copying tends to increase the contrast.

So, to make full use of shadows and to avoid problems with them you need to know: where they occur, what causes them and how they can be controlled. In short, you should be able to play with shadows and make them do exactly what you want.

The shadows from a subject may fall underneath it, onto the surface on which it rests. Such shadows are often unobtrusive because they are viewed obliquely, unless the camera is raised and looking down. Shadows cast by the subject on to a background, on the other hand, being seen "head on" as it were, tend to encroach on the subject. They can sometimes be avoided by moving the background, or by a change in the lighting or shooting angle.

Shadows are also cast within areas of the subject itself. These can only be influenced by manipulating the light reaching the subject – by moving a lamp or diffusing or blocking the light from it.

The size and nature of a light source affects the sharpness and tone of the shadows cast in its light.

A small light source throws a sharp shadow larger than the subject and a large source gives a larger shadow consisting of a dark but unsharp central area surrounded by a blurred outer area of lighter tone (the penumbra).

A point source gives a sharp shadow at any distance between light and subject or subject and background. Only the size of the shadow increases as the lamp and subject are moved closer together or the background further away. If the subject is close to the background the shadow is at its smallest – only slightly larger than the subject. With normal photo lamps which are not point sources, the shadows are sharpest when the subject is close to the background, less well defined when further from it.

With focused lights (spots, projectors) the parallel beam gives a shadow of even tone and sharpness all over which remains the same size whatever the lamp/subject/background distances.

The shape of a shadow alters according to the angle at which it strikes a surface. This surface may be the background or within the subject itself – the same holds true.

Oblique surfaces elongate the shadows cast on them so you can alter the shape of the shadow by this method.

The density of background shadows may be varied with a reflector or additional light. The control of ordinary shadows in the subject has already been discussed.

You can have too many shadows running in different directions or too fussy shadows which distract attention from the subject. Both these problems are avoided if you *keep to simple lighting arrangements*.

The colour of shadows is not so much a question of control in the shooting as the characteristics of a particular film material when underexposed. These days most colour films behave well in this respect when exposed under the light sources recommended for them.

Light, broken up with prearranged "shadows" may be projected with a slide projector in to the subject or background. This rather artificial device may be useful on the odd occasion or for a particular effect but can easily become a mannerism if repeated too often. It is better to have background shadows with some cause for being there and recognizably connected with the subject.

All the abovementioned factors can be juggled about using more than one source. The light from one lamp weakens the shadow from another except where the shadows from the two lamps are superimposed. Then a darker area is formed.

You can cause background shadows to dominate the subject or make them subservient to it. The background shadow can represent not the subject, but something else related to it – e.g. a piece of cheese, with the shadow of a mouse creeping up behind it. There are, however, dangers of falling into crude symbolism with this device, as with all mechanical shadows generated outside the picture area.

Shadows are an almost essential part of composition in photography. They can help to give the picture a sense of visual balance. They can be put in for a purpose connected with later handwork – for example as a background for lettering.
You can shoot pictures consisting only of shadow against a light ground, working up abstract patterns in light and shade.
The main things to avoid, however, in shadows seen in the subject or surroundings are: cross shadows, multiple shadows and heavy solid shadows where they are not desired.
Cross shadows, caused by lamps competing from different directions confuse the shape of a subject, cancel out the effect of texture revealed by any one light and create unpleasant triangular dark areas which have no connection with the subject itself.
Multiple shadows, caused by two or more lamps being set close together, destroy the definition in the picture and cause double or multiple outline shadows for every feature. A proper separation of lamps and the use of diffused illumination will keep your clear of this danger.
Deep shadows most often result from either underexposure or wrong balance between key and fill lights. If an essential part of the subject is lost this is a serious problem. But it is easy to remedy! Rebalance the lighting or give more exposure. Of, if you are using a reflector, bring it closer or use a more efficient one – say metal foil instead of matt white.

Using reflectors

Walls or ceilings in a room can be efficient reflecting surfaces either for a general light dispersing effect or for bouncing light on to the subject in particular areas. But often, you have to move the subject to get the strength or angle of reflection you want.
A movable reflecting screen is more versatile than a fixed wall. It allows you to vary the intensity and angle of reflected light.
Some remarks have already been made on the basic design and function of reflectors (page 68). But there are further points on their use in lighting.

Reflectors are virtually essential with one lamp lighting such as a single flash unit used off the camera (unless it is set for bounced lighting off walls in every shot) because of the excessive contrast given by a single light in all but ideally reflecting surroundings.
A reflector can only reflect light that is already there. To be of any use it must be placed in a position where it receives enough light to reflect for the purpose. From there on it behaves like a light – with its advantages and some of its shortcomings.
All reflectors obey the rules of reflection, so if you want the strongest light from them they must be angled to catch it. The lamp and subject being at the same angle to the surface (angle of incidence = angle of reflection). This is most effective with polished directional reflectors; diffused surfaces far less so. Mirrors follow the rule absolutely.
The light from a diffused reflector, like that from a heavily diffused lamp gives less modelling effect. A large diffusing reflector used too close to the subject and providing a huge flood of reflected light gives the shadow areas a flat, whitewashed appearance. This effect has caused some people to become disenchanted with the idea of using reflectors. Yet the error is only in the technique. The reflector used should be smaller or placed further off. The reflected light should just impart a soft glow to the shadows not cancel them out.
The right reflectors should be chosen and carefully adjusted. Do not overdo the effect or it will look contrived. An adjustment to the angle of the reflector may be the only change needed to reduce or increase its light "output".
For modelling, treat the reflector like a second lamp, shaping the subject with its reflected light. With a shiny reflector or mirror you can introduce catchlights, rim lighting or bright highlights which can add sparkle to the picture or outline a dark edge and increase the plastic effect. With mirrors, as with the lamps they reflect, there are dangers of producing unpleasant highlights or even secondary shadows, so watch out for these.
More than one reflector can be used to assist modelling. For instance, if the subject is lit by a single lamp, a matt reflector placed in a front-side position could make the break from highlight to shadow more gradual while a directional or mirror reflector placed behind

the subject (opposite in the side-back position) gives a rim light effect on the highlight side. More than one reflector suitably arranged on the shadow side and extending from frontal to side-back position can create a long and gradual sweep in tone from highlight to shadow around the far side of the subject. Alternatively, the rim lighting could come on the shadow side defining the edge of this subject against a dark background, with the matt reflector filling the shadows from a side position. The subject would then be moulded in shading from light to dark with a hard glow in the darkest area to denote the shape there. This would give a full rounded appearance to any solid object.

Whatever the effect from reflected light, try to keep it fairly restrained in most pictures and thus within the bounds of probability.

Using Light at Home

For many subjects the average living room or bedroom is an excellent place for taking pictures, whether you use window light, room lighting, flash or photo lamps.

Two main problems prevail, however. The room may be so small that it prevents you from shooting certain subjects without either cutting part of them off, or getting noticeable distortion in the picture from shooting at too close a viewpoint.

The second problem concerns backgrounds. The relative clutter of the average domestic surroundings may be welcome in some pictures as it suggests a pleasant homely atmosphere. In others, the room is, in effect, doubling as a studio. An obtrusive background, even if it is only the pattern of wallpaper, the faintest outline of a doorhandle or a piece of woodwork gives the picture the unmistakable stamp of having been "done at home" when the reverse impression is desired. A domestic background is, after all, quite irrelevant to some subjects.

So before you set up a shot you should think very carefully about choosing the best area of action.

Where to take pictures

Naturally this depends first and foremost on the subject.

If you are taking pictures of a person, or a group, standing up and you want them to appear full length in the picture you generally have to go as far back as possible. You can sometimes gain some extra distance by shooting through an open door. The foreground must be cleared of miscellaneous items of furniture. If you are using photo lamps you may be able to set them up out of sight just inside the door. The long throw from this position will give sufficient evenness of illumination to cover a group quite well. A single flash head, if powerful enough, could be bounced off the ceiling. But with shots from a distance there is generally plenty of space to set up lamps.

With young children you need enough room for their activity and for you to move about yourself fairly quickly without knocking things over.

Head and shoulder portraits need at least five feet shooting range. You should choose an area that allows sufficient space for reflectors or the lamp set up you may need. Alternatively, if you are mixing lamps or flash with window light the position of the windows largely determines the shooting area chosen. You would probably be shooting across the windows (parallel to them, with the subject side lit). The shadow side could be filled by reflectors, flash or lamps. If, on the other hand, you are using the normal household lights you may have to choose a strategic position near a particular light fitting. A second light such as a reading lamp or table lamp must, of course, have sufficient flex to be brought up to serve as a fill in for the shadows. The light source in this case may even be included in the picture.

Flash or photo lamps allow much greater scope. But they do need sufficient throw to give illumination which is not too overpowering, this is especially important if you are lighting a human subject with photo lamps which, after a while, can become a strain. Again, you have to consider the conditions for bounced illumination. Are there large white (or neutral) surfaces close at hand for bouncing flash? Or is there sufficient space to bring in a reflector without having it too close to the subject?

In wide angle shots or general views of interiors, remember that spaces under furniture become very shadowy unless you set up lamps to put light in to those areas.

The smaller the subject and the closer the shot, the fewer difficulties you have with lamps and the easier it is to control the lighting.

Small subjects can be put on the table and lit with household lamps, when shooting in black and white. With colour you might use flash, photofloods or daylight – the latter is particularly suitable when you need diffused, even illumination.

With any of these light sources it is easy to position small reflectors to fill the shadows. A single flash unit used off the camera and a reflector is in many cases all you need. For a blank background you can shoot against a plain painted wall; for a continuous background use a large sheet of paper behind the subject curving round underneath it. This avoids the awkward join of background and working surface. With the light placed to one side of the subject, equidistant from the two flat areas of the paper, the gentle curve of the paper need not be revealed by shadow.

Using the lights that are there

To light a subject in the home you have the choice of flash or lamps. You might use the existing household lights, either *in situ* or moved about to suit the subject.

The wattages most people use these days allow pictures to be taken in well lit rooms with a camera whose maximum aperture is *f*2.8 or larger, with a medium speed or fast film. The limitations are that you always have to take great care with focusing, you have to steady the camera for the slow shutter speeds required and you may have to place the subject quite near a lamp to get enough light. Pictures taken in ordinary room lighting tend to be characterised by extreme contrast effects and rather shadowy backgrounds, particularly if the subject is close to the light source being used. Home lighting is often an excellent source for non-living or immobile subjects which allow weak illumination and lengthy exposures.

More powerful household lamps such as 150–200 W are useful if you intend to take pictures of people. With inanimate objects 60 or 100 W lamps are fine in most instances. In either case no more than three lamps are needed; for the most part say, for portraits and small groups, or static subjects you can make do with two.

If you are photographing a large area, such as a large room filled with people, you would probably be using the existing lighting in the room – one or two central fittings or wall lights. You might consider exchanging the bulbs for others of higher output, provided they do not burn the shades. Removing the shades gives more light but in most cases it would be excessively harsh. Never do this with clear bulbs, as their light is uneven and the film is much more aware of that than you are.

The main disadvantage with using home lighting for large areas is the shallow depth of field produced by the relatively wide aperture you have to use. If you move a lamp closer to a particular area to increase the brightness and allow a smaller aperture you find that you

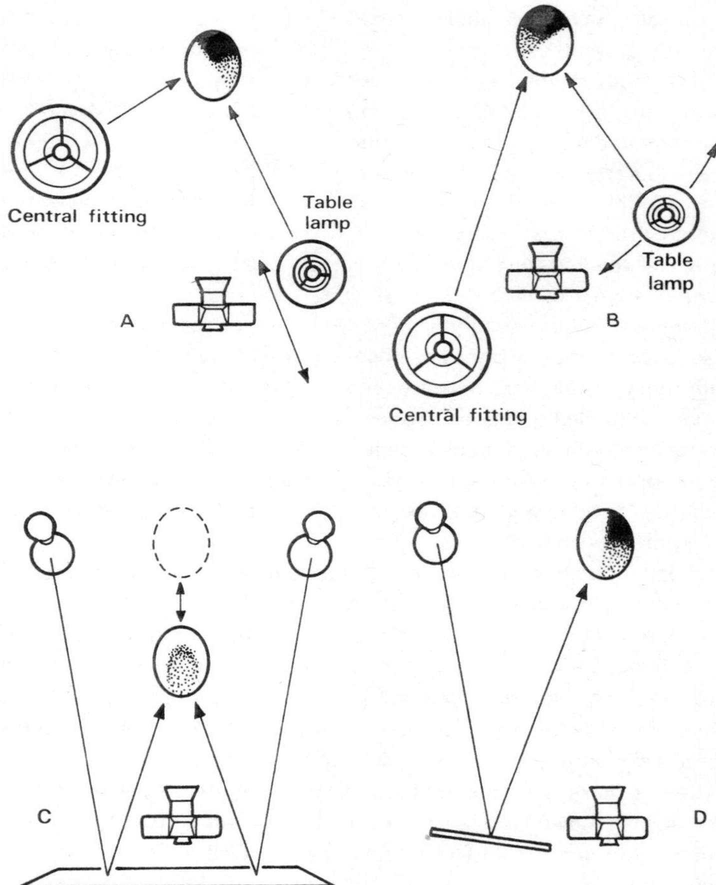

Household lights existing in a room. A. Subject positioned with fixed central light as key, movable table lamp adjusted for distance to give desired filler strength for shadow areas. B. Subject positioned for fixed central fitting as a weak filler for camera position with table lamp (key) closer and its angle adjusted for control. C. Lamp either side of the subject and reflector behind camera so that lighting varies from side to rim light, plus frontal fill as the subject is moved. D. Key and fill from one lamp by mixing direct side light by soft reflected filler from the camera position.

have also increased the difference in brightness between the nearby subjects and those further away. In the resulting picture the light falls off so rapidly that only the foreground subjects are well lit; those just a few feet further off are very shadowy, and others in the background have almost become invisible. Another problem with using existing fittings for large areas is the inevitable "hot spots" of strong light ranged around certain lamps, typically with a central room fitting or standard lamp. If exposure has been based on a general reading for the whole room, subjects placed near to these lamps appear over-lit.

If you are photographing a group you have to carefully arrange individuals so that no one is positioned too close to a lamp. Make sure that they are all more or less equally well lit wherever they are in the room. If the lighting does happen to be very even then you have no problems with large areas except to obtain a sufficiently small aperture for the required depth – which could force you to set very slow shutter speeds and put the camera on a tripod or other solid support.

For most pictures covering large areas you would certainly be better off with special photographic lamps or flash.

Smaller areas or close up subjects are a different matter entirely. If one lamp is enough to cover the subject you can move the subject or lamp to get the result you want. A second lamp could provide the shadow fill in, or you might use a reflector. You could even include the main lamp in the picture. This often gives pleasing effects.

There is more than one approach to home lighting set-ups and not all involve moving the lamps. If you have a central fitting and one or more side lamp (standard, table lamps or wall lights will do) you have the means of producing good, and even interesting lighting. One lamp can serve as the key, and the other as a fill. You can have the subject close to the central light fitting, giving the key lighting, and move up a table lamp until the shadows are filled sufficiently to give the detail needed. Alternatively, the subject could be placed near the table lamp for the key lighting. So, taking advantage of the fact that this lamp can be moved, you can adjust it to give the best modelling effect. The camera angle, and the position of subject and key (table) lamp in relation to it, would be arranged so that the cen-

tral light fitting was behind the camera or on the shadow side of the subject, providing the fill light needed. Although the output of the central fitting might be much the greater of the two it is reduced to a weak fill light because it is so far away. Again, it is a matter of balancing the effect of the two lamps to get the result you want. But it is not difficult – just a question of putting the subject in the right place.
You do not have to confine photography with household lamps to overall "flood", lighting or the classical two-lamp key and fill arrangement. With two lamps, left and right, behind the subject but out of the picture, and sufficient light reflected in to its shadow side from a wall behind the camera, a soft glowing illumination is mixed with hard and brilliant outlines.
As the subject is moved towards the lights and away from the wall, simultaneously the highlights spread around the sides of the subject and the fill light is weakened, darkening the central area between the key lit sides of the subject. Reflected light can be restored to these areas by a substitute such as a newspaper.
When a single lamp is placed to one side or above and out of the picture, or directly behind the subject which blocks it from the camera's view, a reflector placed in front of the subject and next to the camera can provide all the illumination for the subject itself. This could give a variety of effects: for example very soft modelling from one side, or (with a polished reflector or mirror) a hard and direct frontal illumination. A polished reflector must be precisely angled to give the maximum brightness. Existing lamps can be used in numerous other combinations, sometimes giving extremely attractive effects. These are discussed in much greater detail in the companion volume in this series, the *Focalguide to Low Light Photography.*

Quick, fail-safe lighting

One day, you may need some light quickly, and have no time to play about with lights or work out the best style of set-up for a particular subject. You want a dependable set-up that offers reasonable results but avoids the worst lighting faults.

1. *One flash. Soft lighting.* Working with manual flash and with a nearby subject, turn the flash towards your own body but tilted slightly upwards. Shoot by bounced light maintaining constant flash-to-body and flash-to-subject distances once you have set the gun. *For colour, your clothes must be a neutral grey or white*, but for black and white this is unimportant. You must expect this lighting to lack contrast and the background to be severely underlit.

2. *One flash. Direct lighting.* With manual or auto flash and colour or black and white, position the flashgun at least six inches above the lens, set on auto and shoot at any range or use manually and maintain the same subject distance. This lighting is again rather flat for black and white. The effect of troublesome shadows is minimized because the usual outline falls below the subject, where it is least objectionable. If the flash is too close to the camera lens, human or animal subjects may have red eyes; or in black and white pearly-looking pupils. The further the subject is from the flash the more important it is to keep flash and lens apart.

3. *One flash. Diffused lighting.* An alternative to 1, is to cover the flash (but not the auto sensor) with two layers of white handkerchief to diffuse the light – a less reliable expedient than 1.

4. *Two flash heads. Direct lighting.* In colour, you can set the flash heads each at 45° to the subject but one at twice the distance (if they are of equal power), or on half the power if it can be adjusted. There is a risk of subsidiary shadows from the weaker (fill) light. To obviate this set the two (equal power) flash heads at equal distances and cover one with two folds of clean white handkerchief. This arrangement is not too good for black and white work, so for that use arrangement 6 (with flash).

5. *Two flash heads. Diffused lighting.* As 4, but with handkerchieves over each head, one placed half as far away as the first (*not* twice the range). Very soft lighting with two heads can be obtained with bouncing off walls or ceiling but this technique depends on several external influences and is so far from "fail-safe" (unless you have plenty of experience with bounce flash).

6. *Lamps. Direct lighting.* Model and fill. Two floods of equal power; one is at 45° to the subject and the other directly above the camera angle at twice the distance of the first.

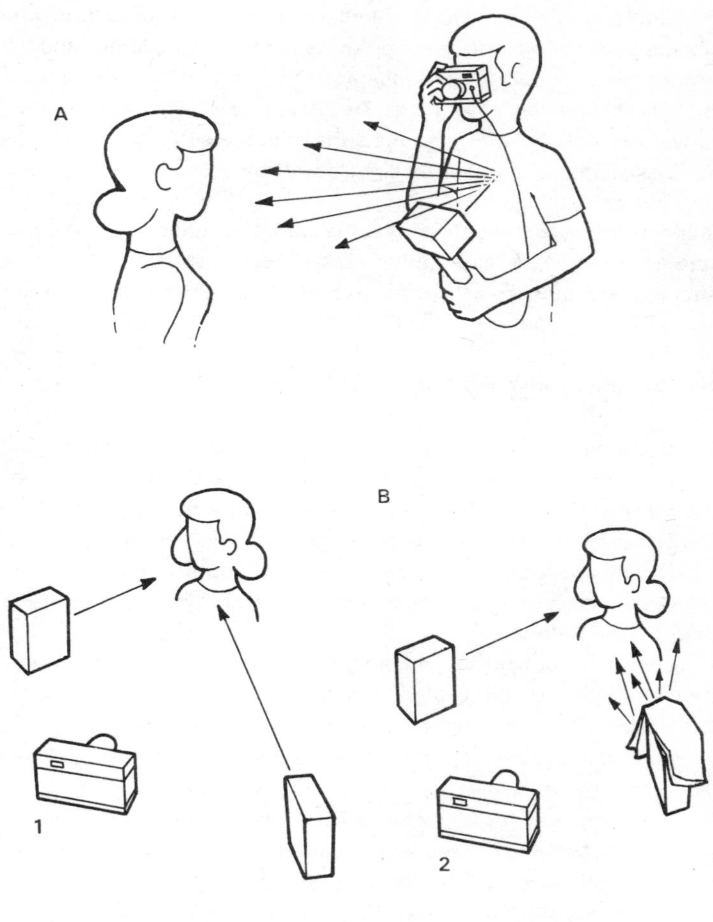

Flash technique. A. Soft frontal illumination by bouncing flash off the photographer's own body. B. Classical two-flash set up with 1, filler at twice the distance of the key and 2, lamps equidistant from subject but folds of handkerchief to weaken and diffuse fill light.

7. *Lamps. Diffused lighting.* Similar arrangement to 6 but with tracing paper or acetate sheet diffusers in front of the lamps and the second lamp at half the distance again of the first.
8. *Lighting for flat copy work.* Two lamps or flash units of equal power each placed at 45° to the surface of the subject. Or, take the subject outdoors and use daylight on an overcast day, particularly for colour.
When using automatic flash avoid very strong reflectors in the picture area such as a large mirror directly behind the subject. (Lamps should never be seen in mirrors, except for deliberate flare effects).

Simple all-purpose lighting

No single lighting set-up can give good results in all situations. If it is just a matter of getting light on the subject regardless of the quality you can put a flash gun on the camera pointing directly at the subject, set the correct aperture and shoot. A single lamp could go directly above the camera. The lighting in both cases will be unpleasant with large specular reflections which give a 'greasy face' effect in portraiture.
Despite the popularity of on-camera flash there is virtually no situation where this would be a good method of lighting the subject. It is considered all-purpose lighting but is really no-purpose lighting. The arrangement is purely for the convenience of having the flash and the camera as one unit.
With colour, the simplest and best one-lamp method for general purposes is heavily diffused frontal lighting. With a flash unit bounce the flash off your own white shirt or blouse. Or, use it pointing directly at the subject, but positioned above the camera and with a diffuser over the front of the unit (but not over the auto sensor). With a photo lamp, use this in the same position but diffused. A large flood with back-reflecting lamp shield will be best.
This lighting will not do for black and white work. Take your single diffused light source about 20° off the camera axis and somewhat higher than the camera lens. As a general rule always keep your lamps above the lens height, *never* below. With the lights placed

fairly high you have a far better chance of getting good modelling; the shadow in the subject is not just to one side but partially beneath it as well, increasing the effect of roundness. Shadows cast by the subject are down behind it. For simple two-lamp lighting use the 45–45 set up given as No 4 above, or set up No 6 which is a better arrangement.

With portraits, when you are using lamps and can see what you are doing, watch the shadow beneath the nose, and try to keep it fairly small. Do not have the eye sockets totally in shade nor a heavy shadow from the hair cast across one eye. You should be able to see two distinct catchlights one (not two) in each eye.

Local lighting for close range

Under this heading we are concerned with improvised close range lighting for shots taken with the minimum preparation. For more serious work where you want the best quality results turn to page 175 where close up photography is discussed in greater detail.

Close range can mean anywhere from head and shoulder portraiture to the point where the subject is reproduced on the negatives at life size or larger.

When a subject is photographed at close range, the camera lens naturally covers a much smaller area than normal. So you do not need the same spread of light. You can bring the lamps forward to concentrate their brilliance just on that area and its immediate surroundings. But you don't have to, of course. You can leave them where they are and shoot with the same illumination as you normally use. But there is an advantage in brightening up the light in close up work. The closer you shoot, the less depth of field is available at any given aperture. The field is often too shallow for the whole of the subject to be focused at once – unless you use a tiny aperture. To maintain correct exposure with this you need either to give a long exposure or have the subject brightly lit. The latter is usually more practicable, especially at extreme close range when you sometimes have to increase exposure anyway to allow for light loss with extension tubes or bellows where these are used. But you have the choice.

When you move a lamp up to a subject as, for example, when you bring a table lamp closer to a person's face, that becomes proportionally much more brightly lit than the background (inverse square law again). That is why table lamp portraits usually have dark backgrounds. This basic fact applies with any subject seen in depth. (For flat subjects, or those which are mostly seen in one plane this is immaterial.) With portraits taken at close range the relative darkness beyond the subject can hide unwanted background features and help keep the background "clean". A simple rough-and-ready method for close up work, especially copying, is to use daylight, outdoors, or through the window. On overcast days it is diffused, and very even.

Failing this, you can set up one or more lamps to imitate it. Bounce your flash off a large sheet of white paper set up to face the subject, but slightly to one side of the camera. Or use a sheet on either side. Photo lamps or domestic lamps can be diffused by placing them behind a broad sheet of tissue or tracing paper, or in front of the reflector. Shield the bulb itself, to prevent any direct rays reaching the subject.

Another method is to place the subject inside a white cloth "tent" and position your flash or lamps outside, lighting through the material.

The fact that you can easily provide *enough* light for close-ups, is apt to make you forget that at close range the same principles of lighting technique apply as for normal work. You want even illumination, you need to shape the subject and you have to fill the shadows to reduce the contrast. Solid objects should be lit with an appropriately angled key, and filled with diffused light from the camera position. Subjects in low relief, such as coins or bas relief medallions need very oblique key lighting, as do any subjects where the surface or texture is important, such as cloth, embroidery or, say, needlework pictures.

When you move the light closer to the subject the contrast increases. Any effect of softening gained by having light originate from a large area relative to the subject is more than cancelled out

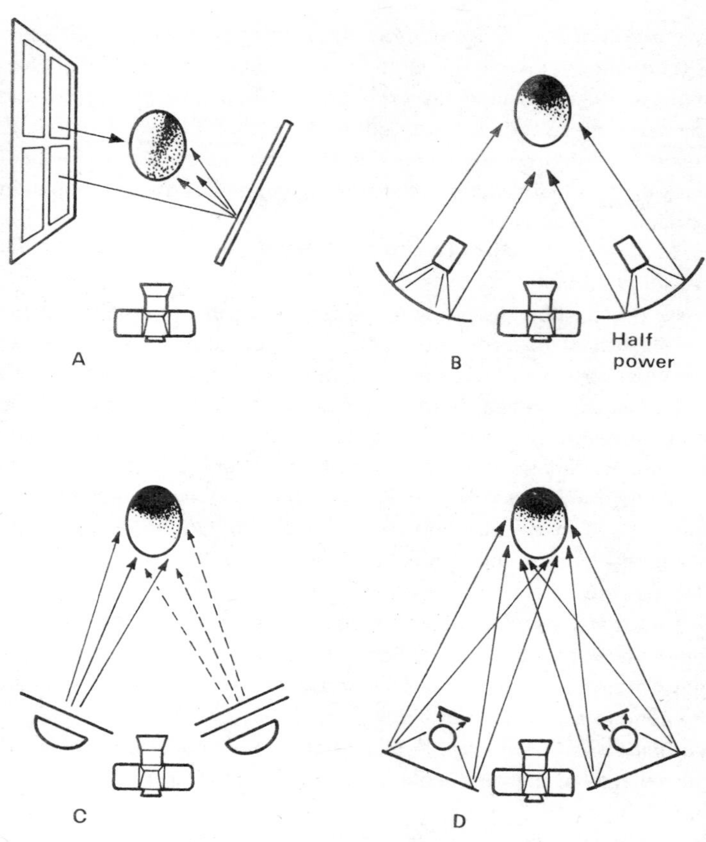

Diffused lighting for close range work. A. Daylight. Windowlight plus reflectors. B. Flash units equidistant either side of the camera facing reflectors and bouncing light at the subject, one at half power as a filler. C. Lamps behind paper and equidistant from subject; one (filler) double diffused with two layers. D. Lamps backed by paper reflectors but swivelled so that only indirect (very soft) light reaches the subject.

by the loss of light reflected from the surrounding walls, ceiling etc. (if there are any) when the lamp is moved in. So, to get full shadow detail you need to increase exposure by about one *f* stop (beyond any extra needed for the lens extension).

Shield the light from the camera lens if it is close by, using a piece of black card. Avoid casting a shadow of the lens on to the subject in extreme close up work.

Watch out for any reflections from the camera itself which may appear in a shiny subject.

If you use flash in close ups make sure it is actually pointing at the subject. Many on-camera units can not be tilted downwards, so wherever possible remove the unit, put it on a sync lead and point it at the subject yourself. Automatic flash still works in close up, giving extremely short exposures. (This can cause a shift in colour balance on some materials). Also, if the subject is of very different tone from the background the sensor could be misled. If in doubt, use the flash manually, if necessary diffusing it with folded handkerchief to reduce the output, and bracket the exposures.

The main things to be sure of in close ups of objects are:

Overall sharpness. Check, where you can, on the focusing screen of the camera, or with depth of field tables. Even the smallest aperture may not give enough depth. To increase depth you may have to take the camera a little further away.

No black shadows. Large detailless shadows should be avoided in close ups, especially if the object of the picture is to convey information.

Correct these by using more fill light than usual, or diffuse light only. Or, keep the light fairly frontal.

Good colour rendering. Use the light source to match the film, avoid having strongly coloured objects nearby that might reflect some light and cause a colour cast. Bracket the exposures, whether or not you are in doubt.

No distortion. If the subject appears to "bulge", move the camera further away and either use a lens of longer focus or enlarge up a smaller part of the negative area.

Even illumination. Move the lights to correct unevenness, or use equal lights at equal range and angle.

Light for larger areas

Ideally, to light a large area you want powerful lamps placed far away and arranged at various strategic angles so that their light falls just where required. Such lighting is unfortunately seldom available outside a theatre or film studio.

Lighting large areas with small resources calls for some cunning. You don't always have to light everything you can see. Sometimes the result is more attractive if parts of the subject are in shade. Often those parts are not even visible in the picture and do not need to be lit. More of that in a moment.

Suppose you have a large interior and you want to light the entire area. You have an electronic flash unit that tells you that you can shoot with it up to a range of 30 ft at a certain aperture. The trouble is that when you expose for the subject at 30 ft, other areas closer to the camera become overlit and faces are washed clean of any features. If you set an aperture for the middle distance, the background may come out dark, and the foreground subjects might still be overexposed. The trouble is that this direct light falls off too quickly to light a whole room evenly *in depth*.

One possible way to light such a large area evenly is to bounce the flash off the ceiling. You aim the flash at a point on the ceiling half way down the room. The main bunch of light rays bounce off and fall on the subjects at the far end. Hopefully, subjects in the middle distance are lit by a mixture of bounced light from the ceiling overhead and some direct rays from the gun, while subjects nearby are lit by oblique rays from the gun. This gives roughly even illumination in depth – in theory at least. But it *can* work, if all the circumstances are right and you are lucky. The same method could be used with the wall of the room instead of the ceiling but is less reliable because the wall is rarely such a good reflector. Or it may be in the picture itself and so appear as an overlit area. Or, again, it may have a gloss paint, mirrors or glass fronted paintings which can cause very perverse reflections if you are out of luck.

Bounced lighting used over very large areas with only one unit is, in more than one way, a leap in the dark. Nevertheless, manufacturers of flash guns often design units with a tilting flash head that may be set at any angle for bounced illumination. But this one-light method is not really practicable for anything but flash, and with large areas only the units with a fairly high output can do it. Even if it is successful, the lighting will not be particularly attractive, though this may not matter to you.

So, to light *in depth*, yet avoid a fall off in illumination with distance, you have to take the lamp or flash round to the side of the subject. You can use it direct. Or, if you bounce it from a side wall or reflector you will get a wider distribution of light. Lit from the side, subjects near or far from you receive approximately the same amount of light, depending on the angle of the light source.

To light in greater depth, place a second lamp or flash further in to the room. But try to keep it out of sight of the camera lens to avoid flare effects. Either shade the light, hide it behind some feature or object in the room, or keep it just outside the picture. Areas of the wall used for bouncing the light should always be excluded from the picture. This is not so important with the ceiling, which is probably white anyway and will not look so different if overlit.

There are quite a number of ways to hide a lamp. It can be placed behind a chair, a chest, a person, or just outside an open door, behind a chimneybreast or even behind the shade of a table lamp. If the lamp is switched on any spill light looks as if it has a good reason for being there and so appears quite natural. Lamps or flash placed in the picture can provide side or frontal illumination, But it would appear more realistic if two lights were used from more or less the same direction. You could use a side-front lighting position for the foreground subjects, having the first flash unit to one side of the camera. The second flash, resting on the mantleshelf half way down the room, could be similarly angled.

There are other methods of lighting in depth. You can light the distant areas with a spotlight, placed sufficiently high for its beam to pass over the foreground subjects. Or a direct flash could be used, calculated for that range (with auto sensor or aperture setting) but shielded from the foreground areas. The foreground could be separately lit from a flood nearby or a separate weaker or bounced flash. The foreground lighting can be arranged to equalize, giving an effect of overall evenness.

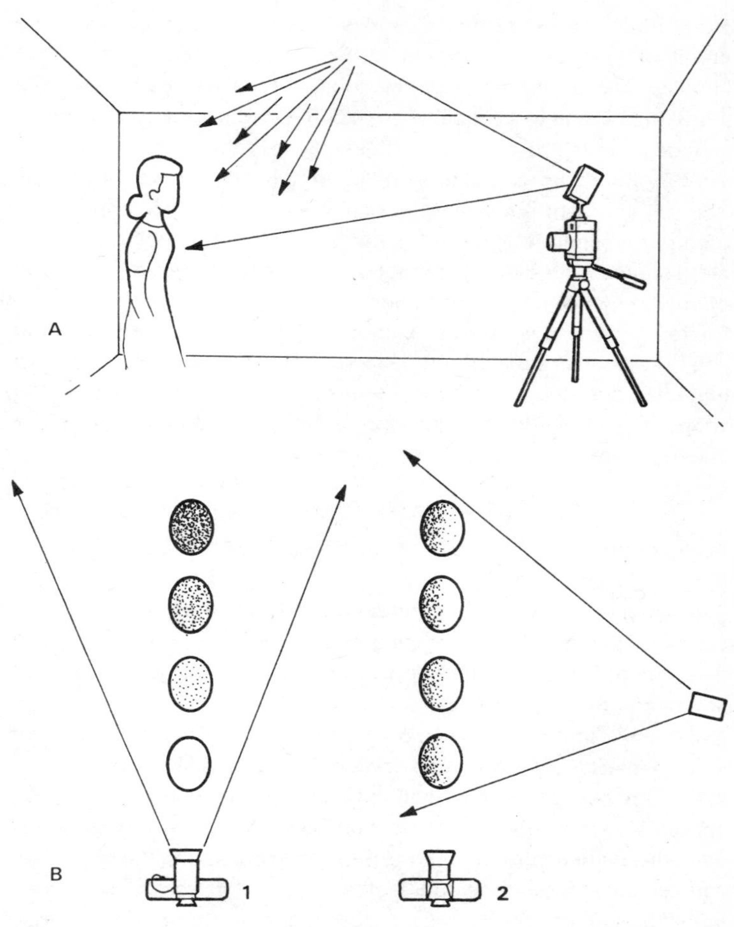

Lighting interiors and in depth. A. Subject across a room lit by flash, angled to bounce soft (key) light from ceiling, mixed with some direct (fill) light from the unit. B. Lighting in depth: 1. Front lighting: Subjects darken with distance. 2. Side lighting: Lights subjects equally regardless of their distance from the camera.

Remember that the further a lamp is from a subject the greater the depth of evenness in illumination. So for this purpose, place your lamps as far as you can from the subject. (This can be difficult in a large room when you probably already have your back to the wall to include as much as possible of the subject in the shot.)

Another approach is not to attempt to light the whole area at all. You can just light the subject, which might be near the camera, and then put a separate light on the background. Forget about the middle distance. The camera cannot see the area in between, so it is often simply not necessary to light it.

Sometimes there is an even simpler solution. You make the lamp itself the central subject and have your subjects suitably placed so that they are all well lit by it. For instance, you could have all the people in the middle of the room seated round the light pool of a standard lamp.

What to avoid

The remarks that follow are not supposed to add up to a complete list of do's and dont's in lighting technique. They are warnings of things to avoid generally when taking pictures at home. Some, if ignored, can be very troublesome indeed.

Avoid using too many lamps; one or two are easier to manage. Add them one after the other, building up the lighting in stages.

Watch the backgrounds as well as the subject. A clear area is a safer background than one filled with household furniture, fittings or ornaments. When photographing people, keep strong horizontal or vertical features (such as door jambs and window frames) well away from the subject. They tend to cut the picture up. Sometimes they look as if they are growing out of the heads of the people you are photographing.

Avoid having mirrors, glazed pictures, gloss painted woodwork or windows without drawn curtains (especially at night) immediately behind the subject and facing the camera, particularly if you are using auto flash, which can be seriously misled by a strong reflection received head-on into the sensor.

Hiding a lamp from the camera. A room offers many hiding places to put a lamp or flash unit in the picture area: 1. Behind a chimney breast. 2. In a doorway. 3. Behind a subject's body. 4. Under a chair. 5. Behind an existing lamp. 6. Behind a chest.

Keep lights clear of strongly coloured reflectors that could throw a colour cast on to the subject.

With groups, keep the lamps far enough away to avoid uneven lighting, or arrange all the people at roughly the same range from the light source.

Pictures by existing indoor light tend to be shadowy, and have high contrast so don't rely on highlight exposure readings only or you will have nothing visible elsewhere in the picture.

With colour film, avoid mixing light sources, unless they are of nearly equal colour temperature, e.g. flash and daylight.

General views of rooms usually contain dark areas in corners, under furniture, etc. unless you put some light in there also. In monochrome, wooden furniture often comes out looking rather dark. Increase the light level or expose for darker woods by the equivalent of at least two whole stops (four times the exposure).

Do not assume that a wide angle shot will necessarily be covered by the lighting. Most flash units quote an angle of illumination; some can be varied. If it is not wide enough, use the flash indirect, say bounced off the wall behind you or off a reflector. Keep flash units from the lens axis by at least several inches, and above rather than beside it, otherwise you could give people in the pictures red eyes. Have the flash further back than the front of the lens; spill light can cause heavy flare or light streaks.

Do not have your light below camera level throwing shadows up behind the subject unless you want that effect. Generally, the lighting is better with the main lamps kept above, even quite high above, the camera level.

But do not put the lamps too high. This can give deep shadows in the eye sockets and lose the catchlights there, deadening the eyes. It also gives long nose shadows.

Too oblique an angle, on the other hand, can cast a bad hair shadow over the face.

Do not put two or more lamps or flash units close together unless at least one of them is sufficiently diffused to remove its shadow, otherwise you get double or multiple shadows. Lights paired to increase the light level are best used indirectly.

Avoid cross lighting from lamps of equal power.

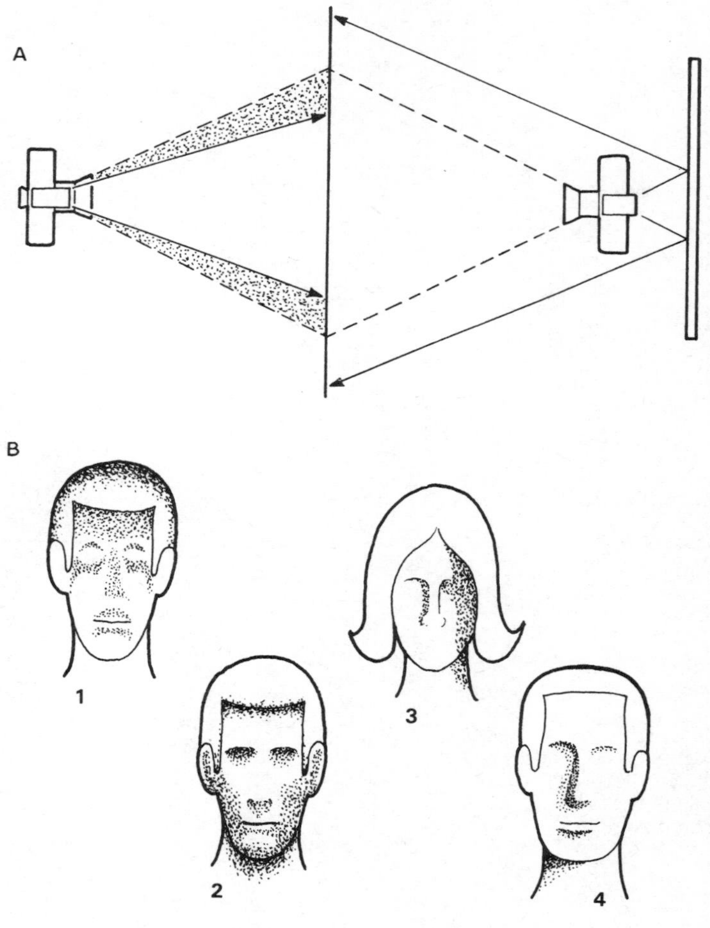

What to avoid: A. The angle included by a wide angle lens can be greater than that covered by the flash, so widen the flash by bouncing it off a reflector. B. Extreme lighting angles: 1. Too far beneath. 2. Too steep an angle over-head. 3. Too oblique an angle casts heavy main shadows across face. 4. Two lamps close together give double shadows.

Out and about with Lights

When you go outdoors to take pictures you may want to take your own lighting with you. There can be several reasons for this. The excessive contrast in a picture taken in direct sunlight can be reduced by using flash as a fill in for the shadow areas. If the background in your picture is much brighter than the subject, you can redress the balance by lighting the subject with flash. Or, if it is a bright day but the sun is not out, yet you want some sparkle in your pictures you can add your own "sun" with a flash from a suitably high angle.

All these uses give you some control over what light falls where – even outdoors. And if you are shooting in colour, of course the flash, bulb or electronic, corresponds in colour temperature with daylight, so it can blend well if used properly.

If you are going to take pictures indoors, in a hall or church for example, the flash is very useful ally. Even if the basic light is actually there, you can use your own to fill dark corners or perhaps to highlight the main subject of the picture. You may sometimes have to rely on it entirely if there is movement in the scene and you can not use a time exposure. Even with time exposures there are methods of using the same flash repeatedly. A small electronic unit is ideally suited to this.

You may decide to use lamps for your interior, perhaps because you like to see the lighting while you adjust it. For this purpose, you could taken two or three lightweight floods, with spare bulbs, a selection of plugs and enough cabling to ensure that you can draw power even from inconveniently placed sockets. A simpler approach is just to take a couple of photoflood bulbs and put them in existing sockets – it all depends what standard of result you are hoping to achieve.

Flash enables you to work inconspicuously and does not require the collaboration of other people unless you want someone to act as a flash stand. You can use flash for candid shots – or, at least, *one* candid shot until you have drawn attention to yourself by firing it! You can take it indoors or out, and you can shoot pictures at night with it.

Indeed, when it comes to mobility and practical scope when you are out and about, the small electronic flash unit wins hands down.

Where you can or can not use lights

Where you are going to set up lamps and draw power, on someone else's property, you obviously need their blessing. But you should have the owner's consent even if you are using your own pocket flashgun. In some cases you will not get permission however hard you try. You may not even be allowed to take pictures. This is often the case with night clubs, and other places giving theatrical or musical performances of any kind. Obviously, flashes could be very disconcerting to an artist concentrating on his act but there is also the question of copyright and the interests of people whose livelihood is to handle the publicity. Amateur performers, politicians and exhibitionists of other kinds however, often welcome the possible publicity you might be bringing to them.

In many instances you are allowed to take pictures on payment of a small fee. Many establishments make a distinction between amateur and professional work and charge many times the fee for the latter – for example if an interior were being used as a setting for fashion shots. But the old prejudice against flash photography is dying now that most people use electronic units and do not leave a litter of spent flashbulbs that are crushed underfoot or ground into the floor. The authorities concerned may stipulate that only electronic flash may be used and not bulbs. (Normally you need special permission in the most lenient places if you want to set up a tripod. But this is because it is a hazard for other people – even in an amphitheatre someone will contrive to fall over it. The same strictures would apply to any lights set up on stands, particularly with the extra inconvenience of trailing power cables!)

Nobody seriously believes that a flash gun used for ordinary photography will damage a painting or the furnishings of a room. (Nor, incidentally does it harm a baby's eyes as people often used to say.)

The main reason for objecting to the use of flash is the one levelled against photography in general – the annoyance caused to other people, or the curtailment of the sales of slides or colour prints which produce revenue for the custodians of a building.

It would be unreasonable of you to flout such regulations deliber-

ately, however petty, as this makes things more difficult for other photographers who come after you.
Nothing can prevent you from using flash outdoors unless you are simply forbidden to take pictures. In the UK this would mainly apply where you were either on private property or in the vicinity of military installations. Normal photography in public places is unrestricted, except in some areas where you may not set up a tripod (such as in royal parks, or certain city zones in the UK) without written permission. By-laws covering public transport property, for example, may prevent you from taking pictures on underground railways.
Some people take pictures where they are not allowed. But a flash would be a very effective way of advertising what is going on!

Using and improving on existing light

You can use your independent light source to improve on the light that already exists in a scene, to predominate over it, or to cancel out its effect altogether. With colour, flash is the natural "mixer" with daylight as they correspond in colour temperature. The most common use of flash outdoors is as a filler for the shadows and this is discussed on page 159. It has many other uses however. The main problems in combining existing and added light are those of adjusting their relative strengths and getting the exposure right.
If you are shooting pictures of people by daylight through a window you can put some detail in to the shadow areas by direct or indirect flash. The same principles apply of course when combining flash or lamps with any existing light source, except that with colour you should take care to use sources of matching colour quality. Window light is a common case where flash can be mixed without such problems. Exposure must be based on a highlight reading taken from the subject as lit by the daylight but at a shutter speed that is also satisfactory for your flash unit. As this is likely to be a fairly slow speed anyway there is no problem with obtaining a wide enough aperture with say, medium speed film.
Base the flash distance on the aperture chosen by dividing the

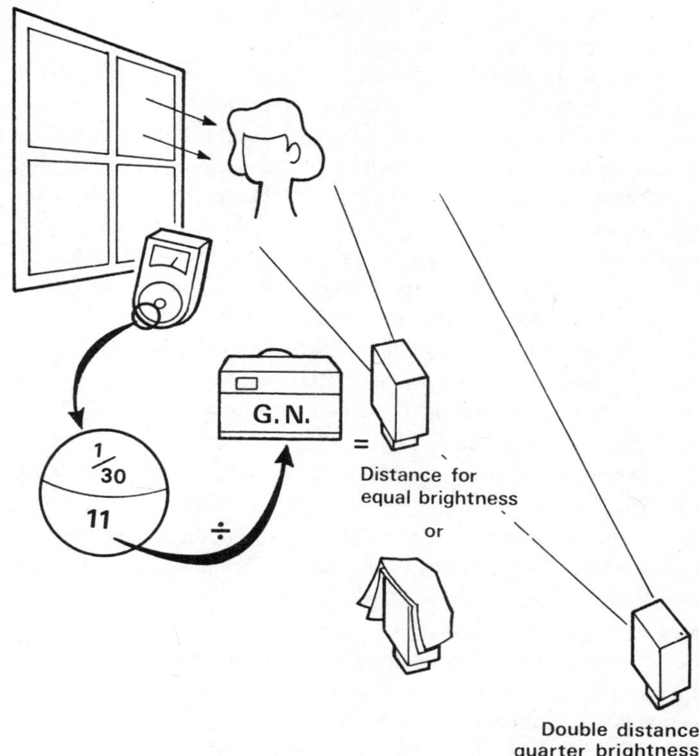

Window light with flash fill for shadows. The highlight reading from the window light determines the key lighting level. Set the camera shutter at a suitable speed for flash, divide the guide number by the aperture in use to find the flash distance for brightness equal to key, then diffuse or move flash away to reduce to normal fill level.

f number in to the guide number quoted for your flash/film combination. This would give you equal illumination for highlight and shadow fill light, which obviously destroys the effect of main illumination coming from the window – it is the basis only. But it enables you to vary the amount of fill light given to the shadows in a predictable way. If you now double the flash distance (or cover it with a couple of folds of clean white handkerchief or similar) you should have highlights from the window light four times brighter than the shadows plus any residual reflected light that is already present in the shadows. In this situation you normally want fairly heavy shadow areas because that is the nature of window lighting.

With automatic flash the routine is a little different. Automatic flash units allow you to set a particular aperture for a given ASA film speed. Some, by regulating their power output offer a choice of stops for each film speed.

But whatever the aperture indicated by the unit, you set the camera diaphragm to two stops smaller, taking care also to compensate with the shutter speed setting in order to retain the correct exposure for the existing light portions of the scene. Thereafter, whatever the distance of the flash it consistently gives one quarter the effective power of the "key" source.

Wherever you want the existing light – daylight or artificial – to predominate, you must set your exposure according to that source. The subsidiary light you bring in must follow that and be suitably restrained if you want it only to clarify shadows.

If you are adding light to boost the total brightness level that is another matter. You can add flash to daylight in this way but remember that if you follow the exposure indicated by the flash unit this may be too little for the general scene, and background areas not reached by the flash will come out darker. Again, follow the basic exposure dictated by the existing light. If you are only concerned with the subject itself and the light is insufficient, you can use the flash, calculating as if the subject were in darkness. Occasionally, if the flash is not quite powerful enough the extra light already in the scene may be just sufficient to push the exposure to the level you want, but much depends on the particular circumstances.

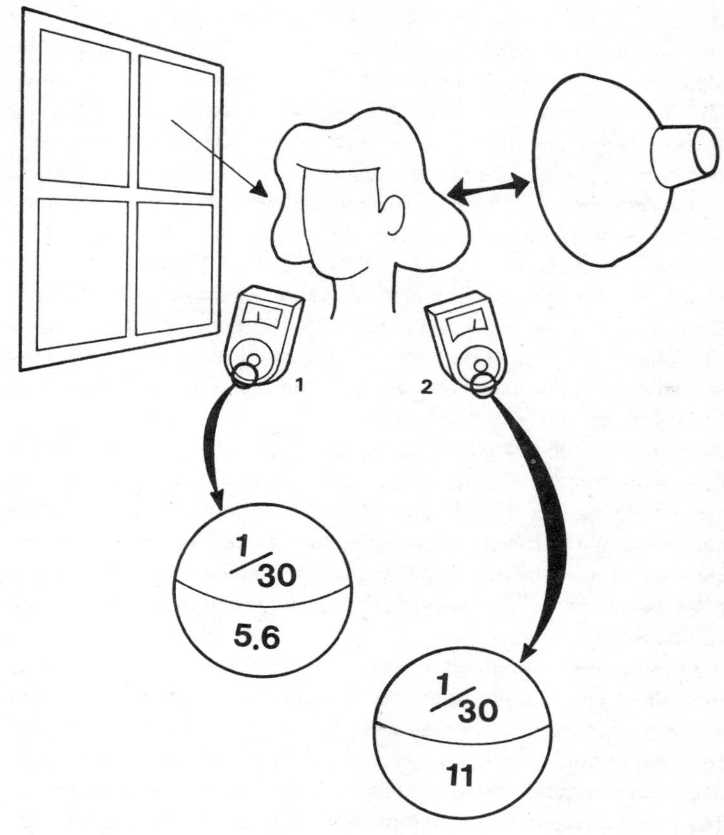

Lamps as main source, with existing light fill in. 1. Take reflected reading from areas of subject lit by existing light. 2. Switch on lamp and adjust its distance until it indicates two stops smaller (at the same shutter speed) with taking a reflected reading from the key lit part of the subject.

If the flash is to be the main key and the existing light the "fill" you set two stops (or what you want) under the exposure reading indicated for those areas already lit and base your flash illumination on the stop you have set. This applies whether you are using automatic or manual flash. If the automatic unit requires you to set a different aperture from the one you have chosen you must adjust this on the camera, making the equivalent shutter speed alteration to compensate. Some focal plane shutters synchronize flash at only slow shutter speeds, however. So, if you are forced to set such a speed use the flash unit manually and move it closer to the subject. Or, if it allows, you could re-set the equivalent power output to give, in effect, more light. Alternatively, you could use a camera with a leaf shutter. If the exposures are long enough, you could even use open flash to fill the shadows.

If you have a moving subject, you could be in trouble. The daylight, even at quite a small stop, may be bright enough to register the image of the subject in addition to that from the flash. So you get a combination of a sharp image and a blurred one. If your camera synchronizes for flash at a medium shutter speed such as 1/125 sec there is less risk of obtaining such secondary images, but they are still possible.

Indoors, lamps are a much more convenient "fill-in" source because they allow you to balance the illumination by inspection. But photo lamps do not match very well with the colour of daylight. If you are shooting in colour, you have to accept a bias one way or the other, depending on whether you choose daylight or artificial light film.

The principles applying to lamps as a fill-in are much the same as with flash. You follow the existing light exposure for all the areas that are already lit and which you want fully exposed in the picture if this is the "key" lighting. You then add your own light where you need it. You can take separate exposure readings in shadow areas where you have added light and adjust its distance, until you have what you want. This might be a quarter of the brightness of highlight areas.

If the existing light is to be the "fill" and the "key" is the lamp you add, take a reading of the areas lit by existing light, then, switch on your lamp and take a reading from an area of the subject lit mainly by that and adjust the lamp distance (or brightness) until it indicates two stops less exposure than the first reading. Set that aperture, or use whatever adjacent aperture you need according to the relative contrast range you want in the lighting – in each case adjusting the lamp brightness to correspond with the aperture set, or by eye.

If they are badly matched, the differing colour temperatures of light sources show up very strongly in colour film. Ideally, you should combine only those sources that are fairly closely related to one another e.g. daylight with flash or tungsten household lights, with photofloods or studio lamps.

The technique of shooting by existing light alone, or combined with flash or photo lamps, is discussed in detail in the companion volume, the *Photoguide to Low Light Photography.*

Flash and daylight outdoors

It is a frequent problem when taking pictures outdoors, particularly in sunlight, for the light to be so strong on one side of the subject that if exposure is correct set for that, the shadow side is unacceptably dark. If on the other hand, exposure is adjusted for the shady parts, the highlight details are "washed away" with over exposure in those areas. These extremes of contrast can be reduced by adding light to the shadow areas with flash, usually placed in a frontal position above or beside the camera. To do this you take an exposure reading of the highlight area and set the aperture accordingly. Then divide that in to the guide number quoted for the flash and film in use and place the flash at twice the distance (in feet) of the resulting figure.

Alternatively, set the flash at the distance calculated and place a couple of folds of handkerchief over the unit.

This is not only reduces the effective lighting power but diffuses the light. Diffused light is often preferable where the flash is not the main source because specular reflections are avoided and the generally raised light level seems more natural, especially in pictures taken outdoors.

You can vary the strength of the fill light but do not overdo it, otherwise the artificiality of the device becomes very obvious. Remember you are compensating for something lacking in the photographic process – not trying for a special effect. You can however, on a suitably dull day, reverse the roles of daylight and flash. The flash, instead of being frontally positioned and close to the camera should be placed high up, corresponding to the position of the sun. You could work to the usual 4 : 1 ratio of lighting intensity as a starting point but take extra shots with the flash placed for the equivalent of say, one stop under and two stops over the basic aperture indicated.

The working aperture is calculated on the basis of the existing light level as before. You take a reading and set the camera to two stops (or two shutter intervals) less than that indicated.

So your highlights, such as they are, become shadows. You then divide the flash guide number by the original aperture indicated in the exposure reading and place the flash at that distance (in feet). This gives you a "sunlight" picture with exposure based on your "sun". It would be preferable not to have a background extending much beyond the subject, otherwise this, too, will come out two stops underexposed.

Alternatively, you can work out the flash distance with the guide number and film speed and, instead of setting the aperture indicated, set two stops less and move the flash unit in to half the original distance.

Another working method would be to expose at the aperture indicated by a normal reading and then deliberately overexpose with the flash by moving it in to half the distance indicated for the aperture dictated by the scene. With auto flash units another expedient would be to place a 2x neutral density (ND) filter over the sensor on the unit (but not over the flash reflector).

Provided you can still synchronise the flash, you may adjust the exposure for the existing light to some extent by altering the shutter speed. This saves you from being uncomfortably confined to one end of the aperture scale or perhaps shooting at a smaller or larger stop than you would prefer. Some possible problems are that the camera may not synchronize at the shutter speed you have chosen and the subject you are shooting may move during the exposure.

Automatic flash units are more limited in their use in this area in that they impose a restriction on the aperture(s) to be set on the camera. But if this is practicable, and does not force you to set a non-synchronizing shutter speed on the (focal plane shutter) camera in order to maintain existing light exposure on subject or background, then if you use the flash on the camera it automatically adjusts the fill light as you move towards or away from the subject.

In practical terms, this is hardly worth exchanging for the restrictions imposed by the automatic unit. For fill in flash then, it is simpler to switch to manual operation and work with guide numbers.

If you are not in particularly bright lighting conditions and you are not too fussy about the quality of the lighting, you can use an automatic or manual flash unit directly, ignoring the presence of any other light source.

Except at long range, say, 20 ft or more (when many automatic units become unreliable and tend to cause under-exposure) the results will probably be quite adequate.

However careful your working method flash does tend to be a rather limiting method of providing shadow fill illumination. The behaviour of automatic units can be quite unpredictable when applied to this task. Individual models differ from one another in the way that they respond under various conditions. The only way to develop a sound working method is to test the reaction of your particular unit with your camera under the conditions in which you wish to use it. There is really no other way, and the answers are not usually to be found in the manufacturer's leaflet supplied with the equipment.

For indoor work in monochrome it is preferable to use lamps or reflectors wherever possible. You can than adjust the balance of the lighting visually. Outdoors you could use reflectors but otherwise you employ flash.

For very long exposures indoors you can use open flash. There are no problems of synchronization, and you have greater freedom in choosing a position for the flash unit.

In some cases you could give more than one flash during the same exposure.

Flash at night

Flash used at night and in the open, tends to give a very flat rendering of the subject, even when the light source is not directed at the subject from the camera position. This is because of the total absence of light reflected from surroundings. The subject takes on the appearance of a placard, having no real volume, no scale and no context if no surroundings are shown, as is so often the case. This is because the output of light from a flash unit is very modest in the spacious surroundings of an outdoor setting. Moreover, because the flash is not reflected from walls, ceiling or other such surfaces it complies unusually well with the inverse square law.

In fact, at night, surrounding features are a positive disadvantage, they mostly come out eye-catchingly overexposed or as murky background shapes – too obviously underlit. Even grass or gravel appear quite unnatural, like imitations made from paper and plastic chips.

The most successful night flash pictures are those in which part of the scene is lit by existing natural sources. They put detail in the background and give a sense of location, even if the subject itself does not appear to be lit by them. The background might be city lights, the evening sky or sunset.

The exposure for such a shot must be based on the light in the scene itself. In many cases this means giving a time exposure and putting the camera on a tripod. Having determined how much exposure is necessary for the scene to be reproduced as you want, adjust the speed and aperture combination so that you give a long enough exposure to allow you time to fire the flash yourself, maybe setting the shutter on "B". Naturally, your aperture must suit both the scene and the flash. To expose, open the shutter, fire the flash at the subject, and close the shutter again. The subject should remain stationary or there is a risk of making a secondary image due to the long exposure.

Any night flash photography done at exposures determined only by the flash itself are certain to have darkened backgrounds, perhaps punctured by a few images of lamps. On the other hand there are locations such as bright city streets where fairly short exposures are possible with a hand held camera. If you can expose for those you can often use your flash for close range subjects without losing the atmosphere of the environment.

If the background is unimportant and there is no other significant light source in the scene you can use your flash to "freeze" the action of a moving subject. The surrounding darkness eliminates the hazard of a double image which would ruin the effect.

Interiors large or small

When you venture out with your camera, you do not necessarily take a huge battery of lights or flash units with you. More often than not, you have only a simple flash unit or perhaps a couple of lamps at the most.

If you intend to photograph large interiors themselves, rather than people or events going on in them, the most useful item of equipment is not a flash unit but a tripod – the best means to successful time exposures. You can not expect to take enough light with you to fully illuminate a cathedral. Nor indeed would this be the best approach. You soon realise how large even quite small public buildings are compared with your own home once you try and light them!

If a picture can be taken satisfactorily without the use of extra lights, then work that way. It is far less complicated. Generally, all interiors should be taken by the light that already exists in them. However, for the perfectionist a method of using lights is described below which, if worked with care, gives results far superior to a straight photograph.

In the *Photoguide to Low Light Photography* a method was described for "dodging" time exposures made in large dark interiors such as churches, halls etc., to overcome the unevenness in distribution of available light in the picture.

This consists of shading brighter parts of the scene with a black card during a time exposure to restrain them and giving the shadow areas a relatively longer time to register on the film.

The greatest problem in photographing interiors is the enormous contrast range. Some parts of a room seem almost impenetrably dark and even if they do not appear so to you, this is how they come out on film. How can you light those dark corners?

Using a flood lamp or an ordinary light bulb in a reflector, you can work the dodging method just mentioned, in reverse – painting the scene with a lamp. You only need a single lamp to give good illumination in quite a large interior. Work as follows.

Use a slow speed film (or an ND filter with a faster one) put the camera on a tripod with the shutter on "B" and set the smallest aperture. (You need this anyway to get the great depth of field desirable in most shots of interiors). Your lamp needs a lengthy black cable and a switch on the reflector, but no stand is necessary. You also need a black cloth, such as a camera dark cloth.

First determine the basic exposure time with the existing light taking a reflected reading with a meter. If the scene is exceptionally dim and the meter readings may be unreliable take your readings off a white card placed in the scene and give three times the recommended exposure. This places the exposure in the middle of the contrast range and ensures reasonably correct register of the highlights without additional lighting.

If you were using one or more photo lamps to light the main part of the room you would fill the shadow areas with a photo lamp also. An ordinary household lamp is used in a photographic reflector if the main lighting is from existing household lights.

Provided you have set a small enough aperture the exposure time should last long enough for you to "paint" the offending shadow areas, with the lamp held in the hand.

To do this, open the camera shutter to start the exposure. Drape the dark cloth over one arm to shield the lamp reflector from direct view of the lens (even the bright edge of the reflector can cause streaks). Hold the lamp itself in your other hand and walk in to the picture (you should be wearing dark clothes) and "paint" the shadow areas with the lamp. Keep it moving all the time, and make sure that it is pointing away from your body so that you do not paint yourself into the scene. If you have weighed up the scene beforehand you will know which areas need more light than others.

Timing the amount of lighting for each area involves guesswork so you should try more than one exposure. But unless you concentrate

Painting with light. 1. Set a small aperture. 2. Set the camera shutter on B. 3. Open the shutter to give time exposure and lock it open. 'Paint' the interior with a lamp, screening it from direct view of the lens with a black cloth.

the light for too long in one particular area you are unlikely to go far wrong. Above all, do not over-correct the shadow areas under tables, in corners, etc. They should still be darker than elsewhere even if full of detail.

The same moving light technique can be adapted to paint the entire scene with your moving lamp as the sole source. You could calculate the exposure on the basis of a reflected reading off a surface lit by the lamp while stationary. If this were say, three seconds, then keep the lamp on the move at approximately that distance but never cover one area for more than two seconds. That allows for a residual exposure giving equal light everywhere from light reflected randomly as you work your way round the room. Obviously this is only a guideline. Much depends on the individual room, the coverage of the lamp reflector and so on.

An advantage of the moving light technique is the absence of well defined shadows in the picture. These are the telltale sign of photographic lighting as opposed to that from the natural direction. So, if you do use additional stationary lights be very careful where you place them in relation to furniture etc. and note particularly where the shadows fall. A lamp shining from the camera position gives least evidence of shadows but it has limited throw.

The same long exposure approach may be used with open flash. You can walk about the room giving flash exposures at the correct distance while the shutter remains open, always keeping the flash unit out of sight of the camera when it fires. But this can lead to patchy lighting in the picture. It is better to flash from some distance to increase the spread, diffusing the unit to avoid definite shadows or edges. You can increase the exposure for any area by giving more than one flash.

"Light-painting" works for any size of room, with flash or lamps. A domestic spotlight for instance could be used to "paint" the shadows in a small house.

Don't expect too much of yourself if you use the method. It is tricky. But it is fun doing it.

Light on the Subject: Inanimate Objects

Lighting for inanimate objects usually follows one of a number of fairly standardized routines which vary according to the kind of subject and the features to be stressed, if any.
Most pictures of inanimate subject matter aim for the best possible photographic quality. They are often shot only to provide a record of the object, so they must contain as much visual information as possible. The lighting can help with this, and there is no room for sloppy technique.
Shooting conditions are in many cases completely under your control, and exposure times do not need to be particularly short. Therefore, for most purposes you could afford to select a slow, fine grain film, unless the greater contrast of such materials is going to be a problem.

Flat copy subjects

When making copies of flat subjects such as maps, prints or other photographs, the camera should be set up exactly square-on to the subject, with the centre on the optical axis of the camera lens. Extension tubes are preferable to close up lenses which may cause barrel distortion, but either can work well.
The camera can be on a tripod pointing down at the subject which is lying on the floor or on a table. But large subjects may not fit between the legs and the camera may be unable to "reach" over to the centre without an attachment bracket, which is also likely to be a little unstable. Lining up is most easily through the camera viewfinder in a single lens reflex. However, any suitable system can be made to work. Tripod legs can also offer an obstruction to the ideal placing of lights, and may cast shadows over the subject. Vertical copying stands with baseboard are available and these are very suitable for copy work up to medium sizes.
A better method for large copy work is to set up the subject vertically so that the camera takes a horizontal view of it. This position also gives complete freedom in the placing of lights. A special copying unit can be constructed with a vertical copy board and sliding camera rail. To centre the camera it is moved up to the centre

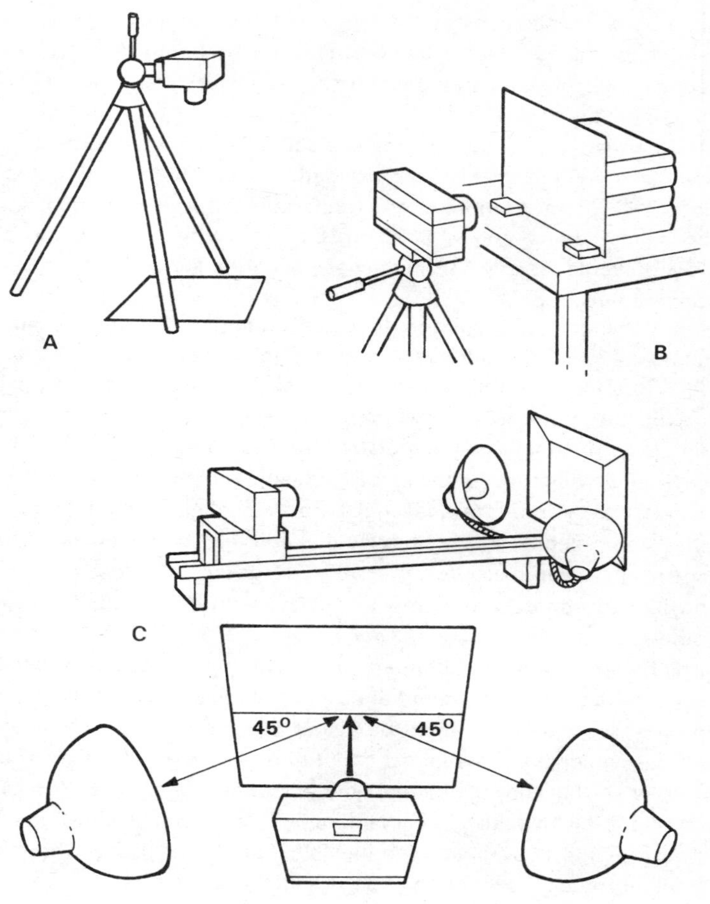

Flat copy subjects. Methods of copying. A. Camera on a tripod looking down on original on floor or table. B. Camera horizontal on tripod facing artwork supported from behind. C. A more permanent set up: a wooden copying bench with the camera sliding in a slot, and lamps mounted on flexible arms. The camera must be centred on the original and parallel with it and lamps at 45° to the surface. Lamps of unequal power are adjusted for distance to compensate.

of the board, adjusted for height, and then drawn back to the shooting position. Lights can be made a permanent fixture of this copy bench, but that arrangement can restrict the distance at which they may be placed.

The easiest way to light a copy subject is to take it outdoors on an overcast day and use diffused daylight. Indoors the normal method is to set up one or more lamps (preferably diffused photofloods or household lamps) angled at 45° to the surface of the copy subject. This prevents directly light reflections from the surface entering the camera lens.

A lamp angled to a surface does not illuminate it evenly because some parts of the surface are closer to it than others, and are therefore more brightly lit. However, the further away the lamp is placed the more even the lighting becomes. If you are using only one lamp, it should be quite distant for this reason.

One lamp will serve for very small subjects if the lamp is placed far enough away from the unevenness to be negligible. Sometimes, if the lamp reflector is angled away this light can be manipulated for sufficient evenness. Alternatively, a good reflector may be positioned opposite the lamp to reflect some of its light from the other side.

It is better to use two lamps of equal power, one positioned either side of the copy board and at the same distance. They should not be placed closer together than the diagonal measurement of the subject being copied. If the lamps are of different powers they must be ranged so that they give equal illumination at the surface. You can check for this by folding a card into a "V" shape and placing it in the centre of the copy area with the fold running vertically. The two sides of the card should be of equal brightness.

To check for surface reflections, look through the camera (through the viewfinder on an SLR). If the reflections are from a lamp, try switching off one, to find the culprit, and then reangle the lamp. Other reflections are probably from the camera itself or some other object nearby. If so, cover the camera front with black tape, a dark card or cloth.

Really troublesome glossy-surfaced subjects must sometimes be copied through a dark tunnel or tube constructed between the camera and subject, leaving just enough space near the surface for the light to reach it from the sides.

The same set-up works with flash. A single unit may be used on "open" flash. You open the shutter, flash the subject first from one side then from the other, and close the shutter again.

(It is safer to give a single exposure rather than retension the shutter, because touching the camera is certain to move it, if only fractionally.)

Copying work that involves the use of extension tubes or bellows also requires a compensating increase in exposure times. However, it is advisable to avoid lengthy exposures (say, more than 10 sec) with colour, as this can upset the colour rendering on ordinary materials. Some artificial light films, though are manufactured for long exposures. They may be characterised as "type L".

The film used should have a contrast range that suits the original. If the subject is a continuous tone one, use a normal film. But if it is a line subject (engraving, printed text, handwriting) you get better results with high contrast materials such as "line" film or, for extreme contrast, "lith" films with appropriate processing.

Texture lighting

The texture of a surface takes on a different appearance according to the way the light strikes it. The roughened surface of a subject is more strongly rendered the more acutely the light falls on it. If the light is frontal (from the camera viewpoint) the effect of texture is suppressed. As the light is moved round and away from the camera angle so the suggestion of texture is increased.

At a very oblique angle a moderate texture can become so exaggerated that the surface appearance is no longer "realistic". That is to say, it no longer appears as we usually see it.

We often observe the texture of a substance under a variety of lighting conditions which, added together, give us a "total" impression of its appearance. If, in a single picture we are to recognize that quality, all its characteristics must be suggested – texture, sheen, colour, and isolated features.

To show their *exact* quality, different textures demand differing lighting treatments. Overcast daylight outdoors is too diffused and working by a window may not allow the precise control you need. A surface may combine more than one surface feature, not only texture. For example an earthenware pot might have a hard gritty surface combined with a crystalline sparkle. A rough metal surface may have a characteristic sheen as well. Some objects have a texture that is also slightly translucent.

All these surfaces have more than one characteristic. To be well rendered you need more than one lamp, carefully placed.

The texture of rough cloth for instance, would be drawn out by an oblique light cutting across its surface, but any folds in the cloth would all be in deep shadow. Therefore you need a second lamp as a "filler" just as with other subjects, to balance the texture key and fill these folds with light. A diffused lamp placed more frontally than the first will serve the purpose. But it also softens the effect of the texture by reducing the contrast generally. You have to regulate these two lamps in relation to one another to get the best effect. Fine texture is best observed by eye while moving the lamps as the viewfinder on a camera can not resolve such fine detail sufficiently well. But you can look through the viewfinder to check the general effect.

A smooth cloth such as emboidered silk or damask needs a different treatment for here a characteristic of the cloth is its surface sheen. An oblique key light will render the fine texture and emphasize the low relief of embroidery. The fill lamp, besides lighting the shadows should reveal the sheen by introducing broad areas of reflection in the cloth. You position this lamp frontally and adjust it until there is a pleasant distribution of tones. Check through the viewfinder that these reflections are as you want them because they move when viewed from a different angle.

Where the texture is combined with a printed coloured pattern do not over emphasize the texture effect or the pattern itself will be lost.

The texture of wood, depending on its surface finish (if any) is another case of combined texture and colour. The more aggressive the texture lighting the less obvious the patterning.

The rougher the surface the greater its response to oblique light. The translucency of some materials is revealed by oblique lighting and this effect is easily suppressed by the frontal fill. So be careful. Machined metal surfaces can be revealed by an oblique light. Very little frontal illumination is needed because even unpolished metal is very efficient at reflecting. So you might need only a piece of white card placed near the camera angle to pick up spill light from the key. Some subjects made from pleasantly textured materials can be difficult to light well. You have to light for good modelling of the subject, yet this lighting probably does not reveal the texture. Where the demands of the subject are, in effect, pulling you in different directions at the same time you have to use several lights, each covering a certain aspect but not cancelling the effect of the other. Leather objects are notoriously tricky to light. A leather article has texture, sheen and a characteristic colour. Yet the subject must also be shown to have volume. Again, with colour there is less need to mould strongly; against this you have the problem of controlling shadow density and highlights so that the colour looks right.

Silver and glass

Silver or other polished metal objects assume many shapes. Flat subjects such as coins and medals are easiest to light because most of the reflections, strong though they are, come off the subject in one general direction. You place one lamp obliquely to model surface features such as incised lettering or relief figures. Then a large diffused reflector lit by a second lamp is angled to reflect in the polished surface when viewed from the camera position.
Reflecting subjects are best seen in contrast to a darker background. Upright silver subjects reflect everything around them. They can be photographed like this but, in a picture, often the reflections confuse the shape and detail of the subject. You can simplify these reflections and deliberately induce broad areas of light by placing large white reflectors around the subject. This prevents dark "holes" appearing in the reflection which eat in to the shape of the subject. One solution is to place the subject on a large white sheet of card

which curves up behind it. You light the background with a flood lamp shielded from the subject, or with a spotlight; then place a second lamp frontally to pick out highlights. Rounded silver subjects can be placed in a tent built up from translucent white material. This is lit by lamps placed outside and arranged as if modelling an ordinary solid subject. But over-efficient elimination of reflections makes the silver look more like earthenware. It is a mistake to try and eliminate all specular reflections or, indeed, to add too many.

Silver reflects the lamps and reflectors etc. around it and even the camera and the photographer himself! The best that you can do is to try to minimize the unwanted reflections by making adjustments here and there and checking their effect from the camera position. Sometimes, placing a strong, specular reflection adjacent to the reflection of the camera or other objects can disguise them. For this, you use a lamp directly, without diffusion. Professionals occasionally employ a special spray to reduce the effect of specular highlights in silver subjects, but it has to be very carefully applied as it, too, can destroy the natural appearance of polished metal.

Glassware, being transparent, is seen partly by the light it reflects, but also by the light refracted within it. When lit, its shape must contrast sufficiently with the background to be seen clearly. If a light background is chosen glass can be shown against it as a dark shape. But the best method is to set it against a dark ground and make the glass sparkle and shine against that. To define the outline you have to allow the glass to pick up the light and transmit it within itself so that it emerges at the edges as a bright line. This leaves the body, or plane surfaces unfilled. Separate lighting can be arranged to cause some reflections in those areas.

With most objects, where there is an irregularity or patterning in the glass the light will refract. Where it is smooth, it favours reflections from outside. You can balance these two factors for the effect you want. The reaction of glassware objects to lighting is highly unpredictable, and this is part of its appeal as a photographic subject. If you light the background only, clear glass will show up against it as a dark shape containing virtually no reflections. Sometimes this gives attractive effects, but the result is usually dull compared with the methods described above.

Coloured or dark glass is more efficient as a reflector than a refractor of light. Often you have to use the light background approach to reveal the colour. Black glass behaves like bronze: giving strong specular highlights but no refractive effect. Some black glass may reveal a dark colour by strong lighting from behind (page 97).
Raw glass is sometimes used for abstract photography, playing with external reflections from the rough surfaces and light refracted by internal faults. Coloured lights may be used for an additional dimension. Moulded glass or plastic are other favourites for abstract work.

Lighting for close ups

The suggestions that follow should be read in conjunction with the remarks on close range photography made on page 139.
Essentially the aims in lighting for subjects seen in close up are similar to those for subjects of any other size. You want to reveal shape and volume by modelling with a key light, and must reduce contrast with fill illumination so that every part of the subject registers on the film as a definite tone. This is particularly important because contrast in close ups tends to be greater than in normal photography.
The main problem is in extreme close-up work. You may not be able to put the light exactly where you want it without the camera itself or its lens getting in the way and casting a shadow across the subject. In this case you have to angle the light as near as possible to the right position, but you may have to settle for lighting that is more oblique than you wanted. If so, diffuse the light as much as possible to make the direction seem less definite. Because the camera is certain to obstruct the light it is even more difficult to get a frontal fill light in the right place than a key. Bouncing light from a reflector placed close to the camera is often risky, because the lamp that provides the light might also cause flare in the camera lens.
The greatest difficulty is in lighting close up subjects which have deep crevices or are otherwise very recessed. Not only does it require frontal illumination but the power of the lighting must be very great to allow a small enough aperture for the maximum depth of field.

It is sometimes possible to change the camera lens for one of greater focal length, move the camera further away yet still get as large an image. Besides possibly improving the perspective of the subject this may give enough extra space for bringing lights to the desired frontal position.

Another solution to the problem of frontal illumination in close ups is the so-called ring flash unit. This is an electronic flash unit with a doughnut-shaped flash tube which fits radially on the camera lens. As the illumination comes from all round the lens, it gives fairly soft lighting with very little modelling effect, though the main features of the subject tend to be surrounded by a shadowy outline. Because its light can penetrate deep inlets in the subject from very close range the ring flash unit has been found very useful in medical work.

Any head-on illumination sets up strong reflections in the subject. These can be eliminated by placing a polarizing screen on the camera lens and another over the ring flash, rotated to a position where the two planes of polarization cross. Thus, only the light from the subject which is scattered at its surface can pass the screen fitted to the camera lens. Direct reflections, being wrongly polarized, are unable to pass (see also page 228).

Close up work often demands that you check the depth of field when the lens is stopped down to a small aperture. But the image is very dim. It is handy to be able to bring in a powerful lamp just to brighten the subject while focusing.

Use of extension tubes and bellows requires an increase in exposure time over that needed with the lens in the normal position. This is because the light emerging from the lens is spread over a greater area and is consequently weaker. This weakening of the light occurs roughly in accordance with the inverse square law. It can be compensated where necessary by moving the lamps closer to the subject in proportion to the exposure increase demanded.

Exposure increases necessary for changes in extension can be worked out for cameras without through-the-lens meters with the following formula:

$$\text{New exposure} = \text{old exposure} \times \frac{\text{New lens extension}}{\text{Old lens extension}}$$

Face in close up. A three-lamp set up with a diffused (umbrella) light in a front side position either side of the camera and a third lamp behind but facing the subject's head, for backlighting on the feathers – *Colin Ramsay.*

Page 178: Profile with soft sidelighting, dark ground and strong backlight. The side light models the face in a realistic tone scale. The hard outline given to the figure as a whole from the light behind, separates it from a background of similar tone and colour – *Colin Ramsay.*

Insects in the natural state leave little time for setting up and lighting. An automatic flash at close range can arrest any movement with its phenomenally short exposure times, even with small apertures that you need for maximum depth of field – *Colin Ramsay.*

Page 179: Side/front lighting with dark ground and the shadow side almost blending. A simple arrangement suited to a child subject – *Peter Stiles.*

Right: The dense texture of an animal's coat can absorb a great quantity of light. But white fur is such an efficient reflector that it is only too easy to overexpose and lose the texture effect – *Peter Stiles.*

When lighting large groups, set the lighting or exposure for an individual in the centre, in depth, of the group. This minimises under and over-exposure for people at the back and front – *Colin Ramsay*.

Right: With powerful effect backlighting a blonde head of hair seems almost incandescent. A soft full, frontal fill light is used here, but spilled rear lighting is sometimes strong enough to allow the front to be filled by reflectors only – *Colin Ramsay*.

Page 184: A metal bracelet with machined surfaces breaks up reflected white light into different colours of the spectrum – *Peter Stiles*.

Shadowless lighting methods

There are several methods of obtaining lighting with little or no shadow, other than using frontal illumination, which only reduces and not eliminates the shadows.

One method is to place the subject on a glass sheet (ideally a glass top table) supported at either end and raised several inches at least above the background, which might be a sheet of white or coloured paper laid underneath. When lights are directed on to the subject, the shadow created falls on to the background. Its position varies according to the placing of the lamps. Sometimes, by choosing the right lighting angle or raising the glass further, this shadow can be moved out of the picture area altogether. With white backgrounds a separate light can be directed at the background to eliminate the shadow. This can give a clean white background and has the advantage that the position of the key light which cast the shadow is not dictated by any need to move the background away. The background light should be shaded to prevent light from spilling into the camera lens. With glass table photography you can also light the subject from behind. In fact, you can have the subject strongly modelled, or hardly lit at all, just as you please.

Another shadowless lighting method uses a moving lamp and you need only one lamp to do it. An opal or pearl household lamp or a photoflood will do. You place the subject on a white sheet and use a film and aperture combination that allows a resonably lengthy time exposure (several seconds at least) when the lamp is close to the camera position. Set the shutter on B, open the lens and, while you count off the exposure in seconds, move the lamp in a nearly complete circle back and forth round the lens. Keep the lamp on the move all the time. Then close the shutter. This gives more or less shadowless lighting but the subject is, of necessity, flatly illuminated.

Other methods for shadowless illumination are to place the subject on a sheet of opal glass or plastic illuminated from beneath, or to put the subject inside the while cloth "tent" mentioned earlier, with a small entrance for the camera lens to look through. Lamps are placed around this tent, lighting it from the sides and front.

If you want a black background you may think of placing your subject on a piece of black velvet or paper. Surprizingly, you can still get shadows! It would be safer to use the glass table method with the velvet or paper laid underneath and the shadow angled out of shot.

Lighting transparencies

The easiest method for duplicating slides is to use a special slide copy attachment designed for the purpose. This is often supplied as an accessory to an extension bellows unit which fits on the lens flange of the camera in place of the camera lens. With such an attachment the slide can be held rigidly, and in the correct position and the lens (remounted on the front standard of the bellows) focused on it. This unit may have a tripod socket which allows it to be mounted on a tripod, which is far more stable than using other methods.

On such copying units the slide holder is usually backed by a flashed opal diffuser. You always copy a side by transmitted light – a lamp placed behind the slide pointing towards the lens. A rigid slide copy unit allows you to use the sky as a light source, but it should be a cloudy day – blue sky will give the copy transparency a cast of that colour.

The light behind the transparency can be supplied by flash. In this case you would reproduce the transparency on daylight film. If you are lighting it with a photoflood you use artificial light film.

It is possible to partially correct the colours of a transparency exposed to the wrong light source. (say, photofloods instead of daylight) by copying with the reverse combination (in this case using artificial light film in the camera but copying by daylight). However, this may produce a rather contrasty result with unsaturated colours.

Improvised copy units must be abolutely rigid and the same requirements of lining up etc. apply as with shooting ordinary flat copy subjects (see page 168). The main problem is with copying a larger transparency. But most people make copies of the same size as the original or a selected part of it.

You can improvise a diffuser behind the transparency with tissue

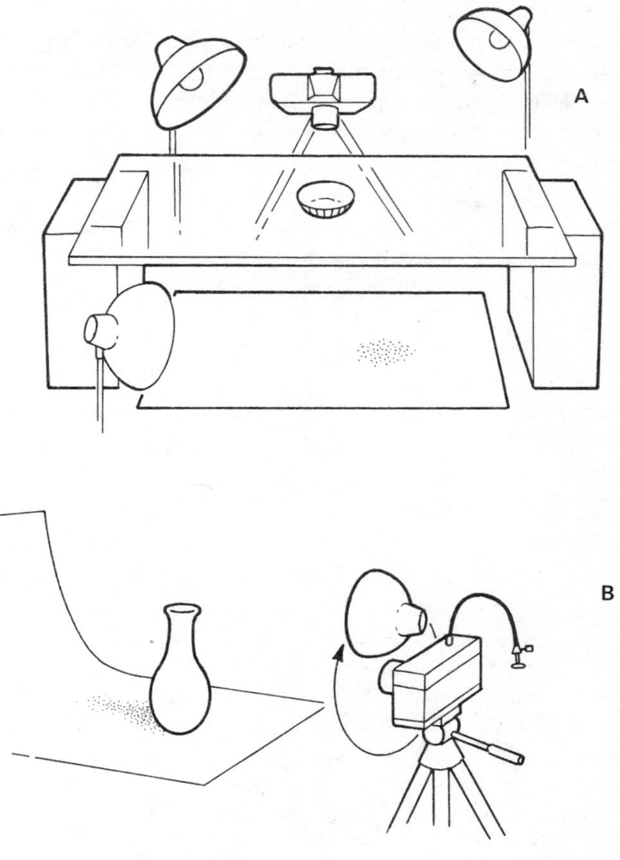

Shadowless background lighting. A. Using a glass sheet supported at either end on which to place the subject, a background sheet is placed beneath. A separate light on this background eliminates any shadows cast by the subject in the key light. B. Another method, with subject on white sheet: A lamp is moved round the camera lens axis during a time exposure. This gives shadowless lighting in background *and* subject.

paper, tracing paper or similar. This diffuser should preferably be placed beyond the depth of field of the camera lens when set at the working aperture, to avoid the risk of the paper "grain" showing in clear areas of the original.

When copying transparencies all light should be kept off the front surface. You can make sure of this by making a black paper tube to span the gap between the lens and the slide.

Copying usually increases the contrast of the image, but there is little you can do to correct this with the lighting.

Lighting People: Portraits and Groups

The home is the centre of family activity, a place where friends and relations can be found enjoying themselves and in a relaxed state of mind. So it is a good place to find subjects of all ages for portraiture. And if you are not too experienced at taking pictures it is just as well to practise on those who know and love you, rather than the unsuspecting and less patient stranger!

Subject and background

The trouble for photographers is that homes are for living in, and they are full of the domestic clutter that we need to be comfortable. Even the most spartan living conditions are very well equipped with odds and ends compared with a photographer's portrait studio. Nevertheless, the home can be a good studio and, indeed, domestic surroundings impart an authentic atmosphere to pictures that is usually missing from the comparable professional studio portrait, despite its well upholstered furniture and background of bookshelves. The problem is that unless the surroundings are watched carefully something can intrude into the picture and so impair the whole effect. Such mischievous items are usually in the background.

Because a background is behind the subject we tend to forget that it is there at all, and possibly full of paraphernalia that the sharp eye of the camera picks out only too efficiently.

One is more aware of the background when taking full length pictures of single individuals than with groups, because of the space around the standing figure. Normally, you can simplify the picture to some extent by removing a few items, though this sometimes just shifts attention on to others. In any case, a totally cleared domestic interior may look rather false.

With full length shots taken indoors the skirting board cuts across the picture with an annoying regularity. As it is so often painted white it is quite difficult to lose in shadow. To avoid it, you can place your subject against a full length curtain but this setting is a well worn cliché and, anyway, gives the picture a ponderous formality. It is difficult to make the subject feel relaxed when pinned to such a target. The best way to avoid the skirting board is to block it from view with the normal furnishings by selecting a good shooting angle. Probably the best plan is to try to use the surroundings as a part of the picture and see if you can make them fall naturally into the composition. If that composition is strong enough, or the person is in a dominant position the surroundings need not interfere too much. But watch out for background features with straight lines or shapes close to, or cutting in to the subject's head, so that, as they say in the movie industry, the subject is "wearing" a lamp or ornament which is behind it.

Most other subjects present fewer problems than the full length portrait in a small room. Young children, for instance, need plenty of space around them to move in and for the photographer to follow them quickly with the camera. Backgrounds are less of a problem. As you are working quite close to a small child the background can be thrown well out of focus. Often the camera is pointed downwards and the child is surrounded mainly by empty floor space. But children also have a natural way of adapting to their surroundings so that props become an accepted part of the picture. Older children can be asked to re-enact a particular pose which you happened to notice a moment before. They are such spontaneous subjects that this approach gets far more convincing results than doing the same thing with adults – where the failure rate would be quite high!

A background can qualify a subject, telling us something about the person in the picture and so make them more interesting. Background interest can include other people, not merely props or furnishings. Or it can just help to make the subject stand out more clearly – a purely pictorial function.

The brightness of the background is very important, and this can be controlled by a choice of the right tones or colours so as to separate it from, or merge with the subject. In most cases you want to avoid a merging effect and, especially in black and white work, you have to take steps to ensure this, possibly with a special light just for the background.

A plain painted wall is a "safe" background; studios use a huge roll of background paper for this effect. But it becomes rather a dull routine. Moreover, plain wall, or paper backgrounds are occasionally of such vivid colour that they steal attention from the subject. The same happens with very insistent patterns, and strongly figured wallpapers should be avoided unless they really "fit" with the picture. A plain white wall is useful inasmuch as you can share it or even throw coloured light or project patterns or shapes on to it with a spotlight or slide projector. Often, light toned backgrounds are chosen for female subjects and darker or more sombre colours for males. But there can be no rules about such matters. In daytime you could use the view through a window as a background, or take the subject outdoors and use frontal flash (page 159). You can also reflect the view through the window via a mirror set up behind the subject.

Definite separation between subject and background gives the picture depth. Normally you separate the two by making the background contrast with all or parts of the subject. A well lit subject is seen against a darker background, or the background is made much lighter.

The background may contrast with individual areas of the subject so that the key-lit side of a person is backed by shadow, and the shady side by light.

Even if you choose a contrasting background you can reduce its relative brightness by moving the main light (which is also lighting the background) closer to the subject or increase the relative background brightness by moving the key further away.

You have greater control with a separate background light, as you can then adjust the background independently of the main illumination to give more detail or a greater feeling of depth. It can also kill unwanted shadows cast by the main light. So it gives greater freedom in the placing of that light. Any shadows it throws on the background can be disregarded.

You may feel that the background light should follow the natural lighting in the scene. But it doesn't have to. The overall effect is the most important thing.

The background light can be included in the picture (if it is, for example, a table or standard lamp) or hidden behind such lamps, furnishings or the subject itself. Preferably, it should be outside the pic-

ture area. Sometimes light may be reflected off the background and on to the subject.
Head-and-shoulder or half-length pictures leave enough space out of the picture for a background light to be placed anywhere. Even with full length pictures a vertical framing often leaves enough space at the sides. If you have the right equipment you might place the background light overhead. A spotlight is ideal because you can position it almost anywhere yet keep the light off the subject itself. You can also adjust the light spread and intensity without moving the lamp. A full spot adjustment could give a splash of light in one area. Flooding, or using flood lamps, could give a soft tone all over the background. But spotlighting one area of the background, especially behind a subject's head leaving the corners dark is a rather old fashioned and theatrical effect. Special backgrounds are available which are already painted with slight variations in tone. These are intended for portrait studio use.
Although the traditional style of studio portrait was years ago largely replaced by a freer approach originating from photojournalism, the studio portrait is again enjoying some favour. This may be part of the natural ebb and flow of fashion, but things are never quite the same the second time. These days the lighting effects demanded are more restrained, more akin to daylight, though we are perhaps on the verge of a revival in the highly wrought and stylized lighting of some pre-war movies.

Lighting the body

In a picture of a person the body is an important element of pictorial design. In some glamour and fashion photography the clothed body is the centre of interest. Sometimes, even in portraiture, the body is posed to make a striking shape. And what a flexible form it is! Not only can the body be arranged in countless ways but the camera angles and perspectives on it seem almost infinitely variable.
It can also, on the other hand, be treated with reticence. A body may be plunged into deep shade, made diminutive by selecting a high shooting angle, hidden behind a prop or cut out of the picture

altogether. The question of posing and arrangement of the human body would fill at least a chapter in itself. We are concerned here only with the question of lighting, considered (if that is possible) in isolation from that of the pose.

Sometimes the full length figure causes problems with excessive contrast, where for instance someone's white dress is so light in tone compared with the surroundings that no details in it can be registered unless so much exposure is given to the film or print that the person's face appears unnaturally dark. Some correction for this is possible in printing by giving extra exposure to certain areas but that can be a tricky operation. Transparencies can not be corrected in this way. You either have to accept a large blank area in the picture or carefully arrange the lighting to fall more strongly on the face than the body. It is better to do this by shading the body rather than risk overlighting the head by placing the key light too high up. That could give deep shadows in the eye sockets, long nose and chin shadows and, in the case of some men, put too much light on a bald head (see page 198).

But in most cases you aim to keep the lighting fairly even. You would also want to avoid underexposing the white dress because a thin negative may make it only printable as a mid-grey. However, often when the modelling light has been carefully placed to light the head and shoulders, the lower part of the standing or seated figure is underlit. A second light placed lower than the first can be directed at this underlit area.

This would be necessary especially if the exact tone or colour (which alters at different light levels) were important.

The body should be modelled with the light to show its form, but not at the expense of good lighting on the face. The body should never be overlit in preference to the face.

One way of escaping a difficult situation in posing, lighting or fitting the figure in to a background is to have the subject seated.

A portrait often has two particularly bright areas, the face and the hands. Traditionally, it is considered desirable to have the hands less bright, as they can draw attention away from the face and, if they are particularly light in tone, may sometimes appear like plaster casts when seen emerging from the dark folds of clothes. (The hands should not be overlooked as a subject in themselves. They are a marvellous model for practising with posing and lighting – quite a challenge when trying to attain fine shaping and a full range of tones without setting up confusing shadows.)

Another approach altogether is to treat the body as a basis for abstract lighting effects, using heavy shadows, rim lighting or silhouettes – all favourite devices in nude photography of that type.

The face

The human head is, from a physical point of view, very roughly a sphere. The facial features – the main evidence of personality – are raised from, or inset into its surface.

In lighting the face you have two main objectives; to show it as a solid shape, topographically as it were, and to distinguish those features which are indicative of character, sometimes by suppressing others.

First, consider the lighting necessary to describe the physical shape: a modelling lamp must be placed at an angle to show that the shape has volume, so the lamp is placed off the camera axis. And to show that it is round, a shadow is created under the chin by raising the key lamp above the camera angle. These movements of the key lamp must be qualified to come extent by the individual face. Additionally, a fill light or reflector puts detail in to shadows created by the key. This may be from the camera position or the side opposite to the key. To avoid double shadows it must be diffused. Its distance is adjusted to control contrast.

An effect lamp may be placed behind the subject pointing towards the camera position but directed downwards on to the top of the hair or back of the head. This undiffused lamp puts some highlight reflection into the hair which can otherwise look lifeless, even under quite bright lighting. (A variation of this is to "set fire" to the subject's hair by directing the light in to the hair from behind creating a halo of light around the head. This is a glamour technique which works best on subjects with fair hair which is combed out.)

Back lighting also sets up a bright highlight around the edge of the head or body – an outline that helps to draw these shapes clearly against the prevalent background tones. If, however, the background is plain white, rim highlighting is omitted as it would "eat" in to the proper outline of the subject. Too much highlighting gives an artificial effect and with colour at least, is not really justified on the grounds of necessity. Effects like this are most easily controlled with a spotlight. You may also want a background light.

The arrangement as a whole is a fairly standardized approach to provide the modelling, contrast control and background separation needed, with three lamps. There are numerous variations. The fill light might be brought closer to reduce contrast, or omitted, to maximise that effect. Highlights on the hair could be created partly by toplighting and partly by the modelling lamp placed in front.

But your main concern should not be with how many lights you can add and what effects (and complications) they produce. Make it a cardinal rule whenever possible to keep the lighting simple, and use the minimum number of lamps.

The critical factor in lighting the face itself is the position of the key light. The face consists of several distinct planes, and the key light shows the shape by casting shadows from the main intersections of these planes.

The eyes are protected by being recessed in the head. A key light must not be at so high or oblique an angle that the eye sockets are filled with deep shadows, and the eyes obscured. They are the principal expressive feature of the face and should be clearly visible.

The cheeks are rounded and the curve of shadow between the front and side is the main evidence of their shape with each individual. Light from a high angle emphasizes high cheekbones for example, but darkens the eye sockets. A balance should be found by adjustment of the key to satisfy these separate needs.

An indication of the muscles in the face of a man could be given by hard light which either models with shadow or just creates strong reflected highlights in these areas. The shape of the chin is shown in much the same way. The lower lip is automatically caught by the high placing of the key. This may be emphasized in shots of women by moistening the lip naturally or with gloss lipstick. Again, such a highlight gives the lip a more emphatic shape.

The chief problem is the nose shadow. It should be neither too large nor an ugly shape. With high frontal modelling lights, the shadow is confined to a small area immediately beneath the nose but the same light also broadens the bridge, which may be undesirable. Moving the light to one side narrows the nose by putting one side in shadow and, if suitably positioned, creates a slight highlight down the centre. The nose then casts a triangular shadow across the face. This can be very ugly.

One way out is to use a very diffused modelling light, which softens the nose shadow. It is better to try to modulate the nose shadow while lighting to shape the other features so that when they are correct, that nose shadow is small but placed under, or to the side of the nose, where it is not too obtrusive. Avoid crossing the mouth with the nose shadow. On the other hand the recommendation that it is should reach a halfway point between nose and upper lip is a bit pedantic.

Placing the light at a low angle centrally, removes the nose shadow from the side but causes a small triangle of shadow reaching up towards the eye. The side and underneath of the nose should be of equal tone. Do not have nostrils highlighted, except when that is an intentionally outlandish effect.

This low lighting angle also highlights the underneath of the upper lip and the area at the top of the eye sockets, except the area immediately beneath the eyebrows, which usually responds to lighting from a higher angle.

The main thing is to light the face as a face and only remain conscious of ugly shadows from the nose, or any other feature, which would draw undue attention to themselves.

All features are made to appear narrower if divided vertically by shadow. Frontal illumination broadens the features. This control can be used as a corrective device or for flattery, broadening a narrow head or nose or vice versa.

When lighting the eyes not only should the eyes themselves be visible but the outward curve immediately beneath – this is part of the natural shape of the eye socket which counterbalances the stronger contour above the eye. If it is flattened or omitted and has neither highlight nor shadow, however slight, the socket has no form and the eyes appear to be stuck in the face like currants in a cake. This is a problem found mainly in young faces. The ravages of time give such a definite shaping in this area that older subjects may seek to have this evidence removed! Bags beneath the eyes are diminished by using very soft and broadly reflected frontal (but not head on) illumination from not too steep an angle.

The eyes reflect the lamps with a separate highlight for each lamp. These catchlights may be missing if the socket is mostly in shadow. Eyes without catchlights look rather lifeless.

If so, add a catchlight to each eye with a frontally placed lamp. This lamp may be doing nothing else and not even be directed at the subject. You can create such a catchlight with quite a weak source. It does not need to be sufficiently strong to register a shadow of its own.

Avoid having more than a single catchlight reflecting in each eye. Also avoid multi-head lighting units, or duplicating the key light. Keep the lighting simple – multiple catchlights give the eyes a somewhat watery appearance. If you use indirect key lighting such as a wide flood or trough light or an umbrella, that shape too is reflected in the eye. On the whole, the pinpoint of a small flood is a more attractive effect.

The appearance of the eye also changes according to whether you use flash or lamps. With bright lamps the pupil closes to a small area and the colour of the eyes is more apparent. In flash pictures on the other hand, where the existing light level is low the pupil is often dilated because it can not react quickly enough to a sudden burst of light. A larger portion of the eye is black and the pigmentation is less evident. Eyes which appear darkened because of dilated pupils can slightly alter the appearance of a person.

Another point to remember when lighting the face is that a bald head can be easily overlit compared with the face. Watch this with lights placed at a steep angle. You can slightly shade the light off this area by clipping a piece of card to the key light or putting such a shader on a separate stand. Shaders are just as useful in portrait lighting as reflectors, and it is useful to have one or two stands around, however improvised, to hold shaders.

There is no "rule" to dictate where the modelling light should come

Groups. For fairly stationary groups. With flash, use bounced illumination reflected from ceiling or wall assessing distance as the centre (in depth) of the group. With lamps, take key far away and raise it. Use a fill light from the camera angle, suitably diffused. Take reflected light exposure readings from a person in the centre (in depth) of the group.

from. Obviously the effect would vary according to the position of the head. If the subject's head is turned away from the camera often the better effects with male portraits is obtained by having the head turned towards rather than away from the light. The strongest lighting is on the narrower side and the side facing the camera is strongly modelled, as it is struck obliquely by the key. The fill light from the camera position chiefly affects the broad side and should be carefully controlled to avoid swamping the modelling effect. If the key comes from the other side a larger portion of the head is brightly lit. The broad side of the face is presented to the main light. The modelling is confined to the side turned away from the camera. The general effect is lighter and softer, possibly more suitable for female subjects. These remarks are of course very generalized, much depends on the individual set-up.

Groups

With groups, especially large groups, your lighting must be spread over a large area. This normally means taking the lamps further away than normal, otherwise the illumination will be uneven. This could be because the lamp does not cover a wide enough angle, or more likely, because in a group some people are closer to the lamp than others, and receive more light – an effect which is exaggerated by the film. (Outdoors, the same applies with fill-in flash; those nearer the flash receive more fill light than those further away.)

When photographing groups you should take three main precautions: Move the lamp as far away as you can because the differences in brightness within the group are then less significant; take exposure readings from a person in the centre (in depth) of the group and not the person in front; and allow a fairly generous exposure with negative films, i.e. over, rather than under the reading. With transparencies, stick as closely as possible to the central reading.

With flash, use the bounced method. Or, if your unit has insufficient output, use it direct (and on manual) basing the aperture on the distance to the centre of the group or slightly forward from that point.

Because the flash unit or lamp is further away more of its light is reflected from the walls or ceiling. So a second (frontal) filler lamp, though useful, may not be essential in this case. If the group is arranged so that all the people are at roughly the same distance from the lamp you have less of a problem (see page 130).

Arranging the lights can be quite tricky with groups because some people may cast shadows on others. You could arrange the people to avoid this but there is a risk that they will become self-conscious and the group as a whole may look too formal. To avoid shadows on faces place the key lamp quite high. The shadows between their bodies may not matter too much. In fact, they can improve the appearance of the group by smothering extraneous detail. If the key light comes from a frontal position then the shadows will be reduced in area. But they may appear more complex, so that the general effect seems rather messy.

Arrange your lighting by eye and check the shadow-effect from the camera position.

Watch that no one moves in to a shadow at the last moment. If you are posing a group it is best, perhaps, to give the people a rough position then allow them to relax and talk. Take the picture later, and without warning, when a natural mood has again settled over the whole group.

Lighting and Action

When you photograph a moving subject you may have one of two objects in mind. You may want to "freeze" the action so that the image is completely sharp and shows no evidence of movement other than the posture in which the subject is caught. Or you may want to show a greater or lesser degree of subject blur to give a feeling of motion in the picture.

Some subjects are suited to either approach. Others can really only be treated in one way. Blurred pictures suggest movement very strongly. It is very appropriate where the subject is making a deliberate violent movement, as in sports, stage performances and so on.

Light level and shutter speed

Accidental blur from movement is rare these days. Unless you are working at low light levels and giving longer exposure than normal you only obtain accidental blur with quite significant movements.

Action across the field of view is more likely to cause blur than movement towards or away from the camera. Intermediate, oblique movements are increasingly likely to produce blur as they become transverse to camera's view.

Assuming that you are using a continuous light source the factors determining degrees of blur from movement are, the speed that the image moves across the film, and the shutter speed. The speed that its image moves depends on the speed of the subject, its direction of movement and distance from the camera. It also depends on the focal length of the lens you are using. The larger the image of a subject, the more it moves for a given subject speed. So movement is greater with close subjects and long focus lenses.

A person walking slowly a little distance away may be "frozen" with 1/30 sec (assuming the camera shutter is accurate and is really giving that speed). To induce a blur effect deliberately you would have to think in terms of 1/15 or 1/8 sec. Blur effects created in an indoor set up should be repeated at several different shutter settings in that region because the precise result is difficult to judge in advance. Too much blur may obliterate the result, while too little looks like an error.

In the majority of cases your aim will probably be to eliminate the effect of blur. Even shots of people at home can cause you problems. Most such movements hardly rate as "action" but the closer the subject is to the camera the greater proportionally is the movement. An arm moving across half the picture area is a bigger movement than the arm making the same movement twenty feet away. So the blur looks correspondingly greater.

Light in the right place

Young children indoors for example, may move about quite a bit. You would not wish to restrict the movement of a child if you want natural-looking pictures but rather, to follow him about with the camera. This can cause difficulties with the lighting. Movement of only a foot or two in one direction may affect the exposure considerably. You can solve this problem by one of two methods.

You can establish a high enough level of lighting generally so that whenever the child moves the light remains acceptable. This can be done by general indirect lighting, or individual diffused lamps set up to "cover" most of the room, avoiding large areas of shadow, if possible. For children the lighting can be placed at a lower level than for adults, as much of the activity is at, or near, floor level. It is less difficult therefore to cover the whole room with light. But avoid too much concentration of top lighting as this will give deep shadows under the eyes etc., unless the floor happens to be an efficient reflector.

Another approach is to carry your light with you, using a flash on the camera or bounced off your own body. Or you could have someone hold a lamp while you shoot, always making sure that it is at a more or less constant distance from the child. The advantage of this method is that once you have set the correct aperture you only need to make sure that you keep shooting at approximately the same range all the time. This approach gives you and the child complete freedom of movement.

Perhaps the easiest approach is to give the child something to do so that its attention is held and it remains in one place for long enough for you to take several pictures.

Problems and potential with movement

When a subject moves about, even in a room, you not only have to make the light level consistent but also keep the subject in focus. When you are working with continuous light sources which are lighting a large area you may be confined to working with a fairly wide aperture, especially if you are relying on the shutter to arrest sudden movement. This allows only limited depth of field.

In room where there are people walking about you have to follow the subject quickly with your focusing and be very accurate when shooting at wide apertures. If on the other hand, you are shooting another kind of "action" subject, athletics in a gymnasium, you may be further away for most of the time and the relative depth of field is greater. (You would, of course, need much more powerful lighting.) But the more violent activity calls for a faster shutter speed, 1/125 at least. This may require you to set the widest aperture even if you are using very fast films, so the depth is again restricted by this factor. Against this, there may be the near certainty that the action will take place in a given spot, especially if the activity is repeated or cyclic.

With a dance sequence you may be able to provide enough light to shoot at, say 1/60 sec. This would confine you to firing the shutter at certain moments in the dance unless you want at least partial blur in the subject. All dances have moments of repose, often containing the best compositional arrangements. There are also the peak moments of activity – a leap for instance, when at the height of the movement the dancer is momentarily stationary. Shooting at such moments is quite common practice among theatre photographers. It requires some sense of timing and it helps if you have seen the dance before so that these movements can be anticipated. Preferably you should see the whole thing round once and shoot on a second performance.

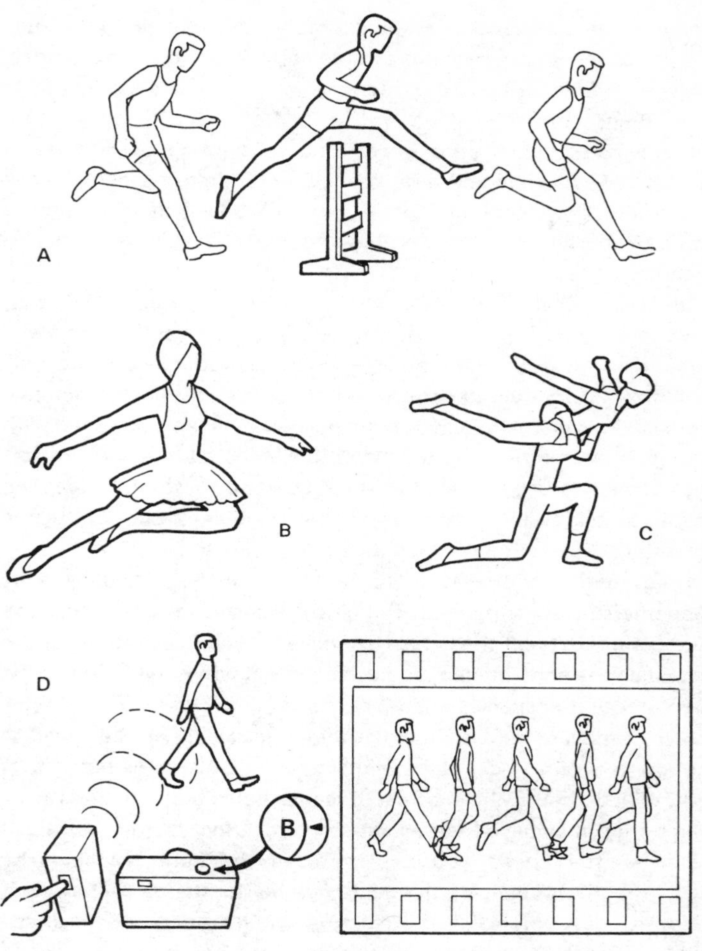

Shooting movement. A continuous light source may confine you to wide apertures giving little field depth, and only medium-short shutter speeds. A. With cyclic action you work at a fixed distance and need not refocus. B. At 'peaks' of movement the subject is momentarily stationary. C. Moments of repose in activity. D. Multiple frozen images of movement by repeated flashes on one frame.

If you are being asked to take pictures for a production you could get the dancers or performers to hold certain striking arrangements while you shoot, or to repeat leaps etc. so that you are more likely to cover it successfully.

All moving subjects shot by continuous lighting set the same problem of balancing aperture, depth of field, shutter speed and film speed and lighting range. Often you are working at the exposure limits of the film material and have to accept results that are less than perfect.

With electronic flash, things are better in several respects. You may have more actual light output at your disposal. This may allow you to set a smaller aperture than your continuous source. But the main advantage is undoubtably the speed of the flash itself. Provided that the flash is overwhelmingly the main source and you can set a high enough synchronizing shutter speed to eliminate any secondary images of the moving subject, you get a good clean, sharp image. The actual speed of the flash is probably anything from 1/600 sec upwards.

On automatic units used at close range the flash lasts for quite phenomenally short periods. The closer the subject the sooner the auto control cuts off the light. This makes it quite easy to arrest the fastest close-range movement such as insect wings, without using a flash unit that is specially designed for that kind of work.

To arrest movement with bulb flash you are relying on the speed of the shutter. With focal plane shutters, this is often restricted to a 1/30 or 1/60 sec at the shortest. Because bulbs burn for a relatively long period they have little action-stopping effect themselves. Each faster shutter speed you use, reduces the light reaching the film – effectively reducing the guide number for the bulb – halving it for every speed interval. If this restricts you too much, you may have to move the flash closer to the subject. But even the most plentiful flash illumination presents problems of maintaining a consistent light-to-subject distance or, alternatively, making frequent changes of aperture. Action pictures taken with flash usually have dark backgrounds because the flash does not carry far enough and the existing light is insufficient to register on the film. (It may cause unpleasant blurred shadow effects anyway.) In a well-planned flash action shot you would probably light the background with a second unit, perhaps triggered by a slave from the light of the first. This would give you arrested action plus apparent depth of illumination even though the light was only on a background wall. In black and white this may confuse the background with the outlines of the main subject, unless you arrange that the background light is weaker. For this, you could move the second unit further away from the background than the main light is from the subject, or put it on half power.

Multiple images

Another possibility with electronic flash is the superimposition of several images of a moving subject by repeated exposures. The ideal method is to have the action take place in a darkened room to avoid secondary images. You then give a time exposure and flash repeatedly with the unit's own button for "open" flash.
Alternatively, you might re-tension the shutter by overriding the double exposure lock on the camera, and repeat the exposure. Where the lock does not disengage on a 35 mm camera you can tension the film on the take-up spool, hold the rewind button down and advance the transport lever. This should tension the shutter without moving the film.
Remember, however, that repeated flashes will gradually build up the background tone. So make it a dark or distant background if possible, with no definite features that can reveal that the camera or film has shifted slightly while you were re-tensioning the shutter. Naturally, a sturdy tripod would be useful to minimize camera movement.

Intentional blur

Using a continuous light source you can shoot at low shutter speeds and take a chance on the amount of blur you will obtain in the picture. Ordinary human movements would blur substantially at shutter settings of 1/15 or 1/8 sec., slower movements at 1/4 sec or more. Another procedure is to plan the movement in the area covered by the camera lens. With a time exposure the subject can move through the lighted area creating a long streak as it goes.

The lights could be filtered for different colours so that as the subject moved into each light the streaks changed colour *en route.* If the lights were narrowed down to cover only certain areas the streaks from a moving subject would be intermittently broken. A human subject could hold a lamp, a lighted match, torch or sparkling firework and make light trails in the picture with these.

Lighting Effects

The appearance of an object is altered by the way light falls on it. We normally accept a fairly wide range of lightings on an easily recognisable subject as "normal". Only when the light comes from a very unfamiliar angle might we hesitate in our identification of what we are looking at. That happens particularly when the odd lighting effect is combined with an unusual viewpoint of the subject or a framing of it from so close a position that certain familiar features are excluded from the picture.

Light angle

To disguise a subject by itself, the light must remove certain information. Roundness, or the depth of objects can be camouflaged by flat lighting. The real volume of an object or its texture may be disfigured by very oblique lighting and the shadows it creates. The camera is more susceptible to this cheating light than are the eyes. It can not see in three dimensions the way we can ourselves.

Very oblique lighting elongates shadows. They grow disproportionately large compared with the mass of the surface of a feature that is casting them. They may even reach over and fall on to another subject, distorting the effect of that, too.

At a certain angle a light can sometimes pick up reflections from the surface of one subject and reflect them on to another.

We have seen that oblique lighting emphasizes texture. If the lighting is even more oblique the shadow creeps up from the deeper areas and gradually engulfs the surface. At a certain position the light may just skim the surface, perhaps creating a myriad lighted peaks. Oblique light often reveals remarkable unevenness in an apparently smooth surface.

The angle of the lighting in a subject tends to carry with it certain associations, assuming that the situation depicted accords with this idea.

Light from directly overhead in a darkened place could suggest that the only access to light or air is through a skylight or grating above – an uncomfortable association giving a disturbing effect in a picture.

High side lighting in a generally well-lit or high contrast situation suggests sunlight in the middle of the day.
Low angle lighting, level with, or a little above the subject with appropriately elongated shadows implies that it is evening light or sunset, whether the light is diffused or direct. In colour, the suggestion is further reinforced if that light has a warm tone – red or orange-yellow.
If you position a lamp beneath a subject you get a theatrical footlight effect. On faces this can look grotesque.
Diffused light from below, mixed with almost equal (diffused) light from overhead in generally light surroundings suggests that the subject could be in snow.
By placing a lamp at an angle near to a window visible in the picture you can give the impression of strong light from the window even though it may be a dull day outside.

Shadow effects

If you want to set up strong shadows use contrasty lighting with little or no fill-in illumination. Mask off any reflecting surfaces such as walls, ceiling, your own clothes etc.
To blur the edge of the shadow, diffuse the light source. To give a sharp shadow, use a focusing lamp, a spotlight or a slide projector working from some distance. Otherwise, choose a small lamp, remove the reflector and use the bare bulb. This should preferably be a clear lamp unless it also throws unwanted patterns from the glass envelope. Take your lamp as far away from the subject as possible. A shadow can be cast on a translucent surface such as a sheet of frosted acetate, or a bed sheet and photographed from the other side. The image will naturally be reversed. Shadow figures can be photographed very efficiently this way.
In any situation where you have the subject set up in front of the camera, the background can be treated separately with highlight and shadow effects. This may be necessary to balance with the subject compositionally or to put a shadow behind a highlight in the subject to reinforce it. The background light would normally be a

separate unit whose light does not fall on the subject itself. The shadows can be manipulated by setting up "flags" or shaders cut to any pattern and placed in the beam of the light. The effect can be checked from the camera viewpoint.

Sometimes it is a little difficult to analyse the main masses of light and shade in a picture because of the multiplicity of other details. One way to obtain a general view if you have a camera with a focusing screen, is to put the whole scene out of focus and then inspect the light and dark areas and see how well they balance. Don't forget to refocus afterwards. Another method is to look at the scene through half closed eyes. This too, divides the scene in to the main highlight and shadow areas. You can do it quickly from any angle and it does not even require a camera.

Shadows may be created in the picture for reasons not connected with improving the composition but to make allowance for some special purpose for which the picture was taken. A dark area can be good background for inserting white lettering for example, or the picture may be intended for joining on to another piece of artwork, or for use in a certain way where a fade to blackness on one edge may be useful.

Double, or multiple-edge shadows can be created within, or beyond a subject by arranging several equal key lamps (preferably spots or focused lights) close to one another. If they are placed wide apart the shadows become detached. If the lamps are at different distances, shadows of various sizes can be made from the same subject, fitting within one another, or spaced apart. A succession of such shadows could be generated from several lamps, though the more lamps you add the weaker the shadows become generally.

Finally, there is the picture generated entirely from shadows. The subject itself may be placed well outside the field of view. The human figure provides a very good means of creating such shadows and these effects often work well in nude photography.

Silhouettes

In a silhouette the subject is in total darkness and is seen against a lighter or white background.

Shadow effects. A. When a lamp is moved close to a subject the shadow can be made much larger than the subject itself. B. An object can be placed behind a translucent screen and backlit to give a shadow background to the main subject.

To make a silhouette you light the background only, and keep all light off the subject itself. It should be placed well forward from the background as this reduces the chance of any spill illumination rim-lighting the edges. If you restrict the lighted background area to just beyond the subject, that further reduces the chance of spill. In negative/positive work, you can extend the white area around a figure by shading this area in printing.

The subject should have a hard outline as if cut out of black paper – the original method of making a silhouette portrait. Most silhouettes of people are profile views as this is usually the most characteristic view for an outline.

A possible arrangement for the lighting is to place a lamp or flash unit on each side, illuminating the background but kept well clear of the subject and shaded to prevent light reaching the edges or front.

Another method is to place a single flash unit or lamp behind the subject and facing the background so that the subject blocks any direct view of this lamp.

A third approach is to light from behind a sufficiently translucent background, such as a thin cloth or diffused plastic sheet. Place your lamps or flash unit directly behind the cloth, masked from the camera lens by the subject outside the area covered by the camera.

You should give the bare minimum of exposure – just enough to print the background as a solid white. The effect of exaggerated contrast natural to photography helps you in this case. Even when you can see some details in the subject yourself, the film will not register them.

Silhouettes of small objects can be made by placing them on a glass topped table and lighting the background underneath, again keeping all light off the subject itself. In this case it is possible to position black card shaders either side of the background area included in the shot to reduce its light diffusing effect to the minimum.

Rim lighting

Rim lighting is an effect in which the edges or contours of a subject are outlined by a thin and brilliant highlight. To achieve this the

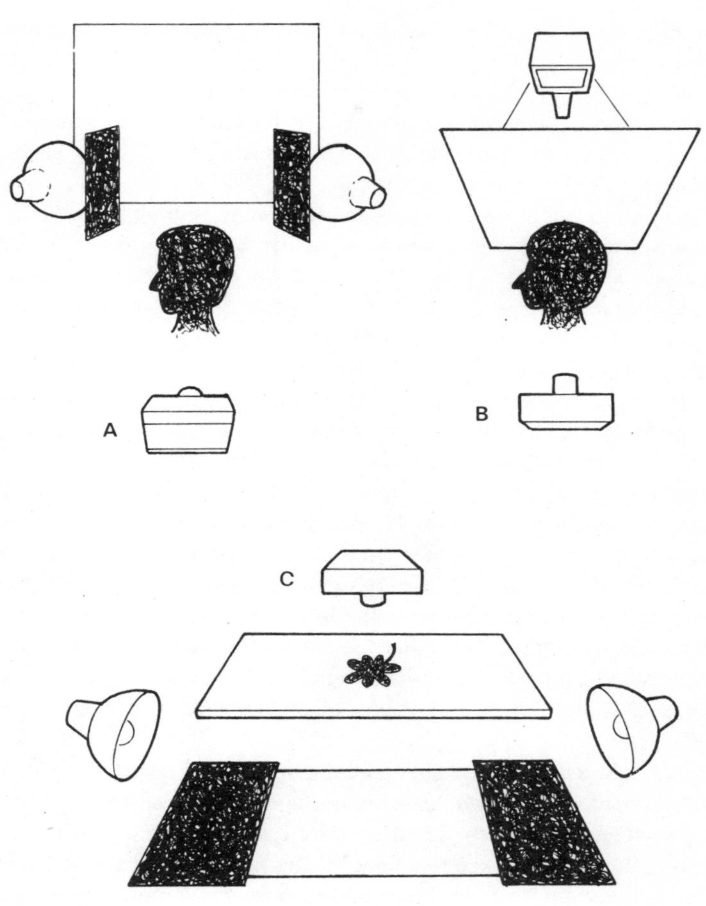

Silhouettes. To make a silhouette, light the white background by a lamp placed at either side, shielding outer margins to prevent spill light from 'creeping' round the subject. B. Or place a flash unit behind a translucent background and directly behind the subject. C. Place the subject on a glass sheet above an illuminated background masked at either side.

illumination must come from a position more or less behind the subject.

Rim lighting has already been mentioned in the context of portraiture and general situations where it is added to a conventional lighting set up, mainly to reinforce the sensation of solidity in the subject, or just to enliven the image.

Rim lighting can also be used as an effect in its own right. This is an extension of the silhouette because, instead of denying the light any access to the front or side of the figure you deliberately induce an oblique highlight tracing around the shape of the subject. Moreover, if the background too, is removed the subject is lit only by the rim light making a shape entirely isolated by blackness.

This rim lighting can be applied to a simple shape such as a bowl, where only the edge of the bowl is seen, or to a human figure where a thin rim of light runs down one side (or both sides if you wish to rim light from more than one direction). A complicated figure like a bowl of flowers could be rim lit, though the more complex the subject the more likely it is that internal reflection would destroy the hardness of this lighting. A patterned object such as a perforated grille can be lit in this way and the result may be quite surprising.

Generally speaking the rougher the surface of the subject the more widespread and diffused the rim light effect. Hairy subjects grow halos of light. Polished surfaces might produce a thin specular reflection.

To rim light a subject you set up a lamp (preferably one that you can control over a narrow angle, such as a spot) behind and to one side of the subject out of the picture. Move it about until you have the effect you want, but keep all light off the remainder of the subject, unless you want it there. You can absorb the unwanted light which passes beyond the subject by placing a black cloth (preferably velvet) in its path.

Flare and halation

Flare is an area of more or less random light which is cast over the image formed by the lens. It can take many forms, light streaks, spots or circles in the picture, or more often, a fog effect over the whole image. The usual cause is internal reflection of light within the lens – between the glass components or the inside of the lens barrel. Modern lenses are fluoride coated to improve light transmission, increase contrast and reduce the likelihood of flare effect to a minimum, even when the lens is pointed straight in to the light source, a classic flare-inducing situation.

Multiple layer coated lenses are claimed to be even more proof against flare, though it is questionable whether the increase in contrast on non-specialist lenses is an advantage.

If you want flare then you might be better off using an old uncoated lens. If your lens will flare and you are seeking the effect, this is the way to go about it: Shoot into a strong light source or have the light just outside the picture area. Give a fairly generous exposure. You can cast about with a reflex camera to see if you can pick up flare, but this is no quarantee of getting it. When the lens is stopped down it is quite likely to remove the flare, especially if it is from a lamp immediately outside the picture area. Or it may alter the flare in some way. Flare may appear very faint in a viewfinder, but much greater in the negative.

In colour, flare evenly distributed across the picture area can give very pleasing effects, softening the colours with a faint haze. When the light "leaks" in to the picture from one corner this, too, can give pleasant effects. Circular or spot flares are less useful and look more like processing faults than deliberately sought effects. The worst effect is a series of coloured diaphragm images scattered across the picture, a freak effect which fortunately does not occur very often.

Halation is an effect in which a bright light source seen in the picture is surrounded by a diffused circle of light. It is caused by the light striking the rear surface of the film and being reflected back into the emulsion layer from behind. As it is normally considered a nuisance, modern films incorporate a special anti-halation backing which reduces this effect to a minimum. So it is now difficult to achieve strong halation effects deliberately.

A certain amount of halation is present in some pictures taken at night that include bright streetlamps. Indoors too, brilliant unshielded lamps or windows with daylight outside can cause

halation. But such effects are very modest compared with the extremes encountered with the unbacked photographic plates that were in use long ago.
Today halation is usually induced artificially by placing an effect screen of one kind or another over the camera lens (see below). But this is really a form of flare.

Lamps in the picture

Light sources included in the picture, if of sufficient brightness, may give rise to the fogging or flare effects noted above. Evenly fogged effects are often caused by dust, bright reflecting surfaces adjacent to the lens or, as we have seen, the scattering of light within the lens.
It is relatively easy to include the even type of flare effect with the light source actually included in the picture area. The uneven effects too are likely to occur with the lamp in the picture but are still difficult to obtain intentionally and to see even when they are present.
Normally, if you are trying to suppress flare effects when shooting directly in to the light you take care to select a coated lens, check that the lens is clean, and use a lens hood to reduce the likelihood of stray light being reflected from surroundings in to the lens (even though the original source of that light is included in the shot).
Obviously to encourage flare in such pictures you do the reverse of these things. Or you can use a diffuser, smear the lens, or preferably a sheet of plastic or glass (or a filter) in front of the lens, with petroleum jelly or a similar substance. Diffusion and flare do not however, appear as quite the same effect.
This approach can create a romantic or hazy atmosphere in a scene, and is especially effective where such light sources as candles, fires and domestic lamps are actually visible in the picture.
Another range of effects is obtained with special cross-screen or starburst screens. These are designed to spread bright lights or the stronger specular reflections in to star shapes with elongated points or other shapes, without affecting the remainder of the picture very noticeably. Such screens are intended for use only where the light

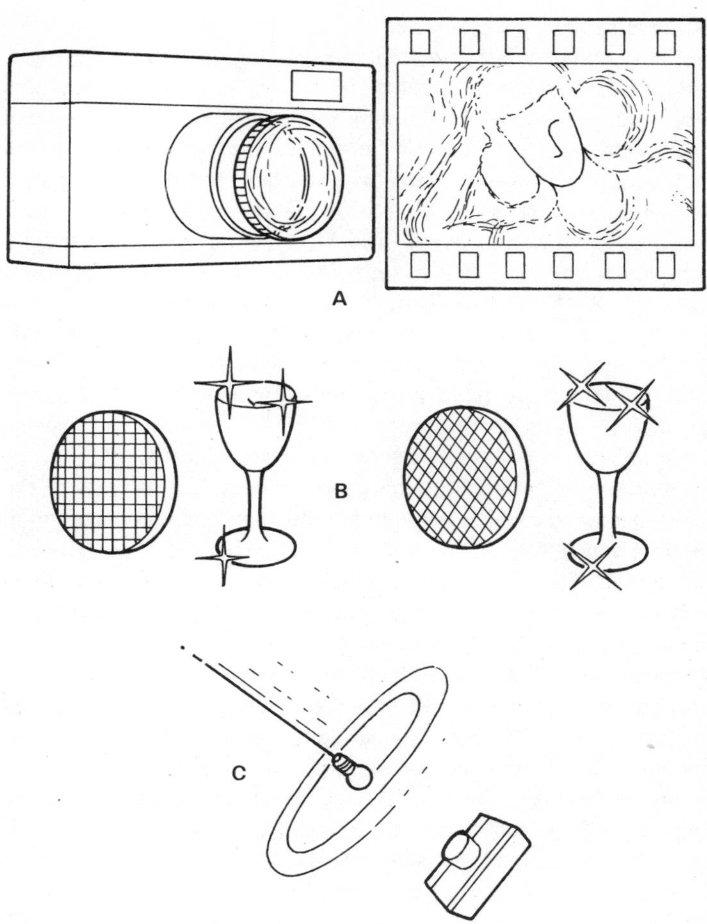

Diffusion. A. Glass sheet of filter smeared with jelly and placed in front of the camera lens. B. Cross-screen gives star-shaped specular highlights which are re-angled by rotating the screen. C. Physiogram made with a lamp swinging from a pendulum above the camera, creating a pattern in light trails.

source is itself in the picture or the reflections from it are very concentrated. It has no effect on ordinary highlight areas of the subject.
Various other effects are possible with a light in the picture. If it is strong source of small area in dark surroundings, light tracings can be made by moving it about in front of the camera whose shutter is open on a time exposure. Under carefully controlled conditions such a small light, when attached to a pendulum can be made to trace out an elaborate and varied system of light trails. The beautiful pattern made in this way is called a physiogram. It can be done with a torch bulb (with its reflector removed) suspended from a long piece of string and swinging slowly above the camera which is on its back pointing upwards. The lines made can be broken intermittently with a shader or coloured with pieces of plastic or filter, or given successive exposures with coloured filters over the camera lens. These images can be photographed in or out of focus.

Numerous other effects can be generated by light tracings in the picture either by moving the light source or the camera itself during the time exposure.

Sometimes a light source in a picture is not sufficiently potent to produce the desired effect of illuminating the subject, yet it is bright enough to photograph well itself. Replacing the lamp (say a domestic lamp with a photoflood) to increase the power may give the right effect on the subject but then cause flare or loss of detail around the lamp. The problem can be solved by retaining the lower powered bulb in the lamp and setting up a second lamp out of the picture to represent the first. This lamp actually lights the subject, doing the job of the first lamp but remaining invisible itself. Thus the light is "cheated" in to the picture by the invisible lamp, which must be appropriately angled. The slight difference in the real and apparent angle of illumination of these two sources is not noticeable from the camera position.

High key, Low key

In a high key photograph the tone scale of the subject is condensed in to a narrow range extending mainly from mid grey to white, with perhaps a single small area of darker tone. No really dark tones appear in such a picture.

High key effects result from carefully controlled lighting, exposure and processing procedures followed up by appropriate printing technique. Printing control does not by itself give the effect. The first step is to reduce the range of tones actually being photographed by selection of a suitable subject. Subjects which lend themselves to high key treatment are those consisting predominantly of medium or light tones, or seen in a particle-laden or light atmosphere which restrains the tonal range by its filtering or diffusion effect.

The high key treatment is often applied to fair haired or blonde female subjects in portraits and nude photography. It is also much used in commercial and advertising work, for stressing the light tones of a product.

The surroundings also must be right. If you are making a high key portrait, for instance, the subject should wear light coloured clothes and be seen against a light toned or white background lit separately to remove any shadows arising from the use of other lights. The background should be lit to a fractionally higher brightness level than the subject itself.

The lighting on the subject should be virtually shadowless; strong, but very soft and from all around, above and below. It is easier to obtain the necessary spread by taking the lamps further away from the subject than normal. (Alternatively, small subjects can be placed inside a "tent" and lit from the outside, with lamps placed all around.) Finally, a principal light, also diffused, is added from the camera position.

With flash, as you lack the visible means of adjustment for shadows etc. use a large broad reflector (such as the "tent" just mentioned or an umbrella) from the camera position. It is difficult to gain the required effect with only a single unit, but if this is all you have, place it immediately above the camera but bouncing off a large white reflector to give the broadest spread possible. Ideally, use a white wall behind the camera. If you have one, a second flash, behind the subject, directed at the background eliminates any shadows present there.

But if you have two flash heads it would be better to place them

both to bounce light from large reflectors placed in a side-frontal position either side of the camera axis.
You should give a reasonably full exposure, though with high key effects on negative film the exposure is not critical. The more exposure you give the less prominent are the mid-tones in the negatives. You can take several shots at different exposures and, with negatives, print the one that is easiest to work with on a soft grade of paper. With colour transparencies however, exposure is just as critical as in normal photography because you have no means of making adjustments later. So in every case bracket your exposures.
It is customary with high key shots to leave at least one area of the picture (such as the eyes) with a reasonably heavy tone. This, as well as forming a focal point in itself, tends to emphasize the general airyness of the remainder of the picture.
Low key requires more or less the reverse treatment. The picture consists mostly of dark and middle tones with perhaps a weak highlight here and there to set off the general effect. You should start with a darker or more sombre-toned subject seen against a dark background. Lighting should be arranged to give a well modelled effect in dark tones but with full detail in the shadow areas. Frontal lighting should be avoided except to insert a few isolated highlights. Likewise, avoid direct side lighting which creates too much shadow and too strong a texture effect. It is essential with low key effects to get exactly the right exposure – enough to give full shadow detail but not to encourage the highlights to become too definite. Very precise control is needed in printing.

Open flash

Open flash, where the flash is fired manually while the shutter is open on a time exposure, can be useful for various effects. It gives the flash unit total independence from the camera during time exposures because no synchronizing lead is necessary. So you can take it as far away from the camera as you please.
If you fire the flash many times at an immobile subject during a time exposure and with the camera rigidly supported you can, as we have

seen, with a solitary unit get the effect of several lights. At night, you can walk in to a scene and create local bursts of light behind subjects, or in front of them, picking up the reflections here and there in the blackness, or firing flare spots in to the lens by turning the flash towards the camera. You can light a large subject piece by piece (page 164). You can fire separate flashes at a moving subject to get superimposed multiple exposures without needing to touch the camera. A special stroboscopic flash unit (or a rapidly flashing lamp of the type used in the entertainment industry) can analyse a movement in a continual series of superimposed static images. This method has been used to study rapid movements such as a golfer striking a ball to help evaluate each stage of the action.

The limitation of ordinary open flash however, is that you have to work in near darkness otherwise the time exposure will produce detail in the rest of the scene and with moving subjects give muddy smears and possibly unpleasant double images.

Projected patterns

A slide projector has a bright enough lamp to project an image or a shadow shape or pattern on to a background behind the subject. It can also project on to the subject itself, provided that subject is of sufficiently light tone to reflect the image. Whirling patterns could be projected on to a nude, or, if straight lines were projected the shape of the body would be described in alternating black and white contours. Graduated shading slides could be prepared and inserted in the projector carrier to give an area of light that gradually fades off in one direction.

Effects can be combined from more than one projector. Masks, coloured filters, slides or objects such as insects trapped between glass may be projected on to the subject for effects in colour or monochrome.

Special filters are produced for display purposes in which coloured patterns or liquid patches move about as the filters are rotated. These may be adapted for photography.

Take care with projector-plus-lamp set ups that you do not swamp the projected images from the projector with light from the other lamps. To ensure this you can use household lamps and shield their rays from the projected areas in the scene.

Infra red flash

Infra red photography requires the use of IR film (available in 35 mm and roll film sizes to special order) and an IR filter either on the camera or over the light source. This filter is needed to absorb the normal visible radiation to which IR film is also sensitive. The camera filter, being optically flat, is the more expensive of the two.
With infra red illumination pictures can be taken of animals or people in darkness without the camera or light source being detected. For such purposes the filter, which sometimes takes the form of a plastic bag, is fitted over the light source, normally flash. When fired, the full red glow of the bulb or tube can be seen, but only if it is directly visible to the subject at the moment of exposure. If, however, the flash is used indirectly, reflected from a wall or ceiling, it becomes completely invisible.
Sunlight and tungsten illumination are among the other sources that can be filtered for use in infra red photography, but fluorescent lighting and other luminants with discontinuous spectra are not suitable.
Another aspect of IR film is its peculiar rendering of tones compared with those we are used to seeing in normal monochrome photography. Sky (except clouds) and water appear dark, deciduous foliage and grass, white, conifers dark and human faces appear pale except for the eyes.
There is also a colour IR film but this is not so easy to obtain. Here the spectral response of the film is translated in to artificial colour renderings instead of tonal values. This film is designed mainly for IR detection work where the differentiation between high and low IR response can be made more clearly visible by these coloured dye "signals" in various parts of the picture. This integral tripack material has one infra red sensitive layer and two layers sensitive to visible light but designed to give false renderings of the subject's colours.

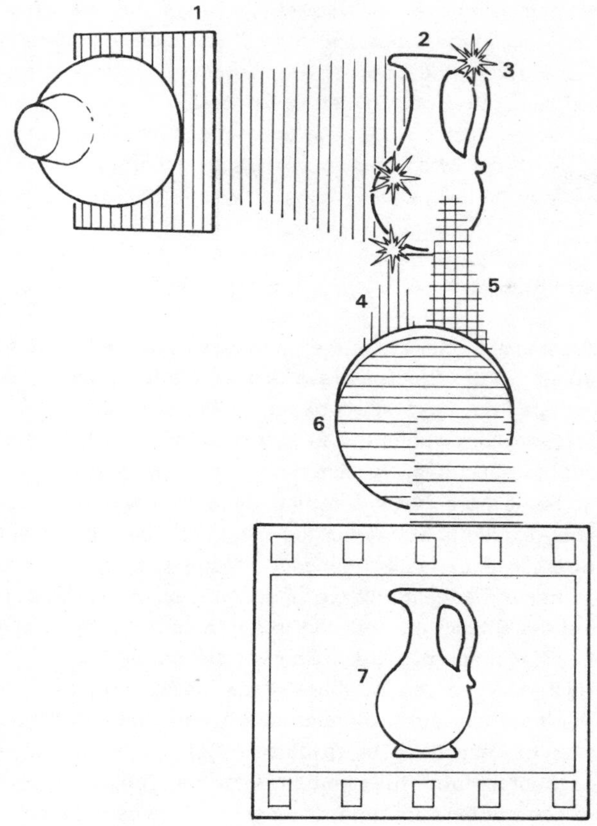

Polarized lighting to reduce specular reflections. A polar screen, 1, is placed over the light source. The polarized light strikes the subject, 2, causing specular or direct reflections 4, plus random or scattered light 5. The direct reflections are eliminated by a pola screen set at right angles, 6, to the plane of the first. Only the random reflections form the image 7, which is therefore free from most surface glare and highlights.

Infra red materials have a short shelf life and should be left in the camera for the shortest possible time. They soon fog through the packing or through the body of the camera. They should also be processed as soon as possible after exposure.
Infra red filtered flash can be used for triggering a slave unit with a second flash head when you do not want light from master flash itself to fall on the subject.

Polarized lighting

If light sources are polarized in the same way as daylight from a blue sky at about 90° to the suns rays and a polarizing screen is also fitted to the camera lens, then direct, or specular reflections from the surface of shiny subjects can be controlled to some extent. If such surface reflections are eliminated not only does the subject appear to be lit more evenly but its colours are strengthened.
A polarizing screen is fitted over the main lamp causing its light to be polarized in a particular plane. A second screen, fitted to the camera lens, is gradually rotated until the specular surface reflections from the subject are reduced to a minimum. At that point the planes of polarization of the two screens are crossed.
Light which is scattered at the surface of the subject loses its polarized property and can therefore freely pass through the screen on the camera to the film. The specular reflections, because they are directly reflected from the lamp, retain their polarization. They therefore can not pass through the screen to the camera lens.
Polarized light may also be used to reveal stress patterns in transparent substances, and to produce an effect of different colours and tones in subjects with a crystalline structure.
Polarizing screens always absorb a proportion of the light striking them and, like many ordinary filters have an exposure increase factor quoted for them. This varies from one make to another but is never less than ×2. So in the case of a ×2 filter you must give twice the exposure to maintain the same image density as you would get when shooting without it. A ×2 screen fitted over a lamp reduces its effective power output to half. Where a ×2 screen is used over the

lamp *and* the camera lens, a total of ×4 applies. So in that case you must give two stops more exposure than you would if you were not using the screens. More information on filters and screens is given in *The Photoguide to Filters,* another book in this series.

Daylight and Artificial Light

There are many advantages to using your lighting equipment in conjunction with daylight, whether you are outdoors or working by the light from windows or open doors.

Daylight gives you the chance to escape (at no extra cost) the monotonous uniformity of pictures taken with a single flash head on the camera. The flash may be the main source, with daylight relieving the shadows. Or daylight may predominate and the flash assume a secondary role. Either way, you can explore the many different qualities of daylight.

Combining sources

Daylight, except direct sunlight, comes from a wide, diffused source – the sky. Outdoors this gives predominantly top lighting. But, because it comes from so wide an angle, it gives the illusion of being an all-round light source. Outdoor subjects therefore seem evenly lit, unless they are actually in the sun.

When skylight comes through the window and lights a room and any subjects in it, the light retains this softness but by restriction, also gains a certain directional quality. If the room itself is not a very efficient reflector a subject near the window is photographed by soft but very high contrast illumination.

One way to reduce the contrast to photographable levels is to introduce an artificial light on the shadow side. Remember, though that in this case the light is introduced for technical reasons – a corrective effect – and not as an effect in its own right. The fill light should therefore accord with the main lighting. If that is very diffused daylight, the fill light should also be heavily diffused. It may be difficult to gain as wide a spread as the daylight, but by using the light indirectly, bounced off a large reflector, you can get near enough to what you need. Often, you can just use a reflector on its own, and reflect the daylight. But this is usually only effective where the reflector can be positioned close enough to the subject to give sufficiently strong reflected rays (diffused rays disperse very rapidly). So, in many instances the only answer is to place the reflector further off and use artificial light.

If the subject is lit by direct sunlight through the window you can sometimes catch its rays on a reflector and direct them back into the subject's shadow side. Often the sun falls at the wrong angle, or too steeply, so that the reflected light would probably be coming from below, which may not be desirable. There again, you can use your artificial light, but the degree of diffusion is not so important, although the light should still be diffused.

If you are not bothered by the quality of the fill light but only its strength, you can use flash or lamps directly. But you risk setting up various pinpoint reflections in certain areas of the shadow side, "greasy" skin reflections with human subjects. You may obtain specular reflections or even a clear image of the lamp itself in polished objects. For corrective effects, the direction from which fill light comes must be consistent with the source, unless you are seeking an effect of two separate sources. If the subject is placed well into a room and sidelit from the window then the fill light too, should be side lighting the subject. The lamp would be reasonably level with the subject it is lighting. Light coming from a steep angle would definitely be identified in the picture as a second source.

The strength of fill in lighting and its balance and control in relation to daylight generally, was discussed in an earlier chapter (page 154).

Daylight and artificial lighting

The differing colour qualities of daylight and (some forms of) artificial light can cause some problems when taking pictures with the two sources combined (page 73).

In black and white photography there are no complications. Although many films are marginally less sensitive to most forms of tungsten illumination than daylight, this does not cause much of a problem. In general work a film rated at 64 ASA in daylight may have a speed of 40 ASA in tungsten. A 160 ASA film drops to 100 ASA. When you mix the sources, you should just remember that a tungsten lamp has marginally less effect on the film than you see with your eyes. So if the subject is lit on one side by window light, and you want to bring up the shadows with a tungsten lamp, you can give a little more light (say half as much again) to the shadow areas than looks correct. On the negative the balance in highlight and shadow should then be as you wanted.

Daylight and artificial light, though both superficially "white" to the eye, can actually differ considerably in colour. Household tungsten lamps, for example, are far "warmer" in colour than the light that comes in through the window. Differencies in colour quality between one light source and another are recorded strongly on colour film. So colour films are often designed to be exposed using either tungsten or daylight, as the source so that the colours then come out looking normal.

The differences in colour content of light sources can be assessed according to their "colour temperature". This is a measurement based on the heating of a theoretical body until it radiates light of a particular quality. As the temperature rises the light changes from red, through orange, yellow and white to blue. The direct relationship in this case between heat and light or, in other words colour temperature, is expressed in Kelvins (K). So we say that the colour temperature of noon daylight is normally 5500 K, for example. The colour temperature of photofloods is only 3400 K; they are much redder. Everyone knows that the more you heat something up the whiter or bluer it becomes, so the higher the colour temperature the whiter or bluer the light. (Oddly enough, we tend to think of redder light as "warm" and whiter or bluer light as "cold" and this is how it is normally described. This is because of other associations such as red fire, blue ice, warm blood, cold sea, and so on).

Some colour films are designed or "balanced" (the colour rendering is biased) for use in daylight. Electronic flash, or blue flashbulbs are near enough in colour temperature to daylight to be suitable for use with the same film.

In the morning and evening, daylight becomes redder. If you are a perfectionist you can filter the flash to match that. Or you can scrape a little of the blue coating off a bulb to increase the warmth of its light output. But this is dangerous unless you have a shield on the gun because without its laquer coating the bulb can shatter on firing.

Alternatively, films are balanced for artificial light sources; some, such as Kodachrome Type A for use with photoflood lamps (3400 K); others including Ektachrome Type B (3200 K) and Agfachrome 50L (3100 K) for photopearl or studio lamps which give a slightly less "cold" light.

Household lamps (2600–2800 K) give light with a much greater red content than either of the two photolamps above. In colour, even with artificial light colour films, these lamps would appear rather orange.

If you take pictures on negative film (for making prints) colour bias caused by shooting with the wrong light source can be adjusted to some extent in printing but the quality of these prints will not be as good as those taken under the correct conditions. Kodacolor X and Kodacolor II film for example, are designed for exposure in daylight, or with flash.

Corrections for colour balance when using the wrong film can be made by fitting a suitable filter over the camera lens. This causes a loss of light and, in effect, a drop in film speed, which must be compensated by an increase in exposure. It is quite common to adjust the colour response of tungsten-balanced film for use in daylight by fitting a Wratten 85 B filter.

It is also possible to filter daylight film for use in tungsten illumination. But the filtering requires such a huge increase in exposure to compensate for the loss of light that it is seldom practicable.

The normal approach however, should always be to use the film designed for the light source you are working with. The question of filtering should only arise where you find you have to use the same film with two different sources because it happens to be the film in the camera.

Mixed-colour lighting

The principal difficulty arises when more than one type of light source is used in the same picture and they are of widely differing colour temperatures. The film can not be chosen or corrected for

both of them, and even with negative film it is not possible to correct in two directions at once.
You can mix flash and daylight quite freely because the difference in colour temperature between these two sources is marginal. If however, you want to mix daylight with the light from tungsten photolamps the difference is very marked.
Generally speaking, you should choose a film according to the light source that predominates. If it is daylight then use daylight film. The tungsten lamp by comparison with this will give a warm light. If, however, tungsten is the dominant light source you can use a tungsten balanced film, but the daylight will appear rather blue. If this is only some light through a window which does not provide much illumination in the scene, then it does not matter.
If neither light source predominates but they play a more or less equal role, then you choose a film according to your personal preference. A daylight film will give a picture with a warm bias in some areas; an artificial light film will tend to give generally colder looking pictures.
If you have to use the same roll of reversal (colour slide) film for pictures taken by artificial light and others taken in daylight, select a high speed artificial light colour film.
To use this film in daylight you have to fit a colour conversion filter (85B) over the camera lens.
Although this brings about a drop in film speed of the equivalent of one full stop (halving the effective ASA speed) you still have plenty of speed in hand because the fast film is now operating at around the rating of a normal colour film.
For details on the use of colour compensating and other filters see the *Focalguide to Filters.*

Light sources and filtering

The following filterings are recommended for correcting colour balance with the light sources most frequently used for photography:

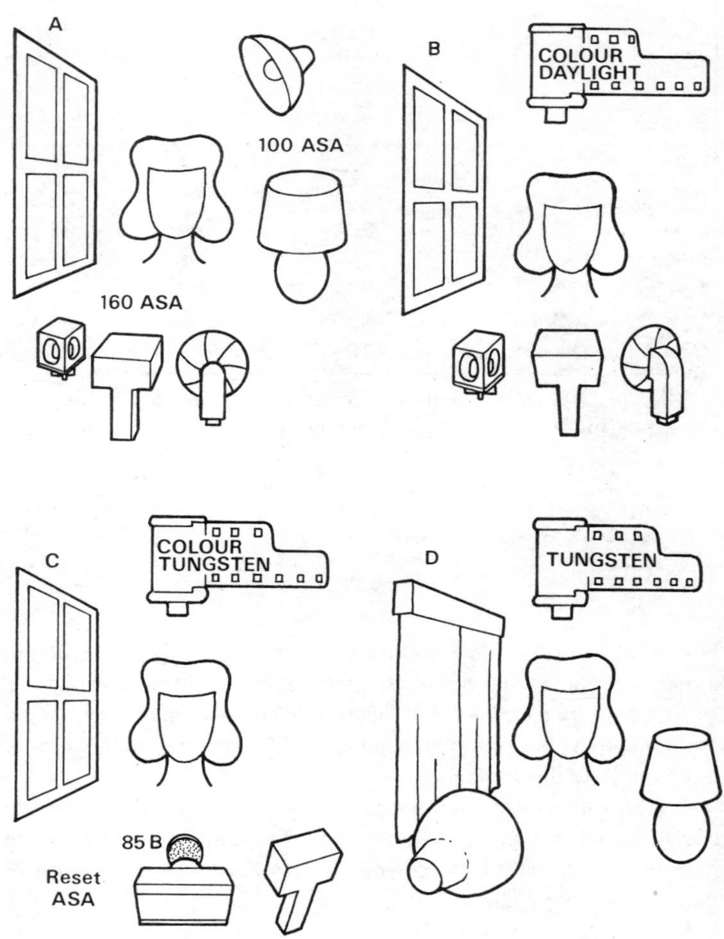

Mixing sources. A. When mixing daylight and artificial light, monochrome may make any marginal allowance required for speed or exposure reading differences. B. Colour, daylight film, blue bulb, cube or electronic can be mixed with daylight. C. Colour Type B tungsten film when used in daylight or with flash added requires an 85B filter on the camera lens. D. Tungsten film indoors without a filter: Draw the curtains. A mixture of photo lamps and household lighting gives a mixture of 'warmth' in illumination.

FILTERS FOR COLOUR BALANCING

Source	Colour film Daylight	Type A	Type B
Daylight	—	85	85B
Blue flash	—	85	85B
Clear flash	80D	81C	81C
Electronic flash	—	85	85B
Tungsten (3200K)	80A	82A	—
Tungsten (3400K)	80B	—	81A
Household lamps* (2900K)	80A + 82B	82C	82B

* Household tungsten lamps vary in colour temperature according to their wattage. The lower wattages are lower in colour temperature.

40 W = 2650 K
75 W = 2800 K
100 W = 2900 K
200 W = 3000 K
(approx)

Other light sources for photography include tungsten halogen lamps, and fluorescent tubes. Some halogen lamps are balanced to 3400 K and are suitable for monochrone film or Type A colour films. Other halogen lamps are balanced to 3200 K and suit monochrome and Type B colour films.

Fluorescent tubes vary widely in colour temperature and range from a warm pinkish-white to a blue-white "daylight" type. Filters are available to correct the main types of tube for use with daylight or tungsten-balanced film.

FILTERS FOR FLUORESCENT TUBES

Lamp type	Daylight film	Tungsten film
Daylight	Filters: 40 M × 30Y	85b + 30m + 10Y
Cold white	Filters: 30 C + 20M	10M + 30Y
Warm white	Filters: 40 C + 40M	30M + 20Y

In each case one stop should be added to the exposure to compensate for the loss of light with these filterings.
As an alternative, some filter manufacturers supply filters designed for the purpose. However, even with these, you need to experiment with particular combinations of film and tube, using colour compensating (cc) filters in addition.

Lighting and Exposure

The best results with any film are obtained only when it is properly exposed. But some films are more tolerant of incorrect exposure than others. The ability of a film to give a good picture when it is under- or overexposed is termed its exposure latitude.

Exposure latitude

Negative films, colour or black and white, generally have greater exposure latitude than reversal (slide) materials, particularly in the direction of overexposure.

The normal method for finding the correct exposure is to take a general reading of the whole scene with the (built-in or separate) exposure meter. This is also what automatic cameras usually do. However, there are shortcomings to general readings. If some parts of the scene are particularly bright, the readings obtained could lead to underexposure of the mid tones and shadow areas of the scene. With negative film you could increase exposure by, say, a stop, to obtain more shadow detail, yet not risk overexposing the highlights. With slide film, however, even though you gain in the shadows, such an increase is certain to result in overexposed highlights. Much of the colour and detail would then be "washed out".

If the contrast is too high for the film to accommodate all the densities, you should increase the light level in the shadow areas. This should not be done by moving the modelling lamp to a frontal position, but by bringing the lamp or reflector which is lighting the shadows closer to the subject, or adding a lamp in that area if there is not one there already.

When you barely have enough light for the subject, try to keep the lighting contrast fairly low, using what light you have to avoid getting any deep shadows. With negative film you can then risk being up to a stop underexposed without loss of detail. With transparencies the slight underexposure will intensify the colour saturation. While there is a little scope on slide film for underexposure with low contrast subjects, remember that this film does not take kindly to great inaccuracies in exposure. Generally speaking, negative film is much easier to use.

Image density

Having seen how it is possible to manipulate exposure and lighting contrast to accommodate all tones on the film, you should now consider how it is best to render those tones. If you have a subject of a particular tone, let us say a mid-grey, you should aim to expose the film in such a way as to give a final image (whether subsequently printed or seen in a slide) of the same grey, otherwise it is not a realistic rendering.

Obviously, varying the exposure can have a lot to do with tone rendering. If you overexpose you may get a tone in the print or slide that is much lighter than in the original subject. If, on the other hand, you underexpose, the tone might come out darker.

The question of tone here, of course, applies in the same way whether in colour or black and white. A mid-grey would correspond to a colour saturation of equivalent density, in the colour transparency or print.

When an exposure meter takes a general reading of a scene it adds together all the different brightnesses and indicates an exposure that is averaged out to give a mid tone. This is fine if the *subject* too averages out to a mid tone; but it is easy to see how this averaging could also lead to wrong exposures. If the subject were mostly very bright, such as a person wearing light coloured clothes and standing in a white room, the meter would read all these light areas and then indicate an exposure to render them as a mid tone – i.e., a mid grey, not the white that they really are. (Skin tones, being that much darker, would come out darker still).

Take an altogether different situation, the classic example of a black cat in a coal cellar. Assuming your meter were sensitive enough, its readings would indicate the exposure necessary to render the black cat and his surroundings as a mid grey when, in fact, we know that they should be black!

To overcome the bias in the meter reading obtained with subjects that are either generally light, or generally dark, you can compensate with the exposure setting. With light scenes you increase the exposure given to the film by say, a stop, whereas with predominantly dark scenes you give less exposure than that indicated – perhaps a stop or half a stop.

Exposure readings

Another approach is to choose a method of exposure reading that is not based on a general view of the whole scene. One way is to take a reading from the mid tone area of the subject. The traditional way of doing this is to go up to the subject and take a reflected light reading from a mid tone area, and then base the exposure on that. Cameras with built in TTL (through the lens) exposure meters are sometimes designed so that the meter takes a reading from only a part of the scene visible in the viewfinder. The tone present in that part of the subject covered by the light reading patch in the viewfinder forms the basis of the reading. So the reading could be taken from a mid tone by placing the reading patch over a mid tone area of the subject. Some meters combine a small reading area with a percentage reading of the whole scene in the viewfinder. There are many variations, and it is at least partly a question of getting used to a particular camera.

Special spot photometers can take a reading from a very small part of the subject. This is useful if the situation forbids your approaching the subject and taking a reading from nearby. The trouble with taking a mid tone reading is that you have to know how to recognize a mid tone – an area lying approximately mid way between the brightest highlight and darkest shadow areas of the subject. This area must also be large enough to make an accurate reading possible.

Another way to make exposure calculations is the "white card" or "artificial highlight" method. You hold a sheet of white care next to the subject and take a meter reading from that. The white card, is, in effect, a synthetic highlight large enough to ensure that the meter reads light reflected from that and nothing else. You then increase the indicated exposure by $2\frac{1}{2}$–3 stops. This should give sufficient shadow detail in all but the highest contrast conditions. The main advantage of the white card method is that you can use it when the light levels are too low for the meter to respond with accuracy – or to read anything at all. But the precise exposure control it allows makes it useful for general purposes. A variation of this practice is to use a grey card which reflects a percentage of the light falling on it.

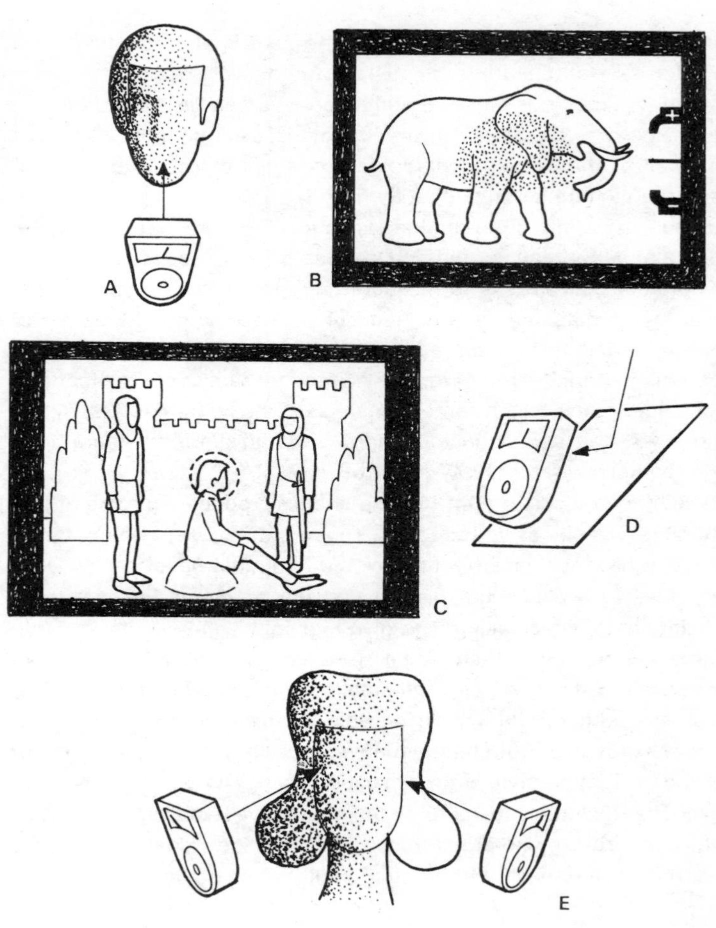

Exposure readings. A. Reflected light mid-tone reading for 'average' settings. B. TTL meter reading from a specific area of the subject. C. Spot photometric reading a very small part of a subject which does not allow close approach. D. Artificial highlight reading from a sheet of white paper – add 2.5–3 stops. E. Average derived from highlight and shadow readings compared.

Any card would do, provided the same card is always used. Once you have determined its reflectance, and by experiment, the factor by which exposures must be multiplied, you can be sure of consistent exposures therafter. To simplify things, use one that reflects 18 per cent of the light (photographic shops sell them). Then you can read the camera settings directly from the meter.

Yet another method of gauging exposure is to take first a highlight, then a shadow reading and find a mean between the two.

A different approach is to measure the light falling on your scene. You have a diffusing cone or hemisphere on your hand-held meter (one manufacturer makes a filter-mount to be fitted on a through-the-lens metering camera for this). Stand close by your subject and point your meter to the camera position. If the lighting is *exactly* the same, you can take an incident light reading from the camera position, pointing directly away from the subject.

Following an incident light reading should produce a picture of just the same density as your subject. Though, of course, if the contrast range is beyond that of your film, then you still have to alter your exposure to produce the picture you want – increasing it to give shadow detail, decreasing it to give highlight detail.

There are however, many other methods and each has its own adherents. But as long as you establish a particular working pattern and stay with it, you should be able to maintain consistently accurate exposures. But you must never lapse into a routine with your set up or lighting style simply because you know what exposure to give. That inevitably leads to an unimaginative handling of subjects, which ignores any potential they might have individually and where a particular approach with lighting could be an advantage.

Long exposure problems

When you are providing your own lighting for a scene and not relying on what already exists, you aim for a light level that allows conveniently short exposures. There are, however, occasions when it is difficult to obtain enough light to avoid lengthy exposure times, particularly when you are relying largely on daylight. This can cause underexposure and poor colour rendering.

The difficulties arise from the breakdown of the law of reciprocity as applied to exposure. The law states that as long as the product of the light intensity and the exposure time remains the same (i.e.; whatever combination of aperture and speed is chosen) the exposure remains constant. This law however, fails to take account of the fact that the film does not respond so readily to light of low intensity as to that of more normal levels. So, unless avoiding action is taken, pictures requiring long exposure times tend to come out underexposed.

The effect various according to the speed of the film. But with most materials the reciprocity law begins to fail at exposure times of longer than one second. So, for these, extra exposure must be given. The table below shows you how much exposure time to add (or the equivalent aperture adjustment) according to the approximate daylight speed rating of the material.

LONG EXPOSURE COMPENSATION

Film	ASA (daylight)	1 sec exp Add	8 sec exp Add
Slow speed	25–5	$\frac{1}{2}$ sec (or $\frac{1}{2}$ stop)	8 sec (or 1 stop)
Medium speed	64–125	1 sec (or 1 stop)	8 sec (or 1 stop)
Fast speed	160–320	1 sec (or 1 stop)	12 sec (or $1\frac{1}{2}$ stop)

With colour films designed for shooting within the range of normal "instantaneous" shutter speeds down to 1 sec, long exposures cause a slight shift in the colour balance. Such films include all the daylight materials and some balanced for artificial light. These films sometimes bear the suffix "S" (denoting short exposures).

Films which do allow for the colour bias effect of long exposures are usually artificial light materials. These may bear the suffix "L" (denoting long exposures). The film is stated to have a neutral balance at a particular exposure time, e.g. 1 sec. On ordinary ("S") materials the shift in colour balance with medium long exposures is not very great, and can be corrected with a colour compensating filter. Kodak issue data listing the filters required with each of their colour film emulsions in such conditions. The filters are for use over the camera lens during the exposure.

Short exposures

Very short exposures can result in a shift in colour balance due to similar causes. But the problem is likely to arise only with the exceptionally brief flash exposures experienced with some older electronic flash units or with automatic flash used in close ups. With the latter, the most practical solution to avoid this problem is to take the flash unit further away or partially mask the flash window.

If an old flash unit proves unsuitable in this way it would be more practicable to consider using an alternative light source such as daylight or photolamps than to experiment with filtering.

Flash and guide numbers

The adjustment of the lens aperture for correct exposure when taking pictures by flash is based on the power of the flash, the speed of the film in use and the distance of the flash unit from the subject. To make calculations quick and simple to do while you are busy taking pictures, the manufacturers of electronic flash units and bulbs issue figures stating the relative power of the flash when used with film of each ASA speed group. This is expressed as a guide number. (This guide number also takes account of the shutter speed.)

The guide number is the product of the lens aperture and the distance (in feet) from the flash to the subject when used with film of a particular speed.

If you have already decided on the shooting distance and want to find the correct aperture to set, you divide the guide number of the flash gun or bulb by the flash-to-subject distance (*not* the camera-to-subject range, which might be different if the flash is used off the camera). For example, in the case of a flash with a guide number (with a particular film) of 40 (ft), which is placed 10 ft from the subject the aperture to set is the guide number divided by the distance:

i.e.: $\frac{40}{10} = 4$. So the aperture is set to *f*4.

Now suppose that for some reason you want to set a particular aperture, say *f*8. The correct flash distance can be found by dividing the guide number by the aperture in use:

i.e.: $\frac{40}{8} = 5$; so the flash should be set at 5 ft.

Any changes in the distance from lamp to subject can be quickly compensated with an aperture adjustment to give the same exposure. As long as the chosen combination of distance and aperture, when multiplied together, come to the same or very nearly the same guide number, exposure is correct for that film.
Guide numbers may be quoted in metres instead of feet. In that case, simply take the flash-to-subject distance in metres.
From the guide number for a particular film you can calculate the equivalent guide number for a film of any other speed. The system takes account of the inverse square law as applied to the intensity of light falling on a subject (whereby the light reaching that subject varies inversely as a square of the distance between light and subject). Thus, the guide number is multiplied by 1.4 for a film of twice the speed, and by 2 for a four times faster film, and so on. But the recommended guide numbers for different film speeds are usually supplied with each flash unit. Some have tables, or calculators which you set on the guide number, that allow you to read off the aperture and distance combinations directly. So then there is no working out to be done.

Automatic flash in practice

Automatic or "computer" flash units are designed to give the correct amount of flash illumination for subjects are various distances without the need for calculations based on a guide number. They do this by adjusting the duration of the flash automatically according to the subject range.

Because an auto flash gauges the exposure according to the amount of light reflected from the subject it also automatically takes in to account the overall lightness or darkness of the scene in front of it. When its light sensor "reads" that the subject has received enough light for the speed of the film and aperture in use, it cuts off the flash.

So, all things being equal, the closer the subject is to the camera the shorter the total flash duration. You just set an aperture to suit your film speed, and keep that aperture for all distances within the flash gun range.

Some auto flash units require that with a given speed of film you must set one particular aperture. Others permit two or more different aperture settings for each film speed. This allows you some choice in the depth of field of your pictures. You may, for example, want the background as far out of focus as possible, and for this you would require a large aperture. Most auto flash units may also be used manually in the ordinary way.

The flash gun usually has a calculator incorporated in its casing. You set the film speed on this and then read off the aperture you must set on the camera for the pictures to be correctly exposed. If the unit has more than one "mode" of operation for auto exposures it will allow you to set alternative apertures. In that case the unit is set to a particular mode and the corresponding aperture is set on the camera. To control depth of field you may choose a particular aperture for the camera, and then set the appropriate mode on the flash unit which regulates the flash for that aperture. (By selecting one mode or another, all that happens is that the light sensor is made to shift its scale of sensitivities in one direction or another.)

From now on the flash unit may be moved towards or away from the subject and the flash duration will be correctly adjusted for the distance.

The mode that allows the largest apertures to be set gives the maximum effective range of the flash unit. In scenes with great depth you usually seek maximum depth of field, the reverse of what you are getting with a wide aperture. But, the greater the shooting distance the less critical is the focusing and, in effect, the greater depth of field available.

If the sensor is independent of the flash head and keeps the subject in line of sight the unit may be used automatically for bounced flash also. If the sensor moves with the head, such bounced flash exposures will not be correct because it is no longer reading the light reflected from the subject but the reflector. In that case the unit should be set on manual operation and the guide number system used, taking the subject range as the distance from the flash to the reflecting surface *plus* the distance from that surface to the subject.

If you are using the auto flash for fill-in with existing light you can set a smaller aperture on the camera than that indicated by the flash unit for the film in use, so that the effect of the flash is reduced. You would have to adjust the shutter speed by the corresponding amount so that the exposure for existing light contribution remained the same. Or, use the flash manually, and double the flash to subject distance indicated by the aperture/guide number combination.

If more than one flash unit is used it is easiest to regulate the exposure manually. Set the units on manual. Base the lens aperture setting on the distance and guide number for the unit being used as the main light. Place the second (similar) unit at twice the distance. Alternatively, choose a lower guide number for this unit.

Flash meter readings

Flash meters are available for reading flash exposures however many flash heads are included in a set up. Readings are taken from the subject position and the flash heads can be triggered by the meter without you having to return to the camera position. These meters are mainly intended for studio work, where the flash heads are positioned independently rather than being held in the hand or mounted on the camera. They can take account of any variation in lighting angle, position etc. They are however, considerably more expensive than the typical CdS or selenium type meter for continuous sources.

Guide Number conversion for electronic flash

The table below allows an easy conversion to be made between the effective power outputs of different electronic flash units when these are not quoted in the same terms, or in terms of the same film speed. Eg: if the flash unit quotes a guide number of 28(ft) at 25 ASA find '28' in the 25 ASA column and read across for guide numbers at other ASA speeds. For metric guide numbers read 'M' line.

	FILM SPEED (ASA)							EQUIVALENT RATINGS	
	25	**50**	**64**	**80**	**100**	**160**	**200**	**W-S**	**BCPS**
Ft.	20	28	32	35	40	50	56	8	300
M.	6	9	10	11	12	16	18		
Ft.	22	32	35	40	45	56	63	10	375
M.	7	10	11	12	14	18	20		
Ft.	25	35	40	45	50	63	70	12	450
M.	8	11	12	14	16	20	22		
Ft.	28	40	45	50	56	70	80	16	600
M.	9	12	14	16	18	22	25		
Ft.	32	45	50	56	63	80	90	20	750
M.	10	14	16	18	20	25	28		
Ft.	35	50	56	63	70	90	100	25	900
M.	11	16	18	20	22	28	32		
Ft.	40	56	63	70	80	100	110	32	1200
M.	12	18	20	22	25	32	35		
Ft.	45	63	70	80	90	110	125	40	1500
M.	14	20	22	25	28	35	40		
Ft.	50	70	80	90	100	125	140	50	1800
M.	16	22	25	28	32	40	45		
Ft.	56	80	90	100	110	140	160	64	2400
M.	18	25	28	32	35	45	50		
Ft.	63	90	100	110	125	160	180	80	3000
M.	20	28	32	35	40	50	56		
Ft.	70	100	110	125	140	180	200	100	3600
M.	22	32	35	40	45	56	63		
Ft.	80	110	125	140	160	200	220	125	4800
M.	25	35	40	45	50	63	70		
Ft.	90	125	140	160	180	220	250	160	6000
M.	28	40	45	50	56	70	80		
Ft.	100	140	160	180	200	250	280	200	7200
M.	32	45	50	56	63	80	90		

W-S = Watt-Seconds (joules) (1 W-S. = 40 lumen sec. approx.);
BCPS (ECPS) = Beam (Effective) candlepower seconds.

Difficult Situations

Bringing light to bear on a subject or situation, besides its obvious advantages, can create problems that were not apparent beforehand. Often these difficulties arise in the handling of the lights, especially if the person using them is uncertain of their *photographic* (as opposed to visual) effect.
Most of these troubles are solved by experience in using lights. No one must expect to get the hang of lighting with the first roll of film they shoot. It could take years to learn to handle lamps with enough confidence to know what they are going to do in every situation. It makes things much easier, of course, if your photography is confined to certain subjects, portraiture, say, or insects.

Too many lamps

This is a beginner's mistake. It comes from trying to do too many things at once without thinking. Remedy: switch off all the lights and start again.
The usual hallmarks of too many lights are: too many shadows (sometimes running in conflicting directions) and multiple highlights.
Think out the lighting in stages, and only use a lamp if you really need it. Because you own four lamps you do not have to use them all for every shot!
Start with the key, and examine the shadows. Adjust the lamp to remove those which seem to you to have an ugly shape or to occupy too large a portion of the picture.
Do the shadows *need* a fill light or do you want an effect of strong contrast? If you want a fill light, position it carefully to actually fill the shadows and not leave a mixture of filled and unfilled areas because of careless positioning. A solitary unfilled shadow can look like a black mark in an otherwise well graduated picture. Make sure the fill light is soft enough. In portraits, avoid a strong secondary catchlight in the eye if possible.
If the background needs a light do not let it spill rays into the camera lens or strike the subject so as to destroy its outline with a broad reflection. Avoid lighting the background to the same tone (in

monochrome) as an adjacent part of the subject. Do not overlight the background and so destroy its colour. You can reinforce a background colour with a filter of similar colour on the lamp.
Only add rim lighting if absolutely essential. It can look very artificial.

Too much light

Light level is, to some extent relative to exposure. But a fully lit scene with many lamps will tend to retain that feeling just as an underlit scene using little light retains its own. So the mood is more the result of lighting arrangements than actual output.
The chief sufferer from very bright continuous lighting is the subject. It can cause people to screw up their eyes and, after a while, show signs of strain. Plants can wilt and some creatures behave erratically or seek refuge in the shade. Juicy subject matter dries up, though a coat of glycerine will preserve a wet look of sorts.
If the light is too strong you may not be able to set a wide enough aperture to differentiate between parts of a subject with the focus, or obtain an out-of-focus background when you want it.
The first remedy is, of course, to reduce the lighting power. But if the best lighting angles can only be achieved from nearby, use a slower film or an ND filter over the camera lens.

The wrong light

Lighting should suit the subject itself, as well as the situation in which it is supposed to be seen. Get the contrast right, and keep the shadows under control. Watch background shadows particularly. They can creep out from nowhere and misshape the composition by adding weight in the wrong places, or confuse with the subject if there is not much separation in tone.
Most human subjects look better in a soft rather than a hard light. Although hard lighting is often recommended for male portraits, the results can be grotesque if overdone, with absurdly prominent pores

in the skin each with its shadow and highlight. Avoid chasing away all dark areas on the head by pursuing them relentlessly with lights. A figure with a highlight on every angle looks comical rather than "well lit". Confine any rim lighting to one side or do without rather than risk a contrived appearance by overuse.

Sometimes, when working in a restricted space, try as you may, you cannot get the lamp into the right position. You could consider reflecting it from a mirror which does fit into the space. This can also put a distance between the lamp and the subject that the cramped conditions would not otherwise allow. Consider opening doors and putting lamps outside the room, or in cupboards or even looking through the window. Or think about bounced lighting.

Never be content with poor lighting on any subject. People looking at a picture with dreadful lighting can only see the results – they can't see your problems!

Too little light

This is a big problem. The shortest answers, if you cannot increase the exposure time or aperture are to: move the lamps closer, or the subject closer to the lamps (that can cause uneven lighting and hot spots, or failure to cover the picture area); use more powerful lamps or flash (if you have them); use a faster film (awkward if you are half way through the film in the camera); boost film development (some films take more kindly to this than others, but the risks are obtrusive grain and poor colour quality); double up the lamps (greater risk of double shadows unless the lamps are placed very close together and well diffused – bouncing would reduce the output); chance under exposure by shooting anyway (you may get an acceptable result).

Reflections in the subject

Strong reflections in the subject may denature the colour, impair the outline, show images of the surroundings (or the camera and photographer) or flare the picture.

Reflections are the natural and inevitable consequence of throwing light on a subject. It is wrong to treat them automatically as something to be eliminated. They only become a problem when they are so aggressive that they spoil the image or reduce the informational value of a record picture.

If, for example, you were photographing a cabinet with glass windows, a reflection of a lamp in the glass would probably cause flare in the picture and loss of detail. If the lamp were moved slightly to one side the reflection may vanish. Always try to adjust the lighting first. Then, if that fails, consider moving the camera or subject.

Sometimes reflections are caused by lamps which have no illuminating function in the picture. Shiny subjects can pick up highlights from all around, even from very weak light sources. So remember to turn off the household lights, or draw a curtain over a window if either of these are causing troublesome reflections. Often the easiest remedy is to remove the reflecting object from the scene, or to re-angle it slightly. This applies to mirrors, polished furniture, television screens, pictures on the wall, ornaments and other such items. With a mirror or picture on the wall it is sometimes only necessary to push a small wedge underneath to alter its angle sufficiently to remove strong reflections.

Shiny subjects can be treated with anti-relection spray. But this is really a last resort, and must be done with great care – enough spray to remove the glare, but not so much as to destroy the reflecting appearance of the subject. Sprays are mainly of use if the reflection is from the actual subject, such as silverware and other polished metal objects.

Dense atmosphere

An ordinarily smoke-laden atmosphere does not so much affect the light reaching the subject as the camera's view through it. Not only is that view obscured by the smoke, but the lights or flash are reflected in it. If you want to minimise the smokey effect shoot from close by and, if possible, position the light close to the subject.

You may choose to retain the hazy effect, or even accentuate it, by outlining light beams against a dark background. You could exaggerate the effect even further by blowing smoke into the light beam.

No lighting problem is impossible to solve. It is largely a question of knowing what the light can do, and then adapting it to the situation, trying as far as possible to see it through the selective eye of the camera.

Index